SIMON PETER

SIMON PETER

*From Galilee
to Rome*

Carsten P. Thiede

Academie
Books Grand Rapids,
Michigan
Zondervan Publishing House

Simon Peter: From Galilee to Rome
Copyright © 1988 by Carsten P. Thiede
First published in 1986 by The Paternoster Press

Academie Books is an imprint of Zondervan Publishing House,
1415 Lake Drive, S.E., Grand Rapids, Michigan 49506.

Library of Congress Cataloging in Publication Data

Thiede, Carsten Peter.
     Simon Peter : from Galilee to Rome / Carsten P. Thiede.
       p.   cm.
     Bibliography: p.
     Includes indexes.
     ISBN 0-310-51561-0
     1. Peter, the Apostle, Saint.   2. Apostles–Biography.
  3. Christian saints–Palestine–Biography.   4. Bible. N.T.-
-Biography.   5. Bible. N.T.–Criticism, interpretation, etc.
     I. Title.
     BS2515.T42 1988
     225.9′24–dc 19
     [B]   88-29196
                                                             CIP

Printed in the United States of America

88 89 90 91 92 93 94 / CH / 10 9 8 7 6 5 4 3 2 1

To Franziska, *my wife,*
who told me that all I needed
was a good Silvanus.

Contents

Introduction

His divine power has given us everything we need for life and godliness through our knowledge of him who called us by his own glory and goodness.

2 Peter 1:3

The tourist who has become accustomed to the pictorial splendour of more famous catacombs, may be disappointed by the gloomy, pictureless, Roman catacomb of *Sant'Agnese Outside the Walls*. But the observant eye will be struck by the sight of a fading graffito: red lines engraved in the wall of a damp, narrow alley show the face of a man. To the right, a name appears in Latin and (incomplete because part of it has been broken off) in Greek. The word is PETRVS. This is one of the oldest known portraits of the Apostle Peter but already it bears the characteristics of later frescos, paintings and statues, representing the Apostle's head, half-balding and round, rather than oval.

We do not possess a single description of Peter's physical likeness in the New Testament, nor in any of the early post-Apostolic writings. Failing this, how can we form our picture of the man himself? What do we know about him, about his life and his writings? May we take into account the portrait of his life in the Gospels, in Acts, and in Paul's letter to the Galatians in assembling a jigsaw which will include the two letters attributed to Peter himself? Today, there is no shortage of studies on every possible aspect of Peter's life (as well as some that seem frankly impossible!) but there seems to be little commitment to the genuine historical Peter.

Yet unlike Paul, who has somewhat overshadowed him in the history of Christendom, Peter remains the most tangible, the most humanly understandable of the apostles. It is Peter, not Paul, who stands out most clearly as a character in his own right, with all his strengths and shortcomings.

All four gospels show us his development from the (married) fisherman to the enthusiastic disciple to the terrified Galilean who denies the Lord three times. In the Fourth Gospel he is one of the first to see the empty tomb, and he receives a prophecy from the risen Christ about his own death as a martyr. Acts tell us how he fulfils his role as first among equals with the other apostles in the weeks after Pentecost. And it is Peter whom Paul chooses to consult when he, the 'one untimely born', finally makes his way to Jerusalem.

However, it is at this stage that Paul seems to supplant Peter. In Acts, Luke's attention moves to Paul alone soon after the Jerusalem Council, but Bible readers and even biblical scholars sometimes seem to forget that conveniently tucked away near the end of the New Testament are two invaluable documents purporting to come from Peter himself.

Beyond New Testament times, the so-called Apostolic Fathers and the Church Fathers contain some information about the end of Peter's life, and the wealth of apocryphal writings of the second century, such as the so-called *Acts of Peter*, supply stories about his journeys and his death in Rome. Although their lack of apostolic authority excluded them from the New Testament, they have heavily influenced later church history and literature—a well-known literary example being Henryk Sienkiewicz's novel *Quo Vadis?* (1886), for which the author was awarded the Nobel Prize in 1905. The title and the central episode of this novel are derived directly from the *Acts of Peter*, written in about AD 180.

This book contains a reassessment of the story of Peter in the New Testament and beyond. It is based on a chronological examination of every reference to the disciple, apostle, letter-writer, and martyr in our earliest sources. Thus, even the two letters are not treated as isolated documents, but as integral parts of an historical process, the legacy of which remains important to this very day.

I am not writing as a theologian, but as a literary historian for whom reading and studying the New Testament as literature and history has been the way to a deeper understanding of the historicity of the Christian faith. The following pages are therefore an attempt to do justice to Peter from a distinctive point of view. Controversial doctrinal questions, such as the primacy of the Bishop of Rome in direct succession to Peter, will not be discussed—the scope of the book ends with the literary and archaeological arguments concerning the martyrdom and burial of Peter in Rome; and all later developments of church history can therefore be left to other studies. I hope that this may contribute to a fresh approach to the apostle. After all, such a book should do more than analyse questions of historicity and authenticity. It should also exemplify what C. S. Lewis, in his customary, thought-provoking way, said about literary criticism: that its sole function is to multiply, prolong and safeguard experiences of good reading.

CARSTEN PETER THIEDE
London
St Peter's Day, 1985

ACKNOWLEDGMENTS

While all deficiencies of this book are my own, I would like to express my gratitude for his invaluable help to Peter Cousins, Editorial Director of The Paternoster Press, and to my parish, St Margaret's, Putney, whose spiritual encouragement was a source of strength at a time when the writing of this book limited my contribution as a Reader.

I

Peter in the Gospels

'And I tell you, you are Peter'

CHAPTER ONE

Background and Calling

I

What are our sources for the life and career of Peter within the New Testament? On the face of it, they are the four Gospels, Acts, 1 Corinthians, Galatians, and 1 and 2 Peter. With varying exhaustiveness, the Gospels portray the period from his call to the first resurrection appearances. Acts takes up the thread where the Gospel of Luke has left it, with the account of Christ's ascension as witnessed by Peter, depicts selected events up to the assembly of the apostles in Jerusalem (the so-called Apostolic Council) and gives no fewer than seven of Peter's speeches. 1 Corinthians tells us of his influence in Corinth, his wife as his travel companion, and his pre-eminence as a witness to the resurrection. Galatians reports Paul's fact-finding visit to Peter in Jerusalem, the quarrel at Antioch, and the apparent allocation of responsibilities to Peter (ministry to the Jews) and Paul (ministry to the Gentiles). Finally, 1 and 2 Peter present themselves as letters written by the Apostle himself, documents from the last years of his life.

For all their omissions—since none of these sources claims to be or approaches being a biography of Peter—the nine documents mentioned above would seem to offer an enviable wealth of contemporary information. 'Contemporary'? The mere suggestion would be rejected by a majority of modern New Testament scholars. Paul's letters, written in the mid-fifties, are regarded as the only reliable sources, while Mark's Gospel may have been written around AD 70, just after Peter's death, and the other three Gospels and Acts belong to the eighties and to the end of the century, while 1 and 2 Peter are late and post-Petrine, with 2 Peter possibly as late as the middle of the second century. This at any rate is the impression given by the 'average' New Testament introduction.

Further investigation shows that the picture is rather more complex. Sweeping statements about 'liberal' scholarship on the one hand and 'conservative' scholarship on the other are no longer appropriate. The evidence will have to be considered in due course. For the purposes of this chapter, however, which deals with the Gospels, a single question needs to be answered at the outset: is it advisable to harmonize all the different (and sometimes apparently discordant) Gospel accounts into one 'story of Peter' according to the four evangelists, as though the existence of four independent Gospels was no more than an accident of history? Or is there good reason for choosing one Gospel as the historical yardstick and starting point?

Such a Gospel exists: it is Mark. Two arguments carry weight in its favour: practically all the fathers of the church who discuss Mark's Gospel link it directly with Peter's preaching. In addition, there is strong evidence from the contents of the Gospel and from its manuscript tradition that Mark's was the first Gospel to be written and that it even precedes the letters of Paul.

The close connection between Peter and Mark's Gospel is witnessed to, with variations of detail, by Papias, Justin Martyr, Irenaeus, Origen, Clement of Alexandria, Eusebius, Jerome and the 'Anti-Marcionite Prologue'.[1] Within the New Testament itself, there may be an allusion to the Petrine authority underlying the Gospel in 2 Peter 1:15, a context first noted by Irenaeus.[2]

These sources all assume that the gospel was written before the watershed of AD 70, the year of the destruction of Jerusalem. If it was written in Peter's lifetime, a date in the late sixties must be the latest possible one. Furthermore, recent research has pointed towards a date before AD 50: the discovery and identification of a papyrus fragment in Qumran Cave 7, containing Mark 6:52–53, papyrologically datable to the period prior to AD 50 (and *archaeologically* no later than AD 68, when the Qumran caves were sealed), can now be said to be safely substantiated.[3] And quite apart from the fact that the destruction of Jerusalem in AD 70 is not even hinted at, the gospel contains further internal evidence that corroborates the witness of the Qumran papyrus to its early date.[4] In brief, then, the Gospel according to St. Mark is our earliest source for the first half of Peter's career, and its historical value is increased by the connection between the writer and the Apostle himself. We shall therefore follow the account of Mark, consulting the other three gospels for additional evidence whenever necessary. The intrinsic value of Matthew, Luke and John is evident: Matthew and John apparently draw upon first-hand material like Luke, the self-confessed historian, who must be taken into account since later we must approach the second half (Acts) of his monumental history (Luke-Acts), in the light of the first half. These three supplement the carefully-wrought sparsity of detail in Mark.[5] Wherever possible we shall in addition consider evidence from archaeology and non-biblical literary sources.

II

We do not know when Peter was born. In view of his death under Nero in the late sixties, and the fact that he was running a fishing business when Jesus met him, we may assume that he was then in his early thirties, born, like Jesus, some time before the turn of the century. The tradition whereby artists portray Peter the disciple as a stout, half-balding, elderly man clearly reflects the influence of his later apostolic authority.[6]

He was a native of Galilee, and never lost his regional roots—so much so, in fact, that the people standing near Peter in the High Priest's courtyard after the arrest of Jesus recognised him as a Galilean from his accent (Mk. 14:70, Mt. 26:73, Lk. 22:59). It is John who specifies his origin in Galilee, saying that Peter, like his brother Andrew, was from the town of Bethsaida (Jn. 1:44). Traces of this locality are only now being rediscovered. However, the village had even been raised to the status of a city by the Tetrarch Philip between 4 and 2 BC, as we can gather from the *Jewish Antiquities* of the historian Flavius Josephus, a comprehensive study published in c.AD 93/4.[7] If Josephus' account is correct (and there is no reason to doubt it), Bethsaida, called 'Julias' by

the Tetrarch, may have been situated on a hill now known as
'et-Tell', to the east of the confluence of the river Jordan with the
Sea of Galilee.[8] It must have been a place of some importance, or
Philip would not have raised it to the status of city, although its
original name means quite simply 'house of fishing'. As Peter had
already left Bethsaida for Capharnaum when we join him in the
Gospel of Mark (1:21, 29), the city would be only of marginal
interest to us were it not for the fact that Peter was brought up
and educated there and that we shall understand his educational
and cultural background much better if we look at life and society
in the area of Bethsaida during the first quarter of the first
century. For too long, it has been asserted that Galilee was a
cultural backwater and that someone like Peter could not possibly
have written the elaborate Greek of the first epistle that bears his
name. Even Peter's antagonists in Jerusalem were deeply preju-
diced against his origins, and indeed against those of Jesus
himself: cf Acts 4:13, Jn. 7:41, 52, Jn. 1:46.

The area of Ituraea and Trachonitis (Lk. 3:1) had been inherited
by the tetrarch Philip after the death of his father, Herod the
Great, in 4 AD. The area lay to the north-east of Galilee proper,
and Caesarea Philippi, established by Philip himself, was its
capital. Bethsaida, at the head of the Sea of Galilee, was the last
city in his territory for the traveller going west; Capharnaum was
just within the territory of his brother, Herod Antipas. Philip,
'reckoned the best of the Herodian rulers',[9] later became husband
of the notorious Salome, the daughter of Herodias, who had
asked for the head of John the Baptist (Mk. 6:21–25).[10]

Philip was a Hellenizer and he furthered Graeco-Roman culture
wherever he could. His territory contained a mixed Greek- and
Aramaic-speaking population, who lived in an international
atmosphere resulting from the presence of important trade
routes, connecting Damascus in the north-east with Tyre in the
north-west, and the 'Decapolis' to the south of the Sea of Galilee.
The area was marked by cultural cross-fertilisation and multilingualism. The north-western shore of the Sea of Galilee was on
the so-called 'Via Maris', or Way of the Sea, an important caravan
route from Damascus to Caesarea in Samaria, mentioned as early
as the time of Isaiah (9:1).

We should not underestimate the importance of such circumstantial evidence. An active knowledge of Greek would have been
obligatory for people like Peter and his co-workers, Andrew,

James and John (Mk. 1:16; Lk. 5:10), who were involved in the fishing industry and trade. They would have heard Peter speaking Greek from childhood days, and refined their linguistic abilities as soon as they had chosen their trade. The hellenistic element in their immediate surroundings is obvious even from their names: Peter's original name, Simon, is Greek with an Aramaic derivative (Symeon—Acts 15:14, 2 Pet. 1:1) and is documented in literature as early as 423 BC, in Aristophanes' comedy *Clouds*.[11] The name of his brother, Andrew, is entirely Greek, and so is Philip, the name of their fellow disciple from Bethsaida (Jn. 1:44, 12:20–22). Apparently, their parents had absorbed enough hellenistic influence to find it quite natural to give their sons non-Aramaic names.

There is in fact ample evidence of Greek in Jewish usage from rabbinical sources of the first century,[12] and both Jesus and his disciples communicated with Greek-speaking people. Our sources mention the Syrian Phoenician woman in Mk. 7:26, a conversation with Pilate in the absence of an interpreter (Mk. 15:2–5), the group of Grecian Jews among the disciples in Acts 6:1, and Peter's dialogue with the centurion Cornelius in Acts 10:25–27—and these are only four examples. Not far from Bethsaida and Capharnaum, on the south-eastern shore of the Sea of Galilee was Hippos, a place renowned for its hellenistic culture, and Gadara, some seven miles further south, had been connected with Greek literature and philosophy since the time of the satirist Menippus, who was born there in the first half of the third century BC.[13] The non-Jewish element in the whole region must have been strong enough since both Isaiah (9:1) and Matthew (4:15) call it 'Galilee of the Gentiles'.

Thus the area in which Peter was brought up and set up business had been thoroughly permeated by Greek language and culture for several centuries, and all strata of society had been influenced by it. He was fluent in Greek—much more so than, say, the average Greek Common Market official today would be in English. With his mother tongue, Aramaic, and Hebrew, the liturgical language of the synagogue and the synagogical elementary school, also at his disposal,[14] Peter must have come close to being what we might call orally trilingual. And it is not unlikely that he would have picked up a phrase or two of Latin from lower-ranking, non-Greek-speaking Roman soldiers in the vicinity and among his customers.[15]

Apart from these linguistic abilities, his educational upbringing would have been similar to that enjoyed by any Jew who had attended elementary school, usually until the age of fourteen: reading, writing and effective memorization techniques were its common features.[16]

III

According to Mark 1:16, Jesus called Peter and Andrew as his first disciples on the shores of the Sea of Galilee and soon afterwards (1:19) called a second pair of brothers, James and John, the sons of Zebedee. All four had been going about their business, fishing, but they did not hesitate for a moment to follow him. Such behaviour strikes us as strange, to say the least, for hardworking, propertied men.[17] So we are not surprised to discover evidence of their earlier acquaintance with Jesus and experience of his authority. Mark passes over this initial encounter, which is mentioned by John (1:35–42), and took place at Bethany 'on the other side of the Jordan' (1:28). Here we find two disciples of John the Baptist who hear him describe Jesus as 'the Lamb of God' (1:36) and decide to follow him: one of them is identified by name as Andrew, Peter's brother.[18] Peter himself does not seem to have been a disciple of the Baptist. Like Jesus himself, Peter was near by, probably as a feast-day pilgrim returning from the Passover festivities in Jerusalem together with Philip and Nathanael.[19] Andrew, at any rate, felt moved to go and find his brother and tell him what they had heard from the Baptist (1:41).[20]

The importance of personal acquaintance with Jesus at the time when he was with John the Baptist is aptly recalled in Acts 1:21–22: the new twelfth apostle, to be chosen as the successor of Judas Iscariot, has to be a man who had been with the disciples from the time of John's baptism. It is none other than Peter himself who pronounces this requirement in his first speech related in Acts.

Luke thus indirectly confirms the account of John. In the Gospel itself, he does not mention the meeting near Bethany, but he records the calling of the first disciples by the Sea of Galilee in 5:1–11,[21] adding, in the story of the miraculous catch of fish, some colour and detail to Mark's terse account. Jesus asks Peter to put out a little from the shore so that he may preach to the crowd who had assembled around him, overlooking his audience. He cannot have been very far from the shore: following the contemporary practice of Jewish teachers, he sits down, and it is unlikely that he would have shouted his message. Thus we may safely assume it

protest but voluntary submission

was a windless morning—otherwise Peter would have found it difficult to keep the boat at rest and in a more or less fixed position.

His preaching ended, Jesus asks Peter to put out into deep water and to let down the nets for a catch (5:4). Peter's reaction to this request comprises what are chronologically his first words in the gospels, and already two of his characteristics are revealed: spontaneous protest and voluntary submission under the authority of Jesus. 'Master,' he says, 'we have worked hard all night and haven't caught anything. But because you say so, I will let down the nets.'[22] This action is all the more remarkable since fishing in deep water during daytime is normally unproductive.[23] Peter's obedience is duly rewarded: he and his men catch such a large number of fish that their nets begin to break, and even the boat of James and John, called to their assistance, is filled to sinking-point. It requires little imagination to understand that these fishermen must have been surprised if not frightened. Such an event runs counter to human expectations and to professional experience. Peter, in the second of his spontaneous reactions, falls on his knees. He realises the extraordinary powers of Jesus, calls him 'Lord', and, conscious of his sinfulness, asks him to 'go away'.[24] Jesus, however, calms Peter and gives him his missionary title: he is to become a 'fisher of men' (5:10; cf. Mt. 4:19). Peter and his partners pull their boats up on shore, leave everything behind them, and follow him (5:11).

Such is the story of Peter's call. He meets Jesus at Passover time near Bethany, where his brother Andrew, a follower of John the Baptist, introduces them to each other. Jesus asks them, as well as John, the son of Zebedee, Philip and Nathanael, to go with him to Galilee. Once there he spends some time preaching on his own and contacts the group from Bethany. When he reaches Caphar-naum, where they have established their fishing business, Peter helps him to preach to the crowd from his boat, experiences the miraculous catch of fish, and is called upon to become a fisher of men. He and his partners, Andrew, James and John (and probably Philip and Nathanael as well) decide to resign from their jobs and become the first disciples of the wandering preacher, Jesus of Nazareth.

IV

For Peter at least, the decision to follow Jesus did not imply an immediate and total tearing-up of his roots. He still had his own house, where he lived with his brother Andrew, his own wife and his mother-in-law (Mk. 1:29–30). It is true that his wife is not mentioned explicitly, but the hypothesis that he may have been a widower is ruled out by 1 Cor. 9:5, where Paul speaks of Peter as taking his wife with him on his journeys during his (later) apostolic ministry. Peter's household appear in the narrative almost as a matter of course. Jesus and some of the disciples went there for supper after service in the synagogue on the Sabbath.[25] Peter's mother-in-law was in bed with a fever, the brothers told Jesus about her illness, he went to her, and healed her, taking her by the hand and helping her up. She was cured immediately and began to prepare and serve supper. Mark's economical account, repeated by Matthew (8:14–15), is modified by Luke in two respects. First, Luke, a doctor, (Col. 4:14), uses the technical term *megas* for the fever and explains that Jesus had to bend over the woman, since she was lying down, probably on a pallet on the ground.[26] Second, Luke shifts the timing of the event: according to him, it happened before the calling of the disciples, not afterwards (4:38, 39). Luke telescopes events in order to recount a typical day of Jesus' work at Capharnaum, his teaching at the synagogue, the exorcism of an evil spirit and the healing of Peter's mother, ending with the healing of the sick in the evening (4:40–41).

In itself, this is a traditional and accepted technique: in respect of Peter, it has the disadvantage that Peter's mother-in-law appears on the scene before the apostle himself is properly introduced.

Peter's house soon became a centre of activity. 'The whole town gathered at the door', Mark tells us (1:33), 'and Jesus healed many who had various diseases.' Jesus, Peter and the other disciples left Capharnaum the next morning so that Jesus could preach in the neighbouring villages (1:38), but they returned a few days later (2:1), and again Peter's house became the base for Jesus' ministry. 'So many gathered that there was no room left, not even outside the door, and he preached the word to them' (2:2). The roof of the house was temporarily damaged when friends of a paralysed man found the crowd barring the way to Jesus and were forced to lower the invalid down through the tiles, which had been hastily removed for the purpose (Mk. 2:2–5; Lk. 5:18–20). The incident tells us something about the architecture of Peter's house. It cannot have been too small, otherwise Jesus, Peter and his relatives and a crowd of 'many' (Mk. 2:2) could not have been accommodated. It cannot have been too high—it was probably a single storey house—or the operation of lowering the paralytic would have been unduly perilous. The roof cannot have been very solid, unless we imagine the men dug their way through it.

Spacious, but simple—this is the idea conveyed by Mark's description; and we can gather further archaeological evidence from a recent discovery at Capharnaum, for it seems that Peter's house has been identified.

Extant literary tradition for the exact site goes back as far as c.381 AD, when the Spanish nun Egeria (Aetheria) described a Christian church in Capharnaum into which the walls of Peter's house had been incorporated. The description occurs in the course of one of the oldest known accounts of a pilgrimage to the Holy Land, an invaluable source concerning what was known about biblical sites during the fourth century.[27] The correctness of her description was established by V. Corbo in 1968.[28] An indisputable identification of the house as belonging to Peter, in the sense that one might have found his name-plate on the door, was and continues to be impossible, but it is evident from the discoveries and details such as a floor renewed several times and a disproportionate number of oil lamps, both dating from the second half of the first century, and also from slightly later fragments or ornaments and inscriptions, that the house received special attention at a very early stage; and it is the only one in Capharnaum to be used—and later on developed—in such a remarkable way. No other house than this, one where Jesus himself had lived and preached, could have claimed such preferential treatment from the first to at least the sixth century, when we find an Italian 'Pilgrim of Piacenza' reporting that he 'came to Capharnaum to the house of St. Peter, which is now a basilica.'[29]

Jesus seems to have settled in Capharnaum, and indeed in Peter's house, for some time (Matt. 4:13, and, as quoted above, Mk. 1:29, 2:1; also 3:20, 9:33; probably also Matt. 9:28–31, 17:25–27). It was the base for his local teaching, to which he would return from the villages in the vicinity time and again. And it was the starting-point for him and his disciples when they finally went south, leaving their homes behind them for good. (Mk. 10:1, 28).

CHAPTER TWO

The Moulding of the Rock

*closer circle
of three
Peter, James &
John*

I

From the moment when Jesus had assembled the twelve disciples until his arrest at Gethsemane, he, Peter and the others formed a close-knit community. They can be seen as a homogeneous group under the authority of one undisputed leader. There are, however, several instances where Peter is singled out, either with some of the others (mostly in the closer circle of the 'three', with John and James) or on his own. And it is the evidence of these passages which we have to consider in our examination of the further career of the man whose house in Capharnaum had been their common starting point.

Even if we did not have any such passages, the three lists of disciples in the synoptic gospels would be indicative enough of Peter's leading role: Mark (3:13–19), Matthew (10:1–4) and Luke (6:12–16) all mention Peter first. Needless to say, they were written with the benefit of hindsight, reflecting therefore the position Peter was to assume during Jesus' ministry and after the Ascension, but their unanimity is in itself a convincing first argument for the reliability of the tradition: there was obviously nothing in the accessible eye-witness accounts and written sources (leaving aside here the question if, among the synoptics,

Matthew could have been an eyewitness) to contradict Peter's pride of place even at this early stage.

It is interesting to note that Matthew and Luke call him Simon, giving Petros, Peter, as his by-name, whereas Mark, the first evangelist, is as it were already one step ahead in his retrospective report, calling him Peter and only then, in grammatically awkward Greek, explaining that this was the (hitherto unmentioned) by-name given to Simon by Jesus. One is almost led to assume that Mark, writing under the long-lasting influence of Peter himself, found it difficult to revert to his mentor's original name. Luke, of course, careful historian that he was, is unobtrusively consistent: having described him as 'Simon whom he named Peter' in 6:14, he simply calls him 'Peter' when he repeats the list in Part Two of his account, Acts (1:13): by then, his 'title-name' had become so natural, that it could be used as the unexplained subtitle.[30]

With Peter as titular head of the twelve disciples, it is not surprising to see him as their representative or spokesman, or indeed as the first of the 'three', even before his confession of faith in Jesus as the Messiah. There are in fact four such incidents. Three of them are of merely circumstantial importance, one each in Mark, Matthew and Luke. The fourth, however, is remarkable for several reasons.

When Jesus walks on the water, an event reported by Mark (6:45–52), Matthew (14:22–33) and John (6:16–21), Matthew underlines Peter's role by adding a highly significant sequence in 14:28–33: Peter challenges Jesus to bestow on him some of his own supernatural power so that he could come to the Lord over the water. This event, inspiring as it has been to artists and poets because of its powerful imagery, has also given rise to questions. Neither John nor Mark mentions it, and whereas John is never greatly interested in Peter's priority anyway, the omission in Mark seems noteworthy. Can the story be authentic? And if so, why is it left to Matthew alone?

There is no doubt about its textual tradition: the passage is or was included in all known manuscripts and codices and its language and style do not betray any of the tell-tale signs of later additions.[31] In other words, it was there from the beginning of the textual tradition of the Gospel as we know it. When this tradition began is of course a different question, but whatever one's position in this debate, it must of necessity remain a matter of speculation. All one can safely say without going into the

Peter walking on water

details of possible redaction, its probability or improbability, is this: the author of this gospel wanted the sequence to be where it still is, and he did so with stylistic and formal consistency. These are the literary facts. The next step must be an assumption which one should not describe as a link in a chain of evidence, but as a possibility in accordance with patristic opinion, seeing Matthew as an eye-witness.[32] The question, how could the incident of Peter trying to walk on the water be depicted by Matthew in such vivid detail, would thus be answered simply: because he was in the boat himself. And even if he was not, the evangelist could and would have asked those who were. Being an eye-witness of an event does not, as we know from many modern courtroom experiences, and indeed from secular historians to this day, necessitate the actual telling of what one has seen. John—assuming again that he, too, was an eye-witness[33]—breaks off before he would have had to tell the story and reserves for himself the later event on Lake Tiberias after the Resurrection (21:4–8). Peter himself does not seem to have placed much emphasis on it, either: we do not find it in Mark, nor in any of the other documents related to his authority. In view of his reticence to stress his foolhardy achievements, this omission is not difficult to understand. The story would not have served a constructive purpose in Mark's gospel which attempts rather to play down his exploits in strength or weakness of faith, preferring instead a sober account based on a balanced amount of information.

Matthew, on the other hand, is interested in the scene not least because it helps him to prepare the reader for Peter's confession of faith two chapters further on. What Luke had done in 5:8–11 (showing Peter as an impulsive human being, everything but a self-assured 'rock', in the account of the miraculous catch of fish) Matthew achieves with another event, also taking place in and near a boat on the sea of Galilee.

Peter is not simply challenging Jesus to prove that he can communicate power. He is also challenging his own perseverance in faith. Our English versions of his first sentence might lead us to presume that Peter wants corroborative evidence: 'Lord, if it is you . . .'. This is not quite what the Greek text implies. Peter knows that it is Jesus. He does not know for sure yet that Jesus is the Messiah—the address, *Kyrie*, is, at this stage, nothing but a conventional courtesy, 'Sir' rather than 'Lord' (compare, for example, even in translation, Matthew 5:33 with 8:6 and our

Peter walking on water

present passage), a form of address given to anyone in authority. But the *ei* in the Greek, conventionally rendered 'if', comes closer to 'since': 'Sir, since it is you, tell me to come to you over the water.'[34] In other words, Peter accepts the privileged position of Jesus and, with characteristic eagerness, wants a share in it.

Jesus takes him at his word, Peter leaves the boat, and he does indeed for a brief moment experience the sensation of walking on the water.[35] It is a fleeting foretaste of things to come—after the Resurrection, Peter, well-grounded in his faith, would perform miracles of a much more impressive nature—but he is clearly not stable enough yet, his concentration slips, instead of keeping his mind faithfully fixed on Jesus, he lets it wander off into an all too natural fear of the fierce wind around him. Not that he had not noticed the wind before: he knew only too well that it was there (v. 24). He was not totally lacking in faith: challenging Jesus and then stepping down from the boat were, after all, expressions of implicit faith. In trying to find out how far Jesus' powers would stretch, he was indeed a man of faith, even if his faith was, as Jesus tells him frankly, little (v. 31). Little, but nonetheless present, even after the catastrophe: the sinking Peter cries to Jesus for help—and how could Jesus help him if he was not powerful enough to do so? What is left of Peter's faith is still strong enough to overcome his fears—he realises that it was his own failure, not any weakness on Jesus' side, that had made him sink, and his cry for help is as much an admission of his shortcomings as a plea for forgiveness.

It was a salutary experience, not only for Peter, who received proof both of the power of Jesus and of his own inadequacy without an undivided, undoubting reliance on this power, but also for the disciples, who, having watched the experience of their spokesman, drew a new conclusion from it: falling at the feet of Jesus, they proclaim him Son of God in unison for the first time.[36] Matthew does not give us Jesus' reaction—it may well be that there was none, as unlike the later scene of Peter's own and much more momentous confession, the proclamation was unsolicited, and therefore, in a certain sense, inopportune.

There is no other event of even remotely similar importance until the evangelists reach Peter's confession itself. Only three times is he singled out by name: twice before the walking on the water (Luke 8:45, Mark 5:37), and once soon afterwards (Matthew 15:15). The first two are both in the same context: Jesus is on his

[handwritten: " inner circle " first mentioned]

way to resuscitate the daughter of Jairus when the edge of his
cloak is touched by a woman who has been bleeding for twelve
years and whose bleeding stops the very instant she touches the
cloak. Jesus, noticing that power to heal has gone out from him,
demands to be told who has touched him. Everyone denies it, but
Luke has Peter offering a common-sense explanation: 'Master,
the people are crowding and pressing around you.' Matthew
does not include this detail in his account of the scene; Mark does
so (5:30–32), but instead of naming Peter, he quotes 'the disciples'
as offering this explanation. This is entirely consistent with his
reticence concerning Peter's role, and one should not read too
much into Luke's identification, either: it is a simple case of *pars
pro toto*, of substituting the spokesman for the whole group. That
this is so is underlined by the textual tradition of the passage:
a number of important witnesses, such as the Codex Sinaiticus,
the Codex Alexandrinus, Latin, Syriac and Bohairic versions, give
'and those who were with him' after Peter's name.[37] Whatever
the original form may be, neither reading shows more than that
Luke takes Peter's position as the disciples' spokesman seriously
enough to put him first when his sources enable him to do so.

It is Mark's turn to name Peter in the same context, soon after
the healing of the woman, when he points out (5:37) that it was
only Peter, James, and John who were allowed to accompany
Jesus to the house of Jairus itself. This is noteworthy because it is
the first, even if the least important, of the scenes where the
'inner circle' of the three is mentioned. *[handwritten: inner circle]*

The last pre-confession passage with Peter, Matthew 15:15,
is again a straightforward example of his role as spokesman.
On behalf of the others ('Explain this parable to us!') he asks for
elucidation, and Jesus obliges, somewhat exasperated by their
slowness ('Are you still so dull?'), explaining what he meant by
talking about the things that go *into* a man's mouth but do not
make him unclean, and those that come *out* of his mouth and
make him unclean.

In the events following the appointment of the Twelve and
leading up to Peter's confession of Christ, Peter is represented in
all three of his pre-resurrection roles: as the disciples' spokesman,
as one of the three, and as the disciple selected for a special
experience and a special position. All these elements are as yet
embryonic; they gain in weight as soon as Peter makes the
decisive step to proclaim his faith in Jesus as the Messiah.

II

We have gleaned fragments of complementary information from all four evangelists. Even where they differ in detail or in the scope of events depicted (as historical accounts tend to do even today), they never contradict each other. It is the next incident in Peter's career which makes this intrinsic agreement even more evident: his confession of Jesus as the Messiah.

Jesus and the disciples are on their way to the villages around Caesarea Philippi, the capital of the Tetrarch Philip's territory (see above, p. 20). The precise setting is of passing interest; Luke (9:18–21) does not mention it. (John's case is quite different; see below p. 43). Being near the capital of a semi-pagan territory when the question about the true identity of Jesus is asked, has of course certain implications. It is intended to settle the matter for the disciples soon enough after their first telling experiences with Jesus, but not too soon before the all-important journey south. They have seen enough to form an opinion, but they have not yet witnessed the conflict-ridden, bewildering scenes near and in Jerusalem. And it shows that hellenized, gentile surroundings are not inimical to the question of his being the Christ—an insight the disciples must have shared, at the latest, when they began their post-resurrection mission.[38] Putting ourselves for a moment in the shoes of someone prone to judging authenticity from the point of view of historical plausibility, we realise that no setting looks more plausible than the one reported by Mark (8:27 f.) and Matthew (16:13 f.).

Why was Peter's confession so important, and what precisely did happen? In Mark's account, the development of the discussion is straightforward enough. Jesus asks the direct question, 'Who do people say I am?' At first this seems merely rhetorical, as Jesus must himself have had a fair idea of what people were saying, but it also confirms that the disciples had independent contacts with the people and had been recognized as followers of Jesus on the preaching tour on which he had sent them some time before (Mk. 6:7–13). The result of this 'poll' among the villagers of Galilee is unsurprising: it is the repetition of popular opinion given in Mk. 6:14–15, where rumours had reached Herod Antipas that Jesus was seen as a risen John the Baptist, or as Elijah, or as one of the prophets 'of long ago'. Strictly speaking, both passages imply that Jesus was seen quite simply as a prophet and that opinion differed only about which prophet he was. It is, however, no accident that John the Baptist and Elijah are singled out by name: John was a forerunner of Jesus by his own admission (Mk. 1:7–8), and Elijah had been regarded as the prophet who would return to announce the Day of the Lord ever since the time of Malachi (Matt. 4:5), i.e. the mid-fifth century BC. For Jews thinking in terms of traditional teaching this was not surprising—and yet it is far less than what 'the evil spirits' had realised immediately when Jesus had begun to act against them (Mk. 1:24, 3:11, 5:7). Jesus' first question is nothing but a prelude to the decisive probing of the faith and insight of the disciples: 'But what about you? Who do you say I am?'

This time we hear only one answer: Peter speaks up, and he declares: 'You are the Christ!'[39] Is he speaking for himself, or is he echoing the view shared by the whole group? Mark is not specific here, but the context suggests that Jesus accepts the declaration as coming from all twelve: 'Jesus warned *them* not to tell anyone about him.' Nonetheless, the contrast between the answers to the two questions must be taken into account: the first question is answered by 'them' (v. 28), the second by Peter alone.

In all probability, and even though everyone present was fluent in Greek and the group was moving about in a hellenized environment, the conversation took place not in Greek, but in Aramaic, their common native language. Peter therefore did not pronounce Jesus 'the Christ', but 'the Messiah'. The two words were synonymous and had been so at least since the Greek Septuagint translated 'Messiah' by 'Christ' (Ps. 2:2 *et al.*) in the third century BC. By Peter's time, the term had acquired a general meaning—a Messiah or Christ was someone sent by God in the last days. More specifically, he was a king, a descendant of David, who would bring peace and divine justice to his people—seemingly not in metaphorical, 'heavenly' sense, but as a ruler on earth. (See Jer. 23:5–6, Is. 55:3–5, Ps. 110:1, 2 Sa. 7:11–16, *et al.*)[40] The Messiah, literally 'the anointed one', was expected to fulfil less a spiritual than a political role. This, of course, did not necessarily follow from the passages concerned—the reverse could be true, as well. If Jesus was sent by God to be a non-political, un-earthly Messiah, one whose kingdom was in the heavens, neither Peter nor any other contemporary Jew could be expected to realise it immediately. Jesus acknowledges Peter's confession—but Peter's and the disciples' understanding of his

Messiahship is far from complete, and he has to warn them 'not to tell anyone about him' (8:30).

This warning leads to a sequence of teaching: Jesus explains his role and predicts his death and resurrection (8:31–32).[41] Peter's reaction is that of an independent, if confused, mind, not at any rate that of a mere spokesman: he takes Jesus aside and begins to 'rebuke' him (v. 32). This is strong language—Jesus himself had rebuked the demons (1:25 and 3:12), and the same Greek work is used in all three passages. The word implies drastic action and is only occasionally used more positively, as in Luke 17:3 where frank, helpful admonition rather than blatant scolding seems to be the sense. How then can Peter 'rebuke' Jesus? For him, a suffering Messiah was a contradiction in terms, incompatible with anything he had been brought up to expect, and his spontaneous reaction must have been one of indignant surprise—having realized that Jesus was sent by God, he now feels constrained to remind him of his obligations, and as this was a decisive moment, we cannot expect Peter to have minced his words. He must have been desperate to make sure that nothing would go wrong—and so deeply rooted was he in the traditional view of the victorious royal Messiah that this attitude reappears in the scene on Gethsemane, where he draws his sword in order to defend Jesus and to evoke the assistance of the heavenly hosts.[42]

Jesus in turn realizes the danger of the situation. His fuller (and indeed true) understanding of his messianic role, supported by far-from-unknown prophecies (Is. 53:4–12, Ps. 22, *et al.*), and not excluding glory and victory, even though of a different, non-political kind (Is. 52:13–15, Ho. 6:1–6, Ps. 110, *et al.*), was under attack by his closest companions, and above all by Peter, whom he had already named Petros, Rock, on the mountain where he appointed the Twelve.[43] The man chosen for a leading role, the consequences of which were not yet fully revealed to him, could not be allowed to perpetrate an incomplete and thus falsifying idea of the Messiah. Peter's attempt to rebuke him is denounced in the strongest possible terms by Jesus, who calls him 'Satan': 'But when Jesus turned and looked at his disciples, he rebuked Peter. "Out of my sight, Satan!" he said. "You do not have in mind the things of God, but the things of men" ' (8:33).

It is probable that the other disciples had witnessed Peter's attack; Jesus had no choice but to reprimand him in front of them. The rendering of his words in the NIV conveys only one of the two possible meanings. The AV and the RSV are closer to the Greek: 'Get (thee) behind me, Satan!'—and this *could* indeed mean that Jesus expects Peter to go away, to go out of his sight. But the Greek word *opisō* is there in the text, and it signifies quite literally 'behind' or 'after'. Mark's use of the word is consistent throughout the gospel: four times he uses it with the genitive personal pronoun (1:17,20; 8:34, and here in 8:33), and in the other three it clearly means to 'follow after', i.e. after Jesus, in the sense of discipleship. There is no apparent reason why the fourth occurrence, our passage, 8:33, should be different. Seen together with the preceding word, *hypagō*, 'to go slowly away', 'to withdraw oneself' (cf. Mk. 6:31, 33, 7:29, 10:52 etc.), it probably means something like 'go and think about what you have said and *do* follow me as a believing disciple.'[44]

Even though this comes closest to what the Greek text implies, it does not yet explain why Jesus calls Peter 'Satan'. The reason, again, lies in the unique fullness of Jesus' own definition of his Messiahship: to distract from this, to try and reverse the declaration of the suffering Christ, is temptation; and temptation, as Jesus knew only too well (Mk. 1:12, Mt. 4:1–11, Lk. 4:1–13), was satanic. Peter is the tempter, and in this he becomes, for a moment, the mouthpiece of Satan. He does not protest against the charge. He realizes that he has gone too far in his attempt to 'persuade' Jesus, and we find a sign of his insight in Satan's workings, based on his own experience, some time after the Resurrection, in Acts 5:3, where he accuses Ananias: 'Ananias, how is it that Satan has so filled your heart that you have lied to the Holy Spirit . . .?'[45]

In the ensuing scene, Jesus takes up the thread of his explanation of the Messianic glory and the cost of discipleship, and he addresses not only the Twelve, but 'the crowd', the wider circle of followers, indicating that his message applied to everyone who wishes to be or to become a believer. But what about Peter's position in the aftermath of this event? Has he lost influence or stature? Has it in fact been an attempt by two of the evangelists (Matthew follows Mark here, Mt. 16:23) to cut him down to size by stressing the embarrassment of the situation?

The contrary appears to be the case: Peter has grown in a very special way, and the uniqueness of his position among the disciples is underlined once again. This does not become obvious immediately for Mark's gospel—but it becomes quite plausible if we keep in mind that Mark wrote in Rome under the influence of Peter's teaching. Thus the inclusion of the scene points towards Peter's matured, humble reflection upon the event (all the more so as he omits the saying about the rock and the keys of the kingdom of heaven found in Mt. 16:17–19), and towards a secured apostolic authority in the mid-first century that would be enhanced, not belittled, by the admission of earlier weakness. A trace of this attitude towards the non-detrimental fallibility of the apostles in general can be found in the early Epistle of Barnabas, written c. AD 75.[46] 'When he (Jesus) selected his apostles, who were to proclaim his gospel and who were lawless beyond all sin, so that he could show that he had come to call not the just ones, but the sinners, he thus revealed that he was the Son of God. For if he had not come in the flesh, men could not possibly have been saved in his sight' (5:9).

The rhetorical exaggeration of Barnabas' description, 'lawless beyond all sin', explicable as it is against the background of Judaeo-Christian thinking, conveys a simple but important message: none of the apostles (and that includes Peter) was chosen for any existing superhuman qualities; they were chosen for their potential in spite of their recurring sinfulness; they were chosen to show to everyone, to this very day, that special gifts of insight and sanctity are no prerequisites for a follower of Jesus; and they were chosen to highlight Jesus' unlimited power to forgive, to heal and to bring about profound and lasting change.[47] The early Christians, and this includes the apostles and their pupils, could therefore look to Peter and his experience as a kind of model—Peter was the *petros*, the rock, not because of his strengths, but in spite of his weakness, 'deputizing' for the weakness of them all.

III

Mark's account is supplemented by Matthew in one important point. He includes the answer of Jesus to Peter's confession, the famous passage where he explains what the by-name 'Peter' signifies and what authority would be linked with it: 'Blessed are you, Simon son of Jonah, for this was not revealed to you by man, but by my father in heaven. And I tell you that you are Peter, and on this rock I will build my church, and the gates of Hades will not overcome it. I will give you the keys of the kingdom of heaven, and whatever you loose on earth, will be loosed in heaven' (16:17–19).

Matthew's account is peculiar for several reasons. He gives a slightly different wording of the answers to Jesus' two questions: in v. 14 the disciples name Jeremiah as one of the other prophets the people saw Jesus as incarnating;[48] and Peter adds the words 'the Son of the Living God' to 'You are the Christ'. This is quite plausible if seen against the background of 14:33 and could well be the full form of a concise version, given by Mark. But Matthew also appears to imply that Simon receives his by-name only here. He seems to overlook that John the Baptist had realized the true identity of Jesus as the Christ before Peter (Mt. 11:2–3), even if in a tentative, questioning way. And there is talk of the 'church' (*ekklēsia*) which seems extraordinary at this early stage of Jesus' ministry, if one does not accept that Jesus could have known what the later result of his teaching and his life, death and resurrection would be, and if one does not take into account what *ekklēsia* and its Aramaic equivalents meant in Jesus' time. In fact, some interpreters have doubted the authenticity of the scene,[49] while others have maintained that it belongs in a different setting, such as the passion narrative,[50] or the immediate post-resurrection period.[51]

None of the numerous attempts to dislodge this sequence from its present place is even remotely convincing. We have already seen that Peter's confession itself is chronologically plausible precisely at this point (see above p. 32). And as Adolf Schlatter put it, the words, 'You are Peter', never belonged anywhere else but next to, 'You are Christ', and there is no reason to suppose that Matthew creates words of Jesus anywhere.[52]

Statement (Peter) and reply (Jesus) form a unity in parallel: Peter's confession is matched by Jesus' blessing. John the Baptist's tentative understanding had been in need of confirmation (Matt. 11:3); Peter is sure of his knowledge, so sure, in fact, that (as Jesus tells him) it was not revealed to him by man (literally: 'by flesh and blood'), but by Christ's 'Father in Heaven'—a formulation that takes up Peter's confession in the literal sense of its wording.

There is no reason to assume that Matthew, seemingly contradicting Mark (3:16), does not describe Simon by his new name, 'Peter' until this scene. Matthew is careful enough to begin by giving the name as '*Simon* (who is called Peter)' in the early stages, i.e. in the sequence of the calling of the first disciples (4:18) and in the list of the Twelve (10:2), where Jesus acts directly in relation to Peter; but the by-name has been in constant and exclusive use in Matthew's narrative ever since the list of the Twelve, and even once before (8:14, the healing of Peter's mother-in-law). What is more, Jesus does not switch to calling Simon by his new name after the allegedly decisive 'name-giving' in 16:18—there is the remarkable passage at 17:25: 'When *Peter* came into the house, Jesus was the first to speak. "What do you think, *Simon*?" he asked.' We are on safer ground if we assume that Jesus used 'Peter' as Simon's by-name, as his honorary title, and that 16:18 is the scene where this by-name is not given, but explained to him.[53] Whenever it was given to him—and the corroborative evidence of Mark and John points to an earlier date—Peter would have had an inkling of one of its possible meanings even before the revelation of the interpretation put on it by Jesus: he must have known Isaiah 51:1–2, where Abraham is likened to a rock, and he may thus have seen his by-name, as yet unexplained, as a confirmation of his figurehead role among the group of the disciples.[54]

In Mt. 16:18, then, Jesus explains the by-name to Peter with a play on words that works both in Aramaic and in Greek. Kēpā, or *Kephas* in Greek transcription, is in fact the form used by John in 1:42 and several times by Paul (1 Cor. 1:12, 3:22, 9:5, 15:5; Gal. 1:18; 2:9, 11, 14). It means 'rock', and is rendered in Greek by *Petros* (see again John 1:42, where the translation is given by the evangelist himself). The preservation of the original Aramaic in Paul's letters, written in Greek for Greek-speaking readerships, is in itself proof of the authenticity of the naming during the Aramaic-speaking ministry of Jesus; so is John's painstaking accuracy in giving the Aramaic form first, and then translating it for his Greek-speaking readers.[55]

But what was Peter, and indeed every reader of the gospel passage, supposed to make of it? For those acquainted with the community of Qumran a text in the so-called *Community Rule* (also called the *Manual of Discipline*), 1QS 8:6–8, may have been a pointer: those verses speak of the Council of the Community which, in the last days, will be solid like a rock that cannot sway. If the community of believers is compared to a rock-like foundation in this interpretation of Is. 28:16, the differences are still more important than the similarities: the Qumran text likens the community to a rock; Jesus in Mt. 16:18 speaks of *Peter* as the rock on which the community will be built. And Peter himself, in his first letter (2:4–6), when quoting Is. 28:16, does not think of applying the passage to his own position: he sees it as referring to Christ, and through him to every individual Christian.[56]

In other words, whereas the idea of a rock-like foundation was not new in itself, from Abraham (Is. 51:1–2; see n. 54) via Isaiah's prophecy (28:16) to Qumran (1QS 8:6–8), its far-reaching application to an individual, ordinary human being in Jesus' time must have been surprising and challenging. With this interpretation of his by-name, Peter receives a special and lasting authority that is based on the inspiration God had given him (Mt. 16:17) and entirely independent of his human weakness (cf. above p. 36). The rock is therefore not a symbol of what he already is, but of what he *will be*: 'on this rock I *will* build my church.' God had given him the revelation that singled him out, and Jesus acknowledges this by lifting him up to his position of privileged responsibility—and, as we will learn from Luke, he keeps praying for him that he may remain steadfast in the faith and strengthen his brothers (Lk. 22:29–31).[57] Peter, even when he succumbs to satanic temptation, is still saved by the personal intercession of Jesus, and although the immediate context of the passage in Luke is the foretelling of Peter's betrayal, it does implicitly refer to previous (and indeed to future) failures, such as Peter's attempt to dissuade Jesus from following the way of the suffering Messiah which earns him that rebuke for being Satan's mouthpiece.

When Matthew uses the Greek word *ekklēsia* for the community to be built by Jesus on the rock of Peter, he is most certainly not putting a later development of Christian self-organisation back into the earlier gospel context. The *translation* of the word here and in 18:17 as 'church' is perhaps slightly unfortunate and at any rate, Peter himself cannot have understood it thus, in the acquired sense of this term. His idea of *ekklēsia* was the one given in the Old Testament: it was God's congregation, originally the people of Israel, a usage of the Greek word preserved in the New Testament by Stephen in his speech (Acts 7:38) and by the writer of Hebrews (2:12).

For Peter therefore, Jesus did not speak of 'my church', but of 'my *congregation*'—it was the new community to be established by Jesus, through the new covenant, that was meant, and the stress is quite clearly on the possessive pronoun. If we want to go on using 'church' in this passage, we can do so only provided we keep in mind that the meaning of the word as used in that dialogue between Jesus and Peter was quite different from what we have become accustomed to see in it. This does not preclude a measure of development, or the existence of certain structures within this *ekklēsia*, even in New Testament times: Paul in 1 Cor. 12:38 uses the word in the context of a primitive organisational hierarchy. But wherever we look, in Acts (8:3, 15:41, 20:28) and in Paul's own letters (e.g. 1 Cor. 7:17, 14:33, 16:19; and particularly in Rom. 16:5, 16:16), the term refers to the mere body of Christians, the congregation as such. Whatever may have happened to this congregation, and to Peter within it, after the Ascension, in Jerusalem, Antioch, Rome and elsewhere, when Jesus uses the word in Mt. 16:17 it is in a Messianic re-interpretation of the Old Testament concept—a reinterpretation, however, that puts Peter unmistakably in a key position.

'The gates of Hades'[58] will not overcome this foundation. In other words, it will survive anything that can threaten it, including death. This promise, pointing to the future, could have indicated to Peter (and to the others) that the new congregation of Christ would continue even after their own deaths. Christ himself was the guarantor of this promise, as becomes obvious from Rev. 1:18: 'I am the Living One, I was dead, and behold, I am alive for ever and ever! And I hold the keys of death and Hades.' (In his first letter, Peter takes up this promise: cf. 3:19, 21–22. It is also there in his first speech in Jerusalem, Acts 2:27, 31 (see below, p. 44 and n. 62).

More controversial than the preceding promises is the final one, 16:19: 'I will give you the keys of the kingdom of heaven; whatever you bind on earth will be bound in heaven, and whatever you loose on earth will be loosed in heaven.' At first sight, it strikes one as conferring unlimited authority on Peter. The kingdom of heaven is seen as a place (the usage is identical with Mt. 7:21!), for which there are keys, as there are keys for Hades. The latter are owned by the risen Christ (Rev. 1:18), but so are the former: Christ can give the keys to Peter only because *he* owns them. This is confirmed by Rev. 3:7 b, where Christ holds the keys of David, a reference to Isaiah 22:22: 'He shall open, and none shall shut; and he shall shut, and none shall open.' The parallel is striking and has of course been duly noted:[59] as God

lays the keys of David on the shoulders of his servant Eliakim
(Is. 22:20–22), so Jesus gives keys of the kingdom of heaven to
Peter. As Isaiah 22:22 suggests, the keys are the signs, the
symbols of the trustee, the steward. Peter will act on Christ's
behalf after the Ascension, not in heaven (it is in blatant
contradiction to the text if Christian folk myth sees Peter
standing at the gates of heaven), but here on earth (Mt. 16:19). He
will have to open the doors of the kingdom of heaven to those
who have accepted the risen Christ as their Lord, and to shut
them to those who have not. Missionary preaching will be his
main tool, of course—and those who accept the message thus
preached will be saved. This in itself, however, is only part of his
special authority, for the same task was given to all other disciples
(cf Mt. 18:18 and 28:18–19) and is still performed by Christian
preachers today. It is thus not the preaching of the Risen Christ
that is a role peculiar to Peter. Whereas missionaries today have
had, and still have, to leave the verdict over the honesty of the
commitment (or final refusal) of their hearers to God, Peter,
during his own mission, was himself the judge who would accept
or reject, bind and loose, and he had Christ's guarantee that his
decision would carry his fullest support in heaven. If Peter
understood the precedent immediately, it must have confirmed
his understanding of *ekklēsia*: both are demonstrations of the
Messianic re-interpretation of traditional concepts. Peter, however, is not the only one to exercise the power that goes with the
holding of the keys: they have been entrusted to him, and he
therefore is in charge of them and bears the responsibility which
their possession entails, but the other disciples have a share in the
daily routine, as it were, of administering it. Mt. 18:18–19 is an
unambiguous clarification of this point prior to the Resurrection,
and in Jn. 20:23 the risen Christ underlines it once again.

Peter is distinguished from the others by the keys with which
he, and only he, is entrusted; in this sense, the first half of verse
19 should be kept apart from the second half. There are two major
indications of the difference between the trustee of the keys and
the other disciples: Peter's authority is closely linked with the
Ecclesia, built on him and victorious over Hades. And his
authority to reject or to accept goes beyond that of the disciples:
his decisions concern not only ordinary, everyday community life
and the power of acquittal, as an application of the rabbinical
usage of 'binding' and 'loosing' already suggests;[59a] they are

relevant in a physical sense as well: Peter exercises the awesome power latent in this charge more forcefully than any of the other disciples: his verdict of death on Ananias and Sapphira (Acts 5:1–11) reflects an authority as unique to him as does his verdict of life on Tabitha (Acts 9:36–42).

The mere 'binding and loosing', on the other hand, is given over to the whole group of the Twelve, and, in Paul's view, to all the apostles including himself: 'For we are to God the aroma of Christ among those who are being saved and those who are perishing' (2 Cor. 2:15). Condemnation as well as forgiveness of sins are the tasks entrusted to the apostles 'under' Peter in Mt. 16:19; 18:18, to be carried out after the Resurrection, when the charge is reaffirmed (Jn. 20:23).

Matthew does not give us Peter's immediate reaction to this appointment; we may assume that he did not grasp its full impact until after the Ascension, when he began to act as the leader of the community; even then he never refers to it himself as the outward proof of his authority. And from the absence of the whole sequence in the Gospel of Mark, it seems that he did not include it in his own teaching about Jesus which he passed on to Mark. In his own ministry, there was no need of this confirmation: it was self-evident from what he did and said.

IV

Luke follows Mark's account with minor differences in the wording, but he omits the 'satanic' interlude and does not mention the precise geographical setting (9:18–20). Both differences are shared by John; as for the omission of the 'Satan' sequence, the reason cannot be that Peter would thus no longer appear in a bad light,[60] for both Luke and John mention the characteristic instance of Peter's human frailty, his denial of Jesus (Lk. 22:54–62, Jn. 18:15–18, 25–27). It is true that Luke has a tendency to soften the shortcomings of the disciples (shared to an extent by John), but to embellish the portrait of Peter by such means would have been useless: Luke, at any rate, knew of the existence of the Gospel of Mark and used it; he must have realized that knowledge of this scene would spread with or without him. And since he does not mention Matthew's sequence of the keys either, which would in fact have performed precisely the function of making Peter appear in a good light, we should perhaps assume that Luke saw no reason for highlighting Peter's role either way; the sober recording of the basic fact, Peter's confession of Christ, was good enough for him here, and as he does not distort the content of the additional material in Mark and Matthew, we cannot accuse him of falsifying the evidence. As for Peter's absolute authority, it is in fact Luke himself who, in the sequel to his gospel, *procures* the evidence.

The case is quite different in John. He leaves it in no doubt that he wants to put the emphasis on other events related to the revealing of Jesus' Messiahship. To begin with, he has Andrew speaking of Jesus as the Messiah as early as the scene on the Jordan (1:40), in a scene which presupposes that his readers recognise the stature of Peter. 'Simon Peter' is mentioned to identify Andrew as his brother in v. 40, even before Peter himself appears on the scene (41–42). Andrew does not speak out of his own insight into Jesus' ministry, but simply reiterates what he has gleaned from the witness of the Baptist, who was, in spite of his testifying to Jesus as the 'Son of God' (1:34), still in need of final confirmation himself (Mt. 11:3). Andrew's statement, important as it is, remains a mere starting-point, on a level with Nathanael's confession in 1:49 (see n. 36) and with the one of the disciples in Mt. 14:33, the scene in the boat. Whether they called him Son of God, or Messiah, or both, such a statement could not have been much more than a precursor to an affirmation based on a fuller insight into Jesus' ministry itself. Even if this was not human knowledge, but God-given revelation (as stated in Mt. 16:16), it still had to be compatible with a day-to-day acquaintance with the living Jesus.

This brings us to Peter's confession as reported by John, 6:68–69. Again there can be no doubt that John is reporting a different occasion. As so often, he omits events recorded elsewhere and uses others—here he does not describe the scene near Caesarea Philippi, but an earlier occasion in Capharnaum (6:59). Some followers were deserting Jesus, because they could not accept the consequences of Jesus' teaching in the synagogue. Jesus is not surprised. In fact, he had expected this and had foreseen even later developments (6:64–65, 66). But he does want to hear what the Twelve themselves have to say. 'You do not want to leave too, do you?' (v. 67). It is here that John gives Peter's confession: 'Lord, to whom shall we go? You have the words of eternal life. We believe and know that you are the Holy One of God.'

The only similarity between this confession and the one in the synoptic gospels is the fact that it is Peter who speaks up: the contents of what he has to say are markedly different. First of all, he is answering a different *question*—the question is not about the true identity of Jesus, but about whether or not to follow him any further; and secondly, the *answer* is not the same: it is a statement in two parts, a) 'you have the words of eternal life' and b) 'we believe and know that you are the Holy One of God'. And thirdly, Jesus' reply does not refer to the necessity of keeping quiet, but to the choice of the Twelve and the existence of a traitor among them. There is no way of reconciling this scene with the three synoptic reports. It is an earlier occasion, identified as such by its locality and its contents.[61]

Peter states that those in the know ('we') do not want to leave Jesus—there is simply no alternative to his teaching (v. 68). There is a subtlety in the Greek text: 'We *have* believed and *have* known that you are the Holy One of God'. The Greek implies that this is no sudden insight, but a developed opinion which the disciples have held over an undisclosed period of time. Yet the identification itself, 'the Holy One of God', is more cryptic than the direct appellation of Jesus as 'the Christ, the Son of the living God' in its fullest synoptic form. To be sure, the Holy One of God is someone very close to God, and indeed closer to God than to man (see Ps. 106:16, of Aaron, and Jdg. 13:7, 16:17, of Samson; but only once is the term used in a prophetic context which could be (and was) interpreted as referring to Messias—Ps. 16:10, where David speaks of the holy one who will not see decay. Strikingly enough, Peter himself quotes this verse in his first speech in Jerusalem, alluding directly to the risen Lord (Acts 2:22–32).[62]

There is thus no reason to doubt the authenticity of the Petrine saying in Jn. 6:69. Spoken prior to the scene near Caesarea Philippi, it is compatible with the latter, as its immediate precursor. Having chosen this incident, John does not have to report the other one—his own particular information about Jesus as the Christ has other additional sources later in the Gospel. As for Mark, Matthew and Luke, they must have preferred the more direct, and more directly provoked scene further up in the north, not least for the sake of *their* readers. But this is another question altogether.

CHAPTER THREE

The Road to the High Priest's Courtyard

1

Having accepted Peter's confession, and having preached to the crowd about his messianic role and about true discipleship, Jesus gives a solemn promise: some of those present will not taste death before they see the Kingdom of God.[63] He begins to fulfil his promise some six days later, when he takes Peter, James and John with him on Mount Hermon.[64]

Mark's account shows a remarkable awareness of the circumstances associated with Jesus' action. Clearly this manifestation of the glory of Jesus is connected with the recent recognition of his status as Messiah. But the interval between the two events is specified: the event takes place, he says, 'after six days', (9:2). Mark does not normally give such details—it seems to point to the presence of an eye-witness, i.e. Peter, who thought the information important enough to pass on to the evangelist. We may therefore assume not only that it did happen 'after six days', but also that this specific length of time had a deeper meaning. In Ex. 24:15–18, when Moses went up on the mountain to meet God, a cloud covered it for six days, and on the seventh day the Lord called to Moses from within the cloud. Mark says that Jesus took the three disciples with him after six days; in other words, whatever happened once he had taken them must have happened later. The six days are the preliminary; the seventh day is the decisive one by implication. And one has to keep in mind that the event probably took place after nightfall, when, according to traditional thinking, the seventh day had already begun.

Matthew follows Mark closely (17:1), but it is interesting to note that Luke chooses to rephrase the dating: according to him, 'About eight days after Jesus had said this, he took Peter, John and James with him . . .'. Did Luke, who knew Mark's text and its reliance on Peter, not trust the accuracy of his source? From another slight alteration in the same sentence, we may infer that this is not the case. Luke has also changed the order of the three disciples: Peter still is first, but then comes John instead of James in second place. Luke prefers to move John closer to Peter, so to speak, as in 9:28 and Acts 1:13; but this is as much a matter of personal shift of emphasis as is the different time: writing as a hellenist for a Graeco-Roman readership, he prefers the eight-day-week; the seven-day-week of the Jewish calendar is thus simply adapted to his needs.[65] Both Mark (with Matthew) and Luke would thus refer to one week.[66]

Mark tells the story in his usual concise manner. Without any background detail (Luke adds that Jesus was praying) he states that Jesus was 'transfigured' and explains graphically what happened: 'His clothes became dazzling white, whiter than anyone in the world could bleach them.' Matthew and Luke note that his face changed, too: it 'shone like the sun', as Matthew puts it (17:2; cf. Lk 9:29). 'Transfiguration' is not a word of everyday usage, but it has acquired a specific meaning in the context of this particular story. When Mark used the Greek word *metamorphoō* (followed in this by Matthew), which the English language has preserved in 'metamorphose' and 'metamorphosis', he used an equally rare term—the Greek Old Testament, for example, does not have it at all.[67] Peter and the other two disciples, as well as the first readers of the gospels, would have thought of another rare phenomenon: 'When Moses came down from Mount Sinai with the two tables of the Testimony in his hands, he was not aware that his face was radiant because he had spoken with the Lord' (Ex. 34:29). And they may have remembered Dn. 12:3: 'Those who impart wisdom will shine like the brightness of the heavens, and those who lead many to righteousness, like the stars for ever and ever.' They may even have thought of Ez. 8:2: 'I looked, and I saw a figure like that of a man. From what appeared to be his waist down, he was like fire, and from there up his appearance was as glowing metal.'[68] And they would have associated the bright and shining white garments of Jesus with the Lord of Heaven, as in Dn. 7:9 (cf. Rev. 1:14). Yet, when this happened, it was new and unparalleled, all the more so as Moses and Elijah suddenly appeared on the scene: 'And there appeared before them Elijah and Moses, who were talking with Jesus.'

No prophetic or apocalyptic text of the Old Testament mentions these two figures together. Elijah, put first only by Mark,[69] was the messenger of the last days, the messenger of the Messiah (as popular belief had it), in the wake of Malachi 3:1; 4:5 (cf. Mk. 8:28 and p. 33 above). Moses was not only the representative of the Law, he was also the symbol of the old covenant which was to be made into the new one by Jesus. And they had something important in common: both had experienced personal contact with God.[70]

They were talking with Jesus, Mark says. Neither he nor Matthew gives us the contents of their conversation; it is Luke who does this. They spoke about his departure, which he was about to bring to fulfilment in Jerusalem' (9:31). This additional information is all the more striking as Luke then goes on to say something else the other two evangelists do not mention: 'Peter and his companions were very sleepy', and only 'when they became fully awake, they saw his glory and the two men standing with him.' If they were very sleepy (or 'heavy with sleep', AV and RSV), how could they later report what was said? Is this why Mark and Matthew say nothing about the conversation—perhaps a Lucan invention? The most obvious source for Luke's additional information is Peter and the other two: For if we look at the Greek text of the passage, we can see that the three were not sound asleep, they were on the brink of sleeping, as is made clear by the word describing their return to full consciousness: *diagregoreō* may mean 'to become fully awake', but it mainly means 'to stay awake'.[71] Luke's sentence could be understood as saying: 'Peter and those with him were so tired that they had almost fallen asleep, but they stayed awake and saw his glory and the two men standing with him.' If this was so, they would still not have grasped everything that was said, and Luke's summary is sufficiently vague to allow the conjecture that when he had read

Mark's account, wanting to find out more, he went to Mark (or Peter, or James, or John) to ask them if they knew anything about the conversation as such and was told that, well, yes, one was rather sleepy at the time, but they had certainly been talking about 'departure' and 'Jerusalem'.[72]

While Mark (followed by Matthew) sees no need to include this kind of information, Peter himself does hint at it quite subtly in his second letter. Before giving his recollection of the event (2 Pet. 1:16–18), he alludes to his own death, employing the same word that is used in Luke's summary of the conversation: *exodos* ('departure' in the NIV and RSV, 'decease' in the AV). This is remarkable above all because *exodos* is a very rare word indeed in the New Testament: it occurs only three times, twice in our passages, Lk. 9:31 and 2 Pet. 1:15, and a third time in Heb. 11:22, where it takes up the Greek title of the second book of the Pentateuch, Exodus, and Ps. 104:38, to refer to the Israelites leaving Egypt. Since Luke and Peter both use the word to signify 'death', it is not unlikely that the unusual expression in Lk. 9:31 goes back to information passed on by Peter himself.[73] It is Peter, at any rate, who takes the initiative once the surprise at the unprecedented scene before his eyes has diminished. 'Rabbi', he says, 'it is good for us to be here. Let us put up three shelters—one for you, one for Moses and one for Elijah.' And Mark adds somewhat cryptically: 'He did not know what to say, they were so frightened' (9:5–6).

For the first time in the gospel—indeed for the first time in any of the synoptic gospels[74]—'Rabbi' is used to address Jesus. Peter advances from the usual and mostly neutral 'Lord' (see above p. 29f. and n. 34), to what may be called a new state of awareness of Jesus' messianic authority: it is plainly more than the everyday courtesy title given to any Jewish teacher of the time.[75] Matthew and Luke, trying to convey the special sense of the term 'Rabbi' on this occasion, have 'Lord' and 'Master' respectively. It has been noted that the first Christian writers had difficulties finding a new term that would approximate the rank Jesus had in their eyes;[76] Peter, on the mountain of the transfiguration, may well have used the traditional address 'Rabbi', but with a special emphasis which made Mark preserve the word in the original language.

'It is good for us to be here', Peter adds in all three accounts. He realizes the uniqueness of the experience and wants to prolong it, particularly as he cannot be sure that he has understood it yet. It is good that they are there also because they could put Peter's spontaneous plan into action: putting up tents, or shelters, one each for Jesus, Moses and Elijah (note that even in Mark, Moses is 'back' in first place here): cf. Mk. 9:5, Mt. 17:4, Lk. 9:33. Peter wants them to stay on and this motif is enhanced by the additional information of Lk. 9:33: Moses and Elijah were leaving Jesus, a good reason to act at once.[77]

Mark's afterthought is interesting: '*He* did not know what to say; *they* were so frightened.'[78] Nonplussed by the happening, Peter says the first thing that comes to his mind and that was to leave later generations of interpreters nonplussed in turn (see note 79). But Mark makes it clear that it was not only Peter who was afraid—all three of them were quite terrified, as the Greek word *ekphoboi*, which occurs only here in the gospels, implies. It was, however, a very special kind of fear that beset them: not the fear of something weird or ominous, but the fear of God—as the only other occurrence of the word in the New Testament, Heb. 12:21, quoting Dt. 9:19, points out: there it was Moses who was frightened on the occasion of the renewal of the old covenant, here it is the three disciples who are frightened when God sends Moses and Elijah and then speaks himself to underline the new covenant in Jesus (cf. Mt. 5:17 and Heb. 8). The disciples' fear is no weakness: it is the appropriate reaction to God's active presence.[79]

And God does act in the most affirmative manner by appearing through a cloud. When Peter, James and John saw the cloud enveloping Jesus, Moses, and Elijah, they would have understood, even before God's voice became audible, that a revelation was imminent: God's use of a cloud for this purpose was, after all, well known since Moses had entered one on Mount Sinai (Ex. 24:15–18, 40:34–35). At first sight, the wording of the sentence in all three synoptic versions seems to suggest that Peter and the other two were also in the cloud; but this is ruled out by the circumstantial fact that they were not, either here or anywhere later during the gospels, given a status as elevated as that of Moses and Elijah, let alone Jesus, to be granted visual contact with God. It may just have been conceivable that Peter, on the strength of his divinely inspired confession and the special rank bestowed upon him by Jesus, could have shared the privilege, but even Matthew does not differentiate between Peter and the other two when the cloud comes, so we infer that he stayed behind with them. This is corroborated by the description of the origin of the voice: Mark, Matthew and Luke are unanimous in asserting that it came *from* the cloud, or *out of* the cloud (*ek tēs nephelēs*), in other words, that it was not a voice the disciples heard while *within* the cloud.

There they were, seeing nothing but that bright (Matthew) cloud, and hearing God's voice speaking to them: 'This is my son whom I love. Listen to him.' (Mk. 9:7; cf. Mt. 17:5, Lk. 9:35).[80] To readers of these three gospels, the message has always suggested an enhanced reiteration of the heavenly voice at the baptism of Jesus (Mk. 1:11, Mt. 3:17, Lk. 3:22). It is not easy to ascertain if the three disciples recognized the reference; however, even if none of these disciples was present at Jesus' baptism, the Baptist himself passed the message on (see Jn. 1:32–34); and the unnamed disciple of Jn. 1:35, 40, most likely the very John who was with Peter and James on the Mount of Transfiguration, would have guaranteed transmission of the message to the others. Nor should we forget Andrew, Peter's brother, who was there, too, when the Baptist told the story.

But even without a clear understanding of the precedent, Peter, James and John would at least have seized the immediate implications: Jesus was the Son of God, and that not in any of the strictly metaphorical senses attaching to the term as it had been applied earlier in Israel's history. This man was 'Son of God' in a unique way. Furthermore, he was affirmed in his prophetic role by Moses and Elijah: see also Dt. 18:15, where Moses himself says to the people that 'the Lord your God will raise up for you a prophet like me from among your own brothers. You must listen to him.' (This 'you must listen to him' is literally the same imperative, in the Greek OT, as the one addressed to the disciples by the voice from the cloud). He was affirmed as the Suffering Messiah whose death was imminent; and he was, in all this, established not merely as a fulfilment of prophecies and promises, but as a unique, majestic entity. Small wonder that Peter, in his second letter, when he wanted to choose a single incident to demonstrate that the apostles had not followed myths, but had been eye-witnesses of Jesus' majesty, selected the Transfiguration.

When the cloud had disappeared, Moses and Elijah were no longer there. Jesus remains the only focal point of the disciples' attention. Descending from the mountain, he orders them not to tell anyone what they had seen (Luke omits the command, but stresses that they kept quiet), until the Son of Man has risen from the dead. This leads to a discussion, first among the disciples themselves, then with Jesus, about the resurrection (not in Matthew or Luke) and the importance of Elijah's coming before the Messiah. Jesus explains; and while he points out that Elijah has already come, Matthew adds (17:13) the thoughtful information that the disciples understood him as talking about John the Baptist.

It is noteworthy that neither Mark, Matthew nor Luke singles Peter out by name in this conversation on the way back to meet the other disciples. Whoever asked the question that would have been on many Jewish minds after the preceding event, 'Why do the teachers of the law say that Elijah must come first?' (Mk. 9:11, Mt. 17:10), he remains unidentified. Tentatively, one might suggest that it was not Peter—otherwise, and in keeping with synoptic usage, he would most probably have been named in connection with such open, direct questioning. After the Resurrection, the remaining uncertainties were dissolved: and it was with the experience and knowledge of the risen Christ behind him that Peter remembered the Transfiguration when he wrote his second letter. It is not irrelevant to look at 2 Pet. 1:16–18 in detail (cf. above pp. 48, 50, notes 73, 80, end).

Peter begins by distancing himself—and his fellow apostles—from ancient myths and from mythical interpretations of the story of Jesus Christ. The 'cleverly invented stories' (NIV) or 'cunningly devised fables' (AV) are 'cleverly devised myths' (RSV). *Myth* is the word used in the Greek text, and it had negative connotations before Peter (and Paul, who is the other NT author to use it: 1 Tim. 1:4; 4:7; 2 Tim. 4:4; Tit. 1:14). Philo, Plutarch, and already Plato (*Timaeus* 26e) had used it disparagingly to denote invented stories, particularly of divine action or intervention. The readers of Peter's letter would have been fully aware of the juxtaposition intended: they may have heard of other so-called gods or godly men, but those stories were myths, and the apostles had not been taken in by anything of the kind: their message was based not on fanciful hearsay, but on a personal experience, on something they had seen and heard themselves. Peter's clear differentiation between myth and the historical authenticity of the events in Jesus' life is something that should be kept in mind whenever the question of 'myths in the New Testament' is debated.

'We did not follow cleverly invented myths when we told you about the power and coming of our Lord Jesus Christ, but we were eye-witnesses of his majesty' (2 Pet. 1:16). Grammatically there may well be, as has been pointed out by many commentators,[81] an instance of hendiadys, where the two words 'power' and 'coming' are meant to describe one thought, i.e. 'powerful coming'. But even so, the two individual words carried their own connotations for Peter. The 'power' was reminiscent of the promise given by Jesus some six days before the Tansfiguration: 'Some who are standing here will not taste death before they see the kingdom of God come with power' (Mk. 9:1). Those who had witnessed the Transfiguration knew what this power was; it could not have been employed to describe the impact of the Second Coming of Christ, the Parousia, the one thing about Christ that was still to happen, at an undisclosed point in time (see 2 Pet. 3:3–10: cf. Mk. 13:32).

They were, Peter says, eye-witnesses of Christ's majesty. There is no need to *name* James and John, the *we* is good enough for his present purposes. The word translated by 'eyewitness', *epoptēs*, is, however, chosen with special care: only Peter uses it in the New Testament, and only he has the equivalent verb, *epopteuō*— and, interestingly enough, this verb occurs twice in his *first* letter (2:12; 3:2), a fact that has been justifiably used to point to the relationship between 1 and 2 Peter.[82] It does not strictly mean 'eyewitness', but rather 'spectator', literally someone who looks upon something—the idea which is behind the use of the word in the Septuagint (Est. 5:1, and the apocryphal 2 Macc. 3:39; 7:35; 3 Macc. 2:21). An interesting possibility concerning Peter's choice of this rare word to tell his readers that he was there when it happened is closely linked with his aim to refute non-Christian myths: we know from inscriptions connected with the mysteries of Samothrake and dated to the first century BC,[83] that it was used to describe initiates of the cult of the Cabiri which had spread over Asia Minor and had, by the time of Peter's letter, become one of the most popular and influential mysteries. Even members of the Roman nobility had been attracted by it, and Peter may thus have had a twofold knowledge of the danger inherent in this particular myth: from Asia Minor itself, where he had been before, and where the letter was sent, and from his stay in Rome, where he wrote it. What is more, the Cabiri were commonly called 'great' (or 'majestic') 'gods', *megaloi theoi*,[84] and it is certainly no accident that Peter goes on to write that he was an eyewitness of Christ's majesty, using the word *megaleiotēs*, the noun directly derived from the adjective.[85] With one touch, Peter not only refutes the thinking of the mysteries as cunningly devised myths, he also shows his readers what the real majesty is: not the one ascribed to those gods, but the one bestowed upon Jesus Christ by God the Father at the Transfiguration.[86]

And to make quite sure that his readers get the message, Peter then calls God 'Majestic Glory', *megaloprepēs doxa*, repeating the word used for Christ's god-given glory, *doxa*, of v. 17, and using a very rare synomym for *megalos* to describe greatness and majesty.[87] Notwithstanding the likelihood that this is a case of 'the characteristically Hebrew avoidance of the divine name',[88] or, much less likely in view of what actually happens, 'a way of protecting the transcendence of God by avoiding the idea that God himself speaks directly'[89] it is Peter's way of saying that he has finally, i.e. after the Resurrection and Ascension, understood what the Transfiguration had implied in terms of the relationship between Father and Son.

He is in fact so thrilled about his insight that he omits a verb in the following passage from sheer eagerness to tell of God's voice as he remembered it (a fact elegantly covered by our translation): 'This is my Son, whom I love; with him I am well pleased' (1:17).

Much has been made of the apparent differences between Peter's account and the wording of the synoptic gospels. They are in fact negligible, to say the least. The problem is basically one of the textual tradition of the passage: however we want to look at the first sentence pronounced by the voice, the actual message is precisely the same in all extant manuscripts. Differences occur only in the order of words: whereas Mark (9:7) has, literally, 'This is my beloved Son', Peter, in the oldest extant papyrus, p72, has (again literally) 'My Son, my beloved one, is this.'[90] Whereas this reading is confirmed by the *Codex Vaticanus* and by some translations, the extant equivalent to Mk. 9:7 is substantiated by *Codex Sinaiticus, Codex Alexandrinus,* and a host of others.[91] Even so, the difference is so unremarkable in Greek that elaborate attempts to turn 'my beloved one' into a second title given to Christ and to find reasons for this[92] are unnecessary. Both versions are saying the same thing, the one found in two early manuscripts of 2 Peter being merely an intensifying of the love of God by means of a repeated *mou* ('mine').[93]

Much more noteworthy is an addition in Peter's version: to Mark and Luke, he adds 'with him I am well pleased' to the words of God. It is, however, included in Matthew's description (Mt. 17:5), and was in Mark's and Luke's versions of the voice at the Baptism (see n. 80 and p. 50, the precedent for the scene).[94]

Equally noteworthy appears to be a subsequent omission: Peter does not give God's command, 'Listen to him!' Or so it seems, for he does in fact give one in his own words, only two verses later (v. 19): 'And you will do well to pay attention to it' (i.e. to the prophetic word)—whereas the original admonition was probably dropped deliberately (along with other features, such as the cloud, the presence of Moses and Elijah, the names of James and John),[95] as it was meant to give authority to Jesus' prophetic teaching about his Messiahship *during his lifetime.* Peter now has to deal with the historical fact of the Risen Christ in opposition to pagan myths; and for this purpose he issues a new and apostolic command: listen to, pay attention to the Old Testament as Messianic prophecy which has so accurately predicted what has happened. Its words have already been made 'very sure'[96] by past events—they will therefore be reliable in view of future events; and this includes 'prophetic' statements by God the Father and the Son Jesus Christ, which takes us back to the context of the Second Coming in v. 16.

Peter, at any rate, concludes the actual retelling of the Transfiguration in v. 18 with an emphasized repetition of v. 16: 'We ourselves heard this voice that came from heaven when we were with him on the sacred mountain.' Note that the (high) mountain of the gospel accounts, has, with the wisdom of hindsight, acquired the status of a holy mountain—but note also that Peter does not intend to turn it into a 'sight': he, too, refrains from identifying it by name.

The Transfiguration, then, is of pivotal importance for Peter to explain God's installing his Son in majesty; Christ's unique role going beyond that of Moses and Elijah; the glory of the Second Coming; and, through all this, the triumph of historical, witnessed events over myths and mythological interpretations. It also serves as a background against which he can underline the authority of true prophecy against home-made interpretations (1:19–21). And it shows us that Peter, during the thirty years and more that had passed since the Transfiguration, had developed a mature understanding of his own experiences and their meaning for his readers. Would anyone but Peter have chosen the Transfiguration instead of the Resurrection at this stage? Peter did, not least because he remembered the glory and majesty (which are not characteristics of the risen Christ in any of the Easter accounts), and knew that it was this power that foreshadowed the Parousia.

II

Peter is highlighted next in a scene which is peculiar to the tax-collector Matthew in his gospel: the story of the temple tax, Mt. 17:24–27. Jesus and the disciples are still in Galilee, they have just returned to Capharnaum, and Jesus is once again staying in Peter's house (17:25; cf., in the context of the following incident, Mk. 9:33; and above, p.25).

It is a scene, which, in spite of its serious message, betrays some illuminating signs of down-to-earth life. Every male Jew from the age of twenty onwards had to pay the annual temple-tax, a half-shekel, which was usually collected on the first day of the month of Adar (February/March).[97] But how to collect it from a wandering teacher? In Capharnaum, when Jesus returns to what appears to have been his only fixed abode, the tax-collectors finally catch up with him. Or rather, they accost Peter, his 'landlord'. 'Does he or does he not pay his temple-tax?' they want to know, and their question may well have been caused by information about that provocative address to the Pharisees on the Sabbath: 'I tell you that one greater than the temple is here' (Mt. 12:6). Peter replies promptly, 'Of course he does', and goes into the house, probably in order to ask Jesus for his half: it was customary for two Jews to give one four-drachma coin—a *stater*, as Matthew knowingly calls it by its fiscal name in v. 27 (he does so again in 26:15).

But when he comes into the house, Jesus is 'the first to speak' (v. 25)—he has overheard the conversation outside and turns the incident into a teaching point. 'What do you think, Simon? From whom do the kings of the earth collect duty and taxes—from their own sons or from others?'[98]

With this question, a highly sensitive topic is broached. It is not a political one, as one might think at first glance, for although the collection of the temple tax was facilitated by the Roman authorities,[99] and although Jesus speaks of the 'Kings of the earth', he is not debating the authority of 'Caesar', as in Mt. 22:21 (in a passage that is concerned with a political issue of theological importance). The money in question *here* is not the tribute payment to the Romans, effected by an offensive official tax coin, the *dēnarion* with the emperor's image, but the inoffensive Jewish temple tax.[100]

Jesus' question elicits the expected answer from Peter: not their own 'sons' are required to pay taxes and duties by the kings, but the 'others', the 'foreigners' or 'strangers', as the Greek word implies. And from this is deduced that the 'sons' are exempt. Which means (or so Peter must have gathered immediately) that the Son of God, and by implication his own followers, his 'family', do not have to pay the temple-tax. A comparatively short time after the Transfiguration, Jesus' logic is stringent—as the Son of God he is above the temple. But it is precisely because he does not want to turn the matter into one of internal conflict (when nothing could be proven to the tax collectors by breaking God's command of Ex. 30:11–16), that he complies with the request. In doing so, he demonstrates to Peter (not to the tax-collectors) that worldly financial worries and obligations are neither a cause of conflict nor a cause of concern to the Son of God; moreover, if he does have to pay a tax to his father, as it were, it might as well come in a heaven-sent way. He tells Peter to go to the lake, take the first fish he catches, open its mouth—and he will find a *stater* to take to the tax-collectors for both their taxes. Whatever the reasons for this 'miracle of the coin', one should not read too much into it. Peter, the experienced fisherman, would have known the fish that could be the vehicle of such a miracle: the John Dory (*Zeus faber*, sometimes called 'Peter's fish' today), a fish with massive jaws that keeps its offspring in its mouth for a while; when they have grown too big for it, it takes a stone in its mouth, so that the little fish cannot remain.[101] Peter may even have caught such fish before which had mistaken a *stater*, dropped accidentally by someone from a boat, for a stone. And Jesus, in fact, may thus have pointed out to Peter that the temple tax was of no greater importance to him than a little stone in the mouth of a fish. But he will also have taught him that in spite of the Transfiguration, in spite of the annunciation of the *ekklesia* to be built upon the Rock Peter, the time had not yet come for an outright rejection of the old temple.[102]

III

It is again remarkable that none of the synoptists mentions Peter by name in their accounts of the disciples' debate about rank (Mk. 9:33–37; Mt. 18:1–5; Lk. 9:46–48). This incident, following the temple-tax story in Matthew's gospel for reasons of narrative structure (it happened on the way back to Capharnaum, as Mark, who has the most detailed report, makes quite clear; 9:33, 34), seems important to our picture of Peter precisely because of the omission of his name. Peter was not particularly concerned about the debate, as his position, especially for the future, had been assured by the commission of the keys. It was the other disciples, who had no such stature, who were uncertain about their future roles. This is underlined by a second such debate, later on the road to Jerusalem (Mk. 10:35–45; Mt. 20:20–28; Lk. 22:24–27) where again Peter remains unnamed.

He does, however, put in a characteristic appearance soon afterwards, just when Jesus has extended the authority to bind and to loose to all the disciples (Mt. 18:18–20). In another brief dialogue, reported only by Matthew, he pursues the question of forgiveness and condemnation in order to make sure that he has understood his responsibility—not just as the 'Rock', but also as a disciple of Jesus: 'Then Peter came to Jesus and asked, "Lord, How many times shall I forgive my brother when he sins against me? Up to seven times?" Jesus answered, "I tell you, not seven times, but seventy-seven times"' (Mt. 18:21–22).

Even Peter's question is already a step ahead of Jewish tradition: it was customary to forgive one's brother more than once, but four times seems to have been the maximum.[103]

The NIV translation 'up to' seven times ('till' in the AV) is not as good as that of the RSV, 'as many as', for Peter's use of the number seven is not a mere allusion to the next highest symbolic number (see, for example, Gen. 21:28, Nu. 23:1). It implies an unlimited number, in the sense of 'as often as necessary'. This is how the word was used by the psalmist (Ps. 119:164), and similarly by Greek authors like Diodorus Siculus;[104] and this is, at any rate, how Jesus wants Peter to understand it: not 'seven times', but 'seventy-seven times' (NIV; AV and RSV have 'seventy times seven') shall he forgive his brother. Whatever the translation (the Greek allows both versions, and even though 'seventy times seven' may be more natural, 'seventy-seven times' seems to be confirmed by the Hebrew original of Gn. 4:24, the only other biblical passage where the word is used), it underlines the message: there is no upper limit when it is a question of forgiving a brother's sins.[105]

Jesus makes use of the occasion to deepen the implications of his answer through the parable of the unmerciful servant (18:23–25). We may assume that this parable is directed to all the disciples present, not just to Peter, who had already received a clear reply to a spontaneous question, and who had already demonstrated an advanced insight into the idea of brotherly love.

IV

With those events after their brief return to Capharnaum, Jesus' teaching in the North has finally come to an end. It is time to go south, towards Jerusalem, to prepare the 'Exodus' announced at the Transfiguration. Peter stresses the importance of the decision to leave their homeland from the disciples' point of view: they are amazed by Jesus' stern attitude towards the rich young man who was not prepared to sell his riches (Mk. 10:17–27), and Peter points out that *they* had 'left everything' to follow Jesus (v. 28).[106] Jesus' reply is a promise, reassuring, but not without ominous intimations. Eternal life is the reward in the end, yet the road towards it leads via persecution. Different kinds of homes, brothers, sisters, mothers, children and fields will even in this present age be given to those who leave everything for Christ and the gospel,[107] but together with all these will come persecutions. It is not unreasonable to assume that this prophecy would have attained its full meaning when the gospel of Mark was written, against a background of anti-Christian persecution in Rome.[108] Even so, the Greek word used, *diōgmos*, had already acquired a somewhat uncomfortable overtone in 2 Macc. 12:23, where Judas Maccabeus' persecution of the sinners led to the death of some thirty thousand men. Mark, incidentally, had used it before in his rendering of a speech of Jesus (Mk. 4:17), as had Matthew in his parallel passage (Mt. 13:21).[109]

Jesus' final sentence is another warning: 'But many who are first will be last, and the last first' (Mk. 10:31). It is one of his characteristic sayings, meant to be remembered and shaped as a chiasmus, a technique of which Jesus was very fond.[110] Here it serves to remind the disciples that they should not count on privileges: the fact that they were the first to have left houses and families for him is, in itself, a prerequisite, but not the complete performance of all that would be asked of them.

Clement of Alexandria, in his remarkable essay, 'What rich man will be saved?', which is a commentary on Mk. 10:17–31 written at the beginning of the third century, gives an interesting interpretation of Peter's question which deserves to be quoted: 'Therefore, on hearing these things, the blessed Peter, the chosen, the pre-eminent, the first of the disciples . . . quickly seized upon and understood the saying. And what does he say? "Lo, we have left all and followed Thee." If by "all" he means his own possessions, he is bragging of having forsaken four obols [about two thirds of a drachma] or so, as the saying goes, and he would be unconsciously declaring the kingdom of heaven a suitable equivalent to these. But if, as we are just now saying, it is by flinging away the old possessions of the mind and diseases of the soul that they are following in the track of their teacher, Peter's words would at once apply to those who are to be enrolled in heaven. For this is the true following of the Saviour, when we seek after His sinlessness and perfection, adorning and regulating the soul before Him as before a mirror and arranging it in every detail after His likeness.'[111]

Clement also has an elegant way of solving the problem of the textual differences between Mark's account and its parallels in Matthew (19:27–30) and Luke (18:28–30): 'This is written in the gospel according to Mark,' he says, 'and in all other accepted gospels the passage as a whole shows the same, concurrent sense, though perhaps here and there a little of the wording changes.' ('What Rich Man', 5:1).

In fact, the only differences worth mentioning here are Luke's omitting of the final saying and the persecutions (omitted also by Matthew), and Matthew's addition of the Son of Man's promise to install the Twelve as judges over the twelve tribes of Israel, sitting on twelve thrones 'at the renewal of all things' (19:28). This prediction that when the last days have come his disciples will be co-judges over God's people, the old Israel as well as the new —the Christian community[112]—is an extension and a reinforcement of the earlier promises given to Peter (Mt. 16:19) and to the others (Mt. 18:18).

CURSE of the fig tree
symbolic V of Israel

We have to wait until after the triumphal entry into Jerusalem before Peter speaks up again as an individual. This episode shows his growing awareness of the deeper meaning of Jesus' actions. After their entry into the city, and after their first visit to the temple, Jesus and the disciples had returned to Bethany, less than two miles (Jn. 11:18) to the northeast, on the eastern slopes of the Mount of Olives, where they spent the night. The next morning, on their way back to the temple, Jesus sees a fig-tree in the distance, approaches it to find out if it has any fruit, finds nothing but leaves, as it is not the season for figs, and says to the tree, 'May no-one ever eat fruit from you again.' And, Mark adds, using Peter's own oral report, 'his disciples heard him say it' (Mk. 11:12–14). Then follows the clearing of the temple and another return to Bethany for the evening. The following morning, 'as they went along, they saw the fig-tree withered from the roots. Peter remembered and said to Jesus, "Rabbi, look! The fig-tree you cursed has withered"' (Mk. 11:20–21).

We can distinguish two main elements in this exclamation: the surprise that Jesus' words did have this very prompt effect, connected with the privileged address 'Rabbi'; and the interpretation of Jesus' action as a 'curse'. The surprise is understandable —one would not expect Jesus' words to have effect overnight, but rather at a later date, when the season for figs had come. More important, however, is Peter's interpretation. Jesus had not literally placed a curse on the fig-tree: all he had said was that no-one would ever eat fruit from it again, which sounds rather like a ban, directed as much against potential fig-eaters coming to this tree as against the tree itself, and there is no hint of its complete destruction in his words. And would not the cursing of a fig-tree that happened to be fruitless at a time when it was in any case not supposed to bear fruit, have been a somewhat wilful action?

It is here that Peter's interpretation, once he has seen the consequences of Jesus' words, points up the deeper meaning of the symbolic action. Peter can call it a curse, because he understands that the fig-tree was used by Jesus to symbolize Israel and the doom of Jerusalem with its temple—and he has acquired this comprehension not least because of the clearing of the temple by Jesus which had taken place on the day between the 'curse' and the 'withering'.

While the fig had been used as a symbol for Israel under God's judgment by some of the prophets (see, for example, Je. 8:13; Ho. 9:10), the withering of the tree had been included in prophecies of judgment over Israel (Joel 1:12, cf. Ez. 17:2–9; Ho. 9:16), even in an eschatological prophecy against all nations (Is. 34:4). Peter clearly has this background in mind when he calls Jesus' action a curse. The very word he uses, *kataraomai*, is not without precedent: God himself employs it when he threatens with his curse the priests who do not honour his name in Malachi 2:2 (cf. Gn. 5:29; 12:3; 27:29; Nu. 23:8; 24:9; Jdg. 5:23; Jb. 24:18; Ne. 10:29; 13:2, 25).

In this sense, Peter acknowledges once again that Jesus is indeed the Christ, the Son of God, whose prophetic warning to Israel will be fulfilled.

There follows an answer by Jesus, not just to Peter, but to all disciples (11:22–25). Since it is expressly described by Mark as an answer, we may be surprised not to find any allusion to the interpretation given above. This, in fact, was not necessary, as Peter had already shown that he had grasped the implications of the fig-tree incident. Jesus therefore concentrates on the power of faith in God. If he, Jesus, had been capable of making that fig-tree wither, so his disciples, through sheer faith and the strength of prayer, if properly related to God's will, would be able to 'move mountains'. It is a theme dear to Jesus: cf. Mt. 17:20 and Lk. 17:6 (see also Jn. 14:13–14; Mt. 7:7; 18:19). As an afterthought, Jesus admonishes his disciples to forgive others when they stand praying, so that God may forgive them themselves. The spirit of forgiveness is a prerequisite for a prayer that will be answered.[113]

VI

Our next encounter with Peter occurs in a sequence which is crucial to the Gospel of Mark: Jesus' prophecy of the destruction of Jerusalem and the Temple, followed by the detailed warning against deception, his longest speech in the whole gospel (Mk. 13:1–37). 'As he was leaving the temple, one of his disciples said to him, "Look, Teacher! What massive stones! What magnificent buildings!" "Do you see all these great buildings?" replied Jesus. "Not one stone here will be left on another; every one will be thrown down"' (13:1–2).

The exclamations of wonder did not come from Peter. For a start, his name is not mentioned; in addition, the title given to Jesus, 'teacher' (*didaskalos*), conflicts with Peter's own usage since the Transfiguration, i.e. 'Rabbi' (Mk. 9:5; 11:21). The enthusiasm, however, was certainly shared by everyone who saw the temple, built by Herod the Great between 20 BC and 12 BC, which must have been one of the most magnificent buildings in the Roman empire; Josephus describes its splendours in breathtaking detail (*War* 5, 5:1–8, cf. *Ant.* 15, 11:3–7); even the Roman historian Tacitus, one of the few secular historians to discuss the Jews and to mention Christ and the Christians, and certainly not a friend of the Jews (he calls them *taeterrima gens*, 'an extremely loathsome people',[114] pays his respects by writing about Jerusalem: 'There is a temple of immense opulence' (*immensa opulentia, Hist.* 5, 8, 1), 'a building erected with a greater expenditure of energy than any other' (*Hist.* 5, 12, 1), and, most tellingly, in his acount of Roman deliberations on the advisability of destroying the temple at all, 'a sanctuary famous above all other works of men' (*aedes sacrata ultra omnia mortalia inlustris, Hist.* frag. 2, quoted by Sulpicius Severus, *Chronicles* 2, 30, 6).

Jesus' prophecy that 'not one stone here will be left on another' must have been hard to understand. The disciples, of course, had an inkling of it because of the earlier fig-tree incident and the clearing of the temple, and they will have remembered OT prophecies, such as Je. 26:18 and Mi. 3:12, where utter destruction is foretold. But even so, when Jesus had reached the Mount of Olives, opposite the temple, as Mark points out (13:3), implying that it was in full view throughout the following scene, those who were with him wanted to know more: 'Peter, James, John and Andrew asked him privately: "Tell us, when will these things happen? And what will be the sign that they are all about to be fulfilled?" '

Here Peter is again mentioned first, followed by James and John, in the same order as in Mk. 5:37 and 9:12. But this time Andrew is added to the list, to give the two pairs of brothers who had been the first to be called by Jesus on Lake Gennesaret. It is unlikely that they would have spoken in chorus; we may safely assume that it was Peter who asked the question—it was he, at any rate, who had already shown an insight into the eschatological elements in Jesus' actions and prophecies. The formulation of the question is a tell-tale indication: it betrays a conscious and partly literal allusion to Dn. 12:6–8, where Daniel is given a prophecy about the end times, which he does not quite understand, but which will be 'sealed until the time of the end' (12:9).

Peter shows that he expects Jesus' prophecy to be closely linked with the end—the plural 'all these things' may even include Peter's recollection of the Transfiguration, where the 'Exodus' in Jerusalem was debated between Moses, Elijah and Jesus. Therefore he and the others can, unlike Daniel, expect an explanation of the precise moment and the 'sign' inaugurating it.

The ensuing discourse answers their questions. In six steps Jesus explains the forthcoming events. He begins by warning them against messianic pretenders and against misinterpretations of events like wars, earthquakes and famines (13:5–8)—these are not signs of the messianic age itself, but only of the period preceding it. He then warns them to be prepared for persecution caused by their preaching of the gospel (which must be preached to all nations before the end comes), and for internecine strife, but tells them that the Holy Spirit will guide their words and that endurance will be rewarded with salvation (13:9–13). In the third section of his speech, 13:14–23, he predicts the sacrilegious destruction of the temple (where Mark adds a helpful parenthesis to alert his readers, v. 14), urging those who will be there to flee to the mountains, in language that alludes heavily to OT prophecies, and warns them once more against false messiahs who might try to dissuade them from fleeing. However, as the fourth section (13:24–27) explains, at an *undisclosed* moment after the total destruction of the temple, the Son of Man will come 'in clouds with great power and glory' to gather his elect from all over the world. Having explained the signs, Jesus hints at the time in his fifth section, 13:28–31. As the leaves on the fig-tree indicate the nearness of summer, so the events that have taken place and are going to happen in Jerusalem need careful observation, as they indicate the decisive moment of destruction which will be witnessed by the disciples' own generation (not necessarily by themselves, v. 30). Christ's own everlasting words will also survive even after the end of the world (which is not implied by the preceding prophecy and is therefore not in contradiction to v. 30). The sixth, concluding section, 13:32–37, is a final exhortation: speculation is idle, no one knows of the day or the hour—therefore, watching and praying is required of everyone, as the short parable of the absent householder (v. 34) helps to explain. The last word sums it all up: 'Watch!' (It is poignant that Mark used the Greek word, *grēgoreō*, only twice more—when the disciples did not watch but fell asleep, at Gethsemane (Mk. 14:34, 37)—on the very Mount of Olives.[115]

Since Peter was one of the communicators of the message, and, as far as Mark's gospel is concerned, the authoritative one, it is interesting to note that Jesus' discourse was not without influence on his two letters. Some of the traces are minor ones—such as the emphasis on the chosen, the elect ones (Mk. 13:20/1 Pet. 1:2), or the repeated call to watch out, impressive not least because it comes from someone who had been caught sleeping and is thus speaking from experience (Mk. 13:5, 9, 23, 33, 34, 36; 1 Pet. 5:8; 2 Pet. 3:17). Although Mark and Peter use different words for 'watching out', the one coincidence is striking—*grēgoreō*, Mk. 13:36, and, as mentioned above, Mk. 14:34, 37, at Gethsemane, reappears in 1 Pet. 5:8. The most noteworthy correspondence occurs in the description of the last days, the cosmic catastrophe that highlights the Second Coming. Without quoting the discourse directly,[116] Peter utilises the same modified Old Testament imagery and interprets it, underlining what Jesus had already said, in terms both of a catastrophe involving heaven and earth, and of the timing of the Parousia which remains incalculable (2 Pet. 3:3–4, 7, 10–12).[117] Leaving aside Paul's underestimated allusion in 2 Thes. 1:8–10 (which implies some knowledge of the contents of Mk. 13:24–26 and a familiarity with OT prophecies such as Zp. 1:18; 3:8, or Ps. 97:3, about destruction by fire), 2 Peter 3 is the only passage in any NT letter where Jesus' prophecy about the Parousia is fully understood and interpreted.

In 2 Pet. 3:1–10, he begins by referring to common, but erroneous expectations of an immediate Parousia (kindled, perhaps, by an all-too-eager misunderstanding of Mk. 13:24–27, 30), before reminding his readers of what Jesus himself had implied (Mk. 13:32, 35) and expounding this. He then takes up Jesus' prediction of what will happen on that day (Mk. 13:24–27), and drives the message home for readers, who, as the whole letter shows, are still quite inexperienced in the faith, and apparently need rather vivid language to make the point clear. So he dwells upon the more terrifying details of the cosmic conflagration which Jesus had only hinted at, as he, unlike Peter, knew that his hearers (and readers) would understand the subtle allusions to OT prophecies. Peter has to fill in the gaps, and he does so most convincingly; Is. 13:10–13 and 34:4 are drawn on more heavily than they are by Jesus, and so is Joel 2:10, 30–32 (quoted by Peter in his Pentecost speech Acts 2:14–21), and he adds other eschatological prophecies which are implicit in Jesus' words, but needed, or so he felt, elucidation: from the Torah, above all, Dt. 32:22; from Is. 66:15–16; Ps. 97:3; and Zp. 1:18; 3:8. He was certainly not giving free rein to his own apocalyptic fantasies. Outside the Old Testament, texts like 1 Enoch 1:5–8; 102:1, Jubilees 9:15 or, at Qumran, 1QH (*Thanksgiving Hymns*) 3:29–36; 6:18–19, show similar perceptiveness. Peter was trying to help his readers understand what was at stake—the Return of Jesus is no tool for false teachers (2:1; 3:3–5), but a matter of serious reality. It is a new beginning, too: new heavens and a new earth where righteousness dwells will follow (3:13), as Jesus himself had intimated when he spoke to Peter and the others about their role at the renewal of all things (Mt. 19:27–28, but see also Mk. 13:27). 2 Pet. 3:2–13 is a striking example of the rock-like qualities of the post-resurrection apostle: Jesus' prophecy has found in him a powerful messenger and interpreter.[118]

VII

Peter had the gift of thinking and acting spontaneously; as we have seen, this led to some early eschatological perceptions which left their matured traces in his own writings. It is therefore all the more remarkable that he appears to have had real problems with the fulfilment of Jesus' role as the suffering Messiah when it actually happened. Was it a conflict of 'theoretical' insight over against the unwillingness of the 'heart' to let it happen? That trait of his character which had become apparent when he had tried to dissuade Jesus from following the path to the cross (Mk. 8:31–33, Mt. 16:21–33; see above, p. 34f.) comes to the fore again when the Passion is near.

The Passover meal is the first such occasion. In the synoptic gospels Peter is not mentioned by name, but he appears in John's idiosyncratic account. The scene, of course, is the washing of the feet, a favourite subject of countless artists throughout the ages—even the twelfth century crusaders' church at St-Gilles-du-Gard in Provence has its middle tympanum adorned by a scene showing

Peter as he rejects Jesus' attempt to wash his feet, tapping his forehead like an irate motorist.[119] The scene in John's gospel (13:3–17), is itself not without an element of exaggeration and involuntary humour, either—on the part of Peter, who is shown as going from one extreme to the other. Yet both extremes depict him as a true 'first among equals', far from denigrating him as a nearly-failed disciple.[120]

The episode begins when Jesus lowers himself to the status of a servant in the most emphatic manner (cf. Abigail in 1 Sa. 25:41). He gets up while the meal is in progress, i.e. between courses,[121] takes off his outer clothing, the *himatia* (the plural, used by John significantly, too, in 19:23, 24, means that he assumed the role of a slave, wearing nothing but his loin cloth), and 'lays them aside' (AV, RSV). For this gesture John uses the same Greek word (*tithēmi*) which he employs no fewer than four times to describe the laying down of Jesus' life (10:11, 15, 17, 18; twice it occurs when Peter offers to lay down his life for Jesus, 13:37, 38; once in the context of Jesus' command to love each other, 15:13; see also 1 Jn. 3:16). He then wraps a towel round his waist—a practical action, but one which again is marked by unusual words: both the term for towel, *lention*, and for 'girding himself', *diazōnnumi*, are used only by John in the New Testament. (*Diazōnnumi* occurs again in 21:7, when Peter puts his garment on to rush towards the Lord from his boat; *lention* here only in the whole Greek Bible.[122])

With a basin of water at hand, Jesus begins to wash the disciples' feet and to dry them with the towel. No one speaks— are they just dumbfounded?—until he reaches Peter. Peter obviously realizes the context of Jesus' action—the symbolism of his self-abasement could not have escaped the notice of the disciple who had already shown evidence of insight into his master's actions. But he thrusts the truth from him; the reality of the approaching end, the 'Exodus', dawns upon him at this moment, and he refuses, against better judgment and knowledge, to play even a passive role in hastening the realisation of the suffering, voluntarily-abased Messiah. As so often, partial understanding proves to be worse than none at all. 'You do not realize now what I am doing', Jesus replies, 'but later you will understand' (13:7). Peter, however, does not want to wait for an explanation—does he not know the reason already?—and promptly refuses the washing of his feet in the most emphatic terms. He is, however, not hopelessly stubborn. When Jesus quite simply tells him that unless he washes his feet, Peter will have 'no part' with him, his mind changes radically. Having a part with Jesus was the one thing that counted—as another Johannine writing makes abundantly clear (Rev. 20:6; 22:16). Affirming how much he desires to have part with Jesus, he goes to the other extreme and asks him to wash his hands and head as well. He realises, of course, that the whole action is symbolic and that the washing of hands and head will not make it more effective, but he is the first among the disciples, and by showing how thoroughly he wants to be cleansed by Jesus, he emphasizes the unlimited extent of his discipleship. This attitude to Jesus and to the other disciples recalls Jn. 6:69.

The lack of enthusiasm in 13:6–8 had been disappointing, but its opposite in 13:9 is excessive. Jesus explains this with the analogy of the man who has been to a public bath and, on his return home, needs only to wash his feet—which would have been soiled by the dust of the road—to be perfectly clean. Like that man, they are wholly clean because they 'have part with Jesus' (see also 15:3). There is no need for repeated 'washing' once this purification has been sealed by the Servant Messiah (cf. Lk. 22:27).

Jesus pursues the teaching sequence by explaining (as he had promised to Peter, v. 7) the future application of the practical aspect of the foot-washing. As he, their Lord and Teacher, has washed their feet, they should do the same for one another. In other words, they should be prepared to do the lowest servant's work—the disciples would remember the OT precedent set by Abigail (1 Sa. 25:41), and both those who had been there and readers of John's gospel would also recall the event depicted in 1:27, where John the Baptist declares himself unworthy of doing as much as untying Jesus' sandals.

The analogy leaves no doubt about the lowliness required of the followers of Jesus in everyday life. This idea of servanthood was understood by Peter: we find traces of it in his first letter (2:13–15, 18–21; 3:1–8; 4:9; 5:5b–6); and in the first verse of 2 Peter he introduces himself as the servant, or rather slave (*doulos*) and apostle (messenger, *apostolos*) of Jesus Christ. This seems to be an application of Jn. 13:16, against the background of the preceding experience: 'I tell you the truth,' Jesus had said, 'no servant (*doulos*) is greater than his master, nor is a messenger (*apostolos*) greater than the one who sent him.'

VIII

A little later, still during the meal, John depicts Peter as asking the 'beloved disciple' to inquire of Jesus who he meant when he hinted at the one who would betray him (13:21, 24). The fact that Peter needed an intermediary has troubled many commentators; one tends, after all, to assume that Peter was given a singular position of honour during Jesus' lifetime. This, however, is not the case, as we have already seen: Peter's elevation to the rank of rock of the *ekklesia* and trustee of the keys is for the future, for the post-ascension community, not for the time of Jesus' own ministry. Whenever Jesus passes on significant teaching or is involved in events of great importance such as the Transfiguration and the Olivet discourse, others are there, such as James, John and (once) Andrew. Peter's unquestioned, privileged role as first among equals and spokesman does not preclude other disciples from acting on their own behalf (see e.g. Mk. 9:38, for John, or Mk. 10:35–41 for James and John; or Jn. 12:22 for Philip and Andrew). Nor does it mean that he could not converse with other disciples in matters of common interest.

If the 'beloved disciple'—identified as John, by unanimous patristic evidence and indeed by most later circumspect exegesis[123] —is addressed by Peter, because he sits closer to the Lord (the debate why Peter did not have one of the 'places of honour' is unnecessary in the light of what has been said above), it merely points to an obvious fact. Other disciples had direct access to Jesus, too; and in a situation where the identity of the traitor was not yet meant to become common knowledge, a quick word between two disciples belonging to the closer circle, one of whom was sitting within whispering distance of Jesus, was only natural. For all that, one should keep in mind that it is Peter who broaches the question: characteristically he wants information. And the other disciple, beloved as he is, does not know more—all he can do is to pass the question on to Jesus.

IX

Whereas his account of the paschal meal supplements the synoptic record with new and important information, John joins them with his report of Jesus' prediction of Peter's denial. Judas Iscariot, identified as the traitor, has left the room. Jesus speaks of his and his Father's glorification, tells the disciples, whom he calls affectionately his 'little children', that they cannot come where he is going, and issues the new commandment of brotherly love for his sake and after his example (Jn. 13:31–35). Peter immediately seizes upon the statement of v. 33, 'You will look for me, and just as I told the Jews, so I tell you now: where I am going, you cannot come.' Jesus had indeed said so twice before. On both occasions (Jn. 7:33–34; 8:21) his hearers had been puzzled. At the time, different interpretations of his words were suggested—a departure from Palestine to teach Greek-speaking Jews elsewhere (8:35), or a ridiculous suspicion of suicide, not taken quite seriously even by those who made it, as the wording suggests (8:22). Although Jesus had hinted at his meaning (8:23–29), the Pharisees did not understand him.

Now Peter, who must have been present on the earlier two occasions, hears the same saying for the third time, and notices that Jesus does not tell them, as he had told the others, that they will not find him. The difference calls for explanation. Jesus gives one of his habitually cryptic answers: 'Where I am going, you cannot follow now, but you will follow later.' Peter immediately grasps one level of this answer: the imminent death of his Lord. And having just made sure that he does 'have part with' Jesus, he wants to retain this togetherness, forgetting, for a moment, about the role he was to play *after* Jesus' death and resurrection: 'Lord, why can't I follow you now? I will lay down my life for you.' We must not doubt the sincerity of this avowal. Only a few hours later, in Gethsemane, he draws his sword and attacks the high priest's servant, thus demonstrating his readiness to fight for Jesus by risking his own life in open combat. But such courage, with sword in hand, is not the courage needed in defenceless dejection, as the scene in the high priest's courtyard would soon show. Instead of glory, it is to be humiliation for the sake of humility. Jesus predicts Peter's denial for the immediate future: 'I tell you the truth, before the cock crows, you will disown me three times!'

This pronouncement in all the solemnity of its double *amēn* (verily, indeed), which marks it as a definitive statement (used twenty-five times in John's gospel),[124] was an unexpected blow after all that had happened before. And it may well be that his attack against the high priest's servant was in part Peter's way of showing his determination all the more vigorously.

In Mark we find no attempt to conceal any of this. Even though his perspective is entirely different from John's, the information he transmits confirms the latter's portrayal of Peter's behaviour. The setting appears to be different—not in the house, but on the way out to Gethsemane, although this is far from certain[125]—and there is a change of emphasis over against John. Jesus begins (14:27) by telling the disciples that they will all fall away and quotes Zc. 13:7 in support of his prediction. He then comforts them by confirming once again that he will rise and by announcing that they will be reunited in Galilee (v. 28). It is at this stage, when, as in John's account, Jesus had already gone on to say something else, that Peter takes up the statement about their falling away. Although John and Mark have chosen different elements of the conversation, both thus agree that Peter was, for once, not rash in speaking. For him, it clearly was a matter of throwing in his very life with that of Jesus—the first time he was faced with such a situation, and we may assume a moment's reflection on how he was to react appropriately, long enough for Jesus to have passed on to the next sentence. 'Even if all fall away', Peter declares, 'I will not' (v. 29). Jesus thereupon predicts Peter's denial for the same night; in Mark's account, it will happen before the cock crows *twice*—a precision, perhaps, which would indicate to his Roman readers that the cock-crows signified an event that would take place before the end of the night.[126]

Peter, however, is not convinced; 'Even if I have to die with you, I will never disown you', he replies—'emphatically', as Mark points out, using a word (*ekperissōs*) which occurs only here in the whole Greek Bible and indicates how shocked and hurt he must have felt. 'And all the others said the same', Mark adds (v. 31), thus underlining Peter's role as their spokesman whose example they see fit to follow.

Matthew follows Mark's account almost to the letter—he adds an interpretative detail (which may well have been there in the first place) in 26:31, 33 and drops the detail of the second cockcrow. It is Luke's depiction of the event that contains some important corroborative information.

Two items concern us here. Luke alone tells his readers that it was Peter and John who were sent by Jesus to prepare the Passover meal (Lk. 22:8–13), an instance which seems to confirm independently the closeness of these two disciples which John illustrates in the incident of the question about the identity of the traitor (Jn. 13:24–25).

Peter + John

Secondly, during the meal, Jesus suddenly addresses Peter: 'Simon, Simon, Satan has asked to sift you as wheat. But I have prayed for you, Simon, that your faith may not fail. And when you have turned back, strengthen your brothers.' (22:31). The emphatic, solemn beginning with the double appellation signifies, as usual, a statement of utmost importance. Peter is addressed, and, as has been customary in Luke's gospel up to this point, by his birth name, Simon. The following 'you' is in the plural: as their spokesman and representative, Peter stands for all the disciples. There can have been no doubt in their minds that Satan was a real, active entity—they will have heard Jesus' words in Lk. 10:18; 11:18; 13:16; and he had been instrumental in turning Judas traitor (Lk. 22:3). Peter himself had every reason to know about Satan's influence (see above, on Mk. 8:33; Mt. 16:23; and also Mk. 4:15). But it is important to note that Satan can only act within the limits set him by God: Job 1:6–12 is an explanatory precedent from the Old Testament.[127] Satan has asked God to grant him the sifting of the disciples: as in the process of the sifting of wheat, the steadfastness of the disciples under pressure of all kind will be subject to satanic temptations, and their faith must be strong if it is not to fall through the sieve.

Jesus, however, has at his disposal a weapon that is stronger than any Satan could employ: his own intercessions. 'But I have prayed for you, Simon', he says, 'that your faith may not fail. And when you have turned back, strengthen your brothers' (22:32b). The 'you' this time is in the singular: not that Jesus would not pray for the others, too, but it is Peter who is singled out for a special task and who is therefore under greater temptation and in need of specific intercession. The terms of Jesus' prayer are remarkable: he does not pray that Peter may be spared, but rather that his faith may not fail, in spite of the inevitability of his succumbing to the Tempter (as the same night would make only too obvious). And Jesus knows that his prayers will prevail: 'When you have turned back', he says to Peter, i.e. when he has shown repentance, weeping bitterly after the denial which Jesus is about to predict. Then Peter will be the one to strengthen his brothers.

It has been noted that this commissioning of Peter on the strength of Jesus' intercession confirms in Luke's gospel what the episode of the rock and the keys had instituted in Matthew's (16:16–19).[128] As Satan's machinations on that occasion did not cause Peter's downfall, so the denial of Jesus at Gethsemane will not remain a triumph of Satan. Peter, temporarily fallen, will be raised by Jesus, through his intercession, and as the strengthened one he will be the rock providing strength for all others. We should not read 'brothers' (*adelphoi*) as a description of his fellow-disciples only: in this passage, the term extends to all followers of Christ (see already Mk. 3:35; Mt. 12:50; Lk. 8:21), and this is how it was understood by the post-ascension community: see 1 Cor. 1:1; 8:12; 15:6; 1 Thes. 3:2, etc., and significantly, 1 Pet. 5:12 and 2 Pet. 3:14 (cf. also 1 Pet 2:17). Peter's role as the rock-like strengthener is one for the whole community, for the *ekklesia*, as Matthew (and Luke in Acts) described it.

Peter, as we know from the other accounts, grasps only half of what has been predicted—and seeks to defend himself against what he understands as a reproach for weakness: 'Lord, I am ready to go with you to prison and death' (22:33). Jesus' reply is marked by an important emphasis: for the only time in Luke, indeed for the first time since Matthew 16:17 in any of the gospels, Peter is addressed not as Simon or Simon Peter, but as *Petros*, Rock. In the prediction of the denial, none of the other evangelists has Jesus addressing Peter by name; it may well, however, be precisely what Jesus did: to shift from his usual way of addressing Peter to the single use of his by-name in order to point out to him with sad, didactic irony that he is, as yet, anything but a rock: that will have to come later, when he has 'turned back'.

Thanks to their variations of emphasis and perspective in detail and outline, all four evangelists contribute to an impressive synopsis of Peter's role on the evening of the Paschal meal. The prediction of the denial was a central event in Peter's career—this weakness that could be turned into strength only by Jesus himself was to become a symbol in the early church, so much so that our earliest extant portrayals of Peter with a symbol, on third and fourth century sarcophagi (still on public display in the Museo Pio Cristiano, a section of the Vatican Museums), do not show him with a pair of keys, but with a cock at his feet and his forefinger pointing towards his chin. Even at a time when the absolute authority of Peter had been established in the Western Church, Peter could still be shown as the one who had denied the Lord—but who had also turned back, conscious of his guilt, in self-imposed penitence.

X

Having left the room of their Passover meal, Jesus and the disciples go to the Mount of Olives (Mk. 14:26; Mt. 26:30; Lk. 22:39), on the other side of the valley of the brook Kidron (Jn. 18:1), where they had a regular retreat (Lk. 22:39; Jn. 18:2) in a garden (Jn. 18:1) called Gethsemane (Mk. 14:32; Mt. 26:36). 'Gethsemane' is clearly used as a proper name by Mark and Matthew. The Hebrew word means 'oil-press', and the place is called an estate (*chōrion*) by both evangelists which means that it was an olive grove used for agricultural purposes, with an oil-press and an area where a group might gather. It may well have been used by Jesus not just as a prayer retreat, but also for teaching his disciples—gardens served for such purposes in Graeco-Roman antiquity[129] as well as in rabbinical circles.[130]

Jesus tells Peter, James and John, the closer group of the three, to come with him into the garden and leaves the other eight behind, near the entrance, asking them to remain there while he prays (Mk. 14:32–33). The three had been singled out before, and twice it had been on mountains—on the Mount of Transfiguration, and, not long ago, on the Mount of Olives itself (where Andrew had been with them), each time in circumstances of special revelation. 'My soul is overwhelmed with sorrow to the point of death', he says to them. 'Stay here and keep watch' (Mk. 14:34). His words allude to Ps. 116:3 (or 114:3 in the LXX, the Greek of which is very close to the Greek of Mark's account), i.e. one of the Passover Hallel psalms that had been sung by Jesus and the disciples at the end of their meal: 'The cords of death entangled me, the anguish of Hades came upon me; I was overcome by trouble and sorrow.' He was alarmed and distressed—a powerful description of his state using two rare New Testament words. The first one, *ekthambeō*, occurs only three times outside this passage, always in Mark: see Mk. 16:5, 6; cf. 9:15; the second one, *adēmoneō*, occurs only three times in total, the other two instances being Mt. 26:37, (Matthew's parallel to Mark's report) and Phil. 2:26.

Jesus knows the hour has come for him to face death, in the words of the Psalm (18:5), 'the dangers of Hades'. This decisive moment, more than any previous one, demands prayer, conversation with his Father. He goes a little further, telling Peter, James and John to stay behind and watch (14:34), and he uses the same word he had used on the Mount of Olives before: *grēgoreite*: watch out, be attentive (see p. 64 above on Mk. 13:34 and 1 Pet. 5:8). The enemy is near—not merely Judas with the Roman cohort and the high priest's henchmen, but also the Tempter who wants to 'sieve' them (Lk. 22:31). The fact that we have a report of the gist of Jesus' prayer (Mk. 14:36; Mt. 26:39; Lk. 22:42) indicates, as it did on the Mount of Transfiguration, that the three did not fall fully asleep (cf. p. 47 above). Their eyes were heavy (14:40); it was the kind of drowsiness we all know from our own experience. Needless to say, this is no excuse for their dismal failure to follow Jesus' request—but it is also characteristic of their reaction in the presence of what one might call 'the holy uncanny' to which they have to be 'woken up' spiritually as well as physically.

As Jesus repeated his prayer three times (Mk. 14:39, 41; Mt. 26:44), they would have grasped its meaning, and not least the striking appellation Jesus gives to his Father, 'Abba', the traditional word used to address the father of the family, but never, not even after Jesus, for God.[131] Only Christians were later encouraged to employ the term: see Rom. 8:15–16; Gal. 4:6–7.

'Abba', Peter and the others dimly hear him pray, 'everything is possible for you. Take this cup from me. Yet not what I will, but what you will' (Mk. 14:36). Two of those present will have recognized the idea immediately: James and John, who had asked Jesus to sit at his right and his left in his glory (Mk. 10:37), had been told about the cup he would have to drink (10:38–39). The image is reminiscent of Je. 49:12, and the fleeting thought that God may take the cup from him, as everything is possible for his Father, is equally based on Old Testament prophecy: cf. Is. 51:22.

But the decisive point is that Jesus submits himself to God's will and even finds the inner strength to remember the three disciples. Three times he returns to them. The first time, he speaks to Peter: 'Simon, are you asleep? Could you not keep watch for one hour? Watch and pray so that you will not fall into temptation. The spirit is willing, but the flesh [body] is weak' (14:37–38). Peter is addressed not so much because it was he who had made the most emphatic vow of discipleship only a few hours before (although this does play a role, of course), but because once again he is seen as the representative of the others: the 'you' in v. 38 is plural.[132]

On the second and third occasions, Jesus addresses all three disciples. In 14:41, what he says to them is translated as a question by RSV and NIV: 'Are you still sleeping and resting/taking your rest?', whereas the AV gives the straight meaning of the Greek exclamation: 'Sleep on now and take your rest!' Both versions convey the same ironic overtone. The AV seems preferable: it underlines the resigned exasperation Jesus must have felt at the weakness of even his three most trusted disciples, and it also supports a reasonable understanding of the difficult next word, *apechei* (AV/RSV: 'It is enough'; NIV: 'Enough!'). The impersonal use of this word, which has several possible meanings, has led to many differing interpretations. The most satisfying direction is indicated by the text of the passage in codices and manuscripts like the Bezae Cantabrigiensis (D05), the Washingtonensis (W032), the Koridethianus (*thēta*038), and several important minuscules as well as some Italian, Syriac and Armeninian versions and Tatian's Diatessaron, all of which add, as a subject to the verb (in one way or another) *to telos*: 'the end', 'the aim'. The evidence of these textual witnesses does not make this the true, original reading, but it makes sense, nonetheless, even if it were merely an interpretation by very early scribes and translators: we could understand the passage as saying, 'The end is fully there', and thus, in context, 'Sleep on . . ., it is all reaching its fulfilment, anyway.' The analogy to Lk. 22:37 is tangible: 'What is written about me is reaching its fulfilment' (*Kai gar to peri emou telos echei*).[133] This reconstruction gains support from what follows (14:41b–42): 'The hour has come. Look, the Son of Man is betrayed into the hands of sinners. Rise! Let us go! Here comes my betrayer!'

The decisive moment finds Jesus in a determined mood. He will not wait for his pursuers. As he sees them arriving, he speaks unambiguously of himself as the Son of Man (cf., for the contrast between future glory and present suffering, Mk. 13:26 with 14:41), and leads Peter, James and John to meet Judas and the others.

Matthew's account follows Mark's closely. He adds the second prayer (26:42), and while the first one differs slightly from Mark's version ('if it is possible', rather than 'everything is possible for you'; and the 'Abba' is only given in translation), the text of the second prayer follows more closely the context of Is. 51:17–23. Matthew, too, reports that Peter was reproached first (26:40), but in his version, his role as spokesman is even clearer: '"Could you men not keep watch with me for one hour?" he asked Peter.' Among the synoptic writers, it is Luke who adds the most intriguing details. On the one hand, the drama with its threefold prayers and reproaches is cut by him to its bare essentials, and Peter is not even mentioned by name. On the other hand, the prayer itself is highlighted in a way that fills in detail without contradicting what has been said earlier: '"Father, if you are willing, take this cup from me; yet not my will, but yours be done." An angel from heaven appeared to him and strengthened him. And being in anguish, he prayed more earnestly, and his sweat was like drops of blood falling to the ground.' (Lk. 22:42–44).

While this description has inspired many artists, it has also caused problems of understanding—sweat-like drops of blood make for colourful brushwork, but complicate medical explanation. The easiest answer, of course, is that this verse, as well as the preceding one, are not original. Some important early manuscripts, including the earliest extant one of Luke's gospel, p75, exclude it, as do most translations and some Fathers who have commented on the passage.[134] But even if the passage is original (which both its style and the cumulative textual evidence strongly suggest), the image is a powerful metaphor: Jesus' agony (only Luke, the doctor, uses the term *agōnia* in the New Testament) was indeed so profound (as we also gather from Mark's and Matthew's description of his state) that his sweat was falling like drops (*hōsei thromboi*). Here is another medical term only used by Luke in the NT—we still have it in words such as thrombosis. By describing his agony in these terms—and one may assume that the basic information came from one of the three disciples present, awake enough to catch such a sight and not to miss the appearance of the angel in v. 43 either (cf. Lk. 9:31), Luke intimates that this prayer marked the beginning of Jesus' sufferings and tortures.

XI

The actual arrest is handled with dramatic restraint by all four evangelists,[135] and not for the first time the four accounts form a mutually supportive picture so vivid that it suggests cumulative eye-witness evidence. Mark (14:43), Matthew (26:47) and Luke (22:47) begin by reminding their readers of the appalling fact that Judas has been one of the twelve. He identifies Jesus with two gestures of reverence, the address 'Rabbi' (Mk. 14:45; Mt. 26:49) and a kiss (Mk. 14:45; Mt. 26:49; Lk. 22:47). This is the sign for the motley group of persecutors, who did not know him by sight, to act. Certainly there were enough people with authority present to supervise the arrest: leading priests (Lk. 22:52), a commanding officer of the temple guard (Jn. 18:12), with servants of the court (Jn. 18:3) and a detachment of the temple guard and temple police (Jn. 18:3/Lk. 22:52), all heavily armed.[136] It is difficult, if not impossible, to give an estimate of their numbers; but whereas there cannot have been too many (one occasionally reads estimates of 1,000 people!)—a potential uprising by alarmed followers in the city had to be avoided. Judas would have told the Sanhedrin that the group itself was unlikely to use their weapons— if any—in revolt (which was probably one of the reasons why he had left them in the first place), and we know that the temple guard alone consisted of twenty-one men (Mishnah Midd. 2:1), which may suggest a conservative estimate of some fifty people.

Jesus expressly confirms Judas' identification, and does so in words which underline his unique status. 'I am' he says (John 18:5), *ego eimi*. On the surface this is a way of saying 'It's me', but is an obvious reiteration of similar statements on earlier occasions: Jn. 8:24, 58 contain an unambiguous allusion to Dt. 32:39 where God says of himself *ego eimi*—cf. Ex. 3:14. Such a declaration is the last thing the henchmen had expected from a hopelessly surrounded trouble-maker. Overawed, they step back and fall to the ground (Jn. 18:6). Question ('Who is it you want?') and answer ('Jesus of Nazareth') are repeated, and again Jesus states that he is the one and adds that they should let the disciples go free (18:8)—which, as John explains, happened in fulfilment of an earlier word (Jn. 17:12; cf. 6:39, 10:28).

The armed men proceed to arrest him, but while they are doing so, Peter draws his short sword. *Machaira* was a technical term for a long knife or short sword, although it had already been a synonym for the proper long sword, the *rhomphaia*, in the Greek OT—it is at any rate the same word and thus the same type of weapon as the one used for the weapon carried by the guard. He attacks the personal servant of the high priest and cuts off his right ear (Mk. 14:47; Mt. 26:51; Lk. 22:50; Jn. 18:10).

Only Luke and John mention that it was his right ear and only Luke that Jesus healed the wound—a medical point of characteristic interest to a doctor with a hint of Jesus' care for a victim of violence even in such a moment. John alone gives the names of the attacker and the servant, Malchus. This is one of John's usual touches of informed detail; Peter's does not come as a surprise, as he was the one who, more than anyone else, had felt the obligation to act, to try and do something, to prove himself to Jesus and by doing so perhaps even to reverse the whole situation with the assistance of the legions of angels (see above, p. 34 and n. 42). After all, as he saw it, it was the very last chance to turn the Suffering Messiah into a glorious victor. Whatever his motives, this was not a thoughtless, impulsive action: he knew that he risked his life—drawing the sword was provocative enough, and using it was tantamount to rebellion. It must be said that of all those surrounding Jesus, including the guards, Peter was the only one to show actual physical courage.[137]

It may seem surprising that Mark (copied here by Matthew) and Luke do not give Peter's name. They would have known it, of course,[138] and the reason for the omission is obvious: both Mark and Luke were writing for Roman readerships, Mark in Rome and in all probability during Peter's lifetime, Luke also during Peter's lifetime and (Lk. 1:1; Acts 1:1) to a high-ranking Roman civil servant. Nothing could have been more counterproductive to their interests than naming the man who had used a sword in open revolt against the state authorities and who had, by the time they wrote, become the pillar of the community in Rome.[139]

There may be more than mere chance in Peter's cutting off the servant's ear. It has been held that this was merely accidental, as Peter was no expert swordsman,[140] but with a short sword, not a battle weapon, even a fisherman would be able to choose his target from close distance. As the whole action was deliberate in the first place, the cutting off of the ear may well have been the most efficient way of achieving the desired impact short of killing the man. Josephus reports in his *Antiquities, 14,* 13:10, that cutting off the ears was a way of preventing someone from exercising priestly office, as 'only flawless men are admitted by the law'. For Peter, Malchus was the representative of his master, the High Priest, whom he attacked through the servant, thereby effectively provoking the highest religious authority with one stroke. There is OT precedent for this kind of vicarious action in 2 Sm. 10:4.[141]

Jesus, however, cannot condone Peter's action; with remarkable patience he explains that he has to go the whole way (Jn. 18:11), that the use of the sword would only lead to Peter's own death (Mt. 26:52, an impressive reminder of Gn. 9:6), and that he could have summoned the angelic legions himself if that had been his

Father's will (Mt. 26:53–54). Rebuked for what he thought was glowing proof of his faithfulness to his Lord, Peter disappears. His last attempt has failed, he is at a loss what to do now—what does the Lord expect of him to do to prove worthy of his status as rock? Peter is one of those who learn from experience, as we have seen, even if slowly, so he flees from the confused, incomprehensible scene (Mk. 14:50; Mt. 26:56). But unlike the others (with one exception) he stays nearby, to follow developments from a safe distance (Mk. 14:54; Mt. 26:58; Lk. 22:54; Jn. 18:15).[142] This, again, is a courageous decision. Peter is clearly rock-like in his discipleship, even though his understanding is imperfect.

By the time he writes his first letter, understanding has come, and he passes it on to his readers in unambiguous, encouraging words: cf. 1 Pet. 2:19–21; 3:9–14, 17; 4:14–19. Suffering with the suffering Messiah, not revolting against the cost of true discipleship, but being assured of the inheritance of God's blessing (1 Pet. 3:9)—this, Peter says, is one of the most important characteristics of the Christian whose faith and hope are in the God who raised Christ from the dead and exalted him (1 Pet. 1:21) in glorious victory.

CHAPTER FOUR

From Denial to Reinstatement

I

'And Peter followed him at a distance, right into the courtyard of the high priest. There he sat with the guards and warmed himself at the fire' (Mk. 14:54). How did Peter get into the courtyard, into the lion's den, as it were? Explanation is provided by John who offers, at this stage, one of his stimulating but puzzling 'inside' reports. 'Simon Peter and another disciple were following Jesus', John writes (Jn. 18:15). 'Because this disciple was known to the high priest, he went with Jesus into the high priest's courtyard. But Peter had to wait outside at the door. The other disciple, who was known to the high priest, came back, spoke to the slave girl on duty there and brought Peter in.'

The passion accounts of the four evangelists are, it seems, full of mysteriously unnamed people. But again, there are some telltale indications—the most obvious and most helpful one being the fact that this second disciple is described in the same way as the 'beloved disciple'; as *allos mathētēs*, the 'other disciple': cf. Jn. 20:2, 3, 4, 8. The other, the 'beloved disciple', had close contacts with Peter (Jn. 1:40; 13:23–24; cf. Lk. 22:8–13; cf. p. 68

above), and this appears to be corroborated by the present passage. Even if there is no alternative to identifying the disciple of Jn. 18:15 with the disciple of Jn. 13:23–24 and Lk. 22:8–13, the question remains, why this John is suddenly presented as an acquaintance of the high priest. For this, the evidence is well known, though highly circumstantial. Historical sources begin with a letter sent by Polycrates of Ephesus to Victor, the first Roman bishop to convene a synod and to work for Roman supremacy over the other Christian communities. In his letter, written c. AD 190, and quoted by Eusebius (*HE* 3, 31:2–4), he states that 'John, who leaned on the Lord's breast', was 'a priest wearing the plate, a martyr and teacher, and he sleeps at Ephesus', (i.e. he was buried in the very city where Polycrates was bishop, only some eighty to ninety years after his death). What Polycrates, whose letter suggests a thoughtful, self-critical Christian mind, wanted to say, is clear: John was a descendant of the family of Aaron, the Levite and first high priest of the hereditary priesthood. In Lv. 8:9, Aaron receives the plate (*petalon*, the same Greek word as in Polycrates' letter) from Moses, as a sign of his investiture. This golden plate had in turn been prescribed by God as part of the priestly uniform (Ex. 28:32/ 29:6). Polycrates' statement was evidently based on earlier information, most likely going back to John himself. Only one question remains: does this tally with what the New Testament has to say about John's background? The circumstantial evidence seems positive: Mk. 15:40 and Mt. 27:56 together indicate that John's mother was Salome. Salome was the sister of Mary (Jesus' mother): cf. Jn. 19:25 with Mk. 15:40. Mary in turn was a relative of Elizabeth (Lk. 1:36) who is described as a 'descendant of Aaron', Lk. 1:5. It follows that there is at least a link in the New Testament between John and the family of hereditary priests.[143]

John was thus entitled to free access to the high priest's quarters; indeed he was entitled to carry out priestly duties at the temple.[144] Two things are noteworthy here: John, for the first and only time in the course of his discipleship, makes use of his privilege, and he does so in order to help Peter, whom he apparently acknowledges, despite the desperate hour, as the one disciple with a special role. Mark, Matthew and Luke do not mention John: in the context of their accounts, his action (which could after all be seen merely as a factor in the story of Peter's predicted denial) could be omitted.

Once inside, Peter joins the servants and officials of the high priest at the fire (Mk. 14:54/Lk. 22:25/Jn. 18:18). There is a difference in the order of events, or so it seems: in John's account, Peter's first denial seems to happen at the door, when the servant-girl lets him in, whereas the others appear to locate it by the fire. We need not assume any conflict. Since Mark, Matthew, and Luke have omitted John's intervention, they have no need for a servant girl *at the door*. Even so, John does not say that the girl *asked him* at the door; all he says is that it was the girl who had been at the door, literally 'the door-girl' (*hē paidiskē hē thurōros*), who later seemed to recognize him and wanted to make sure. This is precisely what the other evangelists say: this girl (all four agree it was the servant girl who elicited Peter's first denial) approached Peter; it is indeed unlikely that she asked him immediately at the door, as the other disciple (who disappears soon afterwards!) would still have been there (Jn. 18:16b)—and Peter would most certainly not have denied the Lord in the presence of his trusted fellow disciple, the beloved one (or of any other disciple, for that matter). The servant-girl's question makes sense only at a moment when the other disciple was no longer present, i.e. at the fire, where he is not mentioned any more (Jn. 18:18).

More intriguing are the contents of the conversations. They are, once again, striking examples of the reliability of eye-witness accounts differing (as any modern jury or historical research committee would confirm[145]) precisely in those small details of wording which make them all the more trustworthy as independent confirmation of an event whose form and historicity can be said to be safely established.

Mark is to the point, as usual. Having 'introduced' Peter as present in the high priest's courtyard, he gives his account of the hearing before the Sanhedrin and then returns to Peter's denial, making it quite clear that these events are simultaneous. He does not spare Peter—or rather, in view of Peter's authoritative influence on the account, Peter does not spare himself. There is a certain aggressiveness in the tone of the dialogue between the girl and Peter. 'You also were with that Nazarene, Jesus', she says (Mk. 14:67), having looked at him closely.[146] Peter's first denial is indirect. 'I don't know or understand what you're talking about.' To emphasize that he wants to be left alone, he begins to move towards the forecourt. At this moment, the cock crows for the first time.[147] We should remember that Peter's mere presence must have caused suspicion: the group around the fire in the courtyard consisted of servants of the high priest, so that he was the odd man out before he so much as opened his mouth. The girl may have seen him before, on an earlier occasion somewhere in Jerusalem, or perhaps she simply had a hunch that the reason for the man's otherwise inexplicable presence was his association with 'the Nazarene', and accosted him on the off-chance that he would give himself away. This interpretation is strengthened by the wording in John's account, where the girl does not make an explicit statement, but asks an equally explicit leading question: 'Surely you are not another of this man's disciples?' (Jn. 18:17). His 'I am not' answers the question in the expected way: the girl is not entirely convinced herself, and Peter does not encourage her.[148] (When John says that Peter was warming himself at the fire—and that he was still there when the second question came, he does not contradict the move towards the forecourt in Mark's account: the NIV translation of Mk. 14:69 is misleading. The girl did not 'see him *there*', i.e. in the forecourt, but she 'observed him', which is the proper translation of '*idousa auton*'; and before he could even get to the forecourt, the second question stopped him in his tracks. He tried to get away, but he did not succeed).

The second approach is shared by others in the group. Peter has become an object of general curiosity: Mark says that the same girl now alerts those standing around (14:69), and that Peter denies the charge again. Matthew, who seems to imply that he did reach the forecourt, has another girl speaking to the people there (26:71—apparently Matthew's attempt to explain how anyone could involve Peter in a second denial *there* is a thoughtful but unneccesary development of Mark's account). John (18:25) has the group, i.e. someone from the group, asking the second question. Luke, who, like John, does not mention the forecourt at all, singles out a man—one who has taken up the girl's initial approach. The differences in detail confirm the basic fact: it is not just a dialogue between the girl and Peter any more. If he had tried to brush her off at the beginning, he had failed: now they have all taken notice.

And worse is to come—a third time the question is put, the accusation is made: members of the group at the fire have recognized his Galilean accent, and as it was known that Jesus and his followers had come from Galilee, they can press Peter even harder: 'Surely you are one of them, for you are a Galilean' (Mk. 14:70). Matthew, again interpreting Mark, says 'Surely you are one of them, for your accent gives you away' (26:73). Luke, who even gives a time interval ('about an hour later') has the statement in an indirect form (22:59), and John identifies this third speaker as a relative of Malchus (18:26) who thinks he recognizes the swordsman from the olive grove: it is not unnatural for John, who had taken such an interest in Malchus before (he may indeed have known him personally through his contacts with the high priest's household), to choose this utterance over against the Galilean give-away mentioned by the synoptics.

Further details are supplied in the accounts of Peter's third denial, which is emphatic—he swears (Mk. 14:71; Mt. 26:74—in Matthew's account he has sworn already at the second denial) and he curses (Mk. 14:71; Mt. 26:74). Mark leaves open who or what is cursed: with the grammatical object missing, it could be a general curse, whereas Matthew, at least in the RSV and the NIV, but not in the AV translation of 26:74, seems to imply that Peter cursed himself (in the sense of 'May I be damned if I am not telling the truth'). This is not warranted by the Greek words. Both Mark's *anathematizo* (only here in the gospels) and Matthew's *katathematizo* (only here in the whole Greek Bible) are strong words for cursing, but are used without an object in both instances.

Luke adds a puzzling detail in 22:61: 'The Lord turned and looked straight at Peter.' How can the Lord appear so suddenly, immediately after the crowing of the cock, the very moment his prediction is being fulfilled? Again the facts mesh together when corroborative evidence is taken into account. John (and he alone) points out that Jesus was sent first to Annas (18:13), still called by his old title (18:19), and then by Annas to Caiaphas (18:24). But he also points out that they shared the same palace, namely that of the high priest, Caiaphas (18:5). It appears that they were living in two different wings and that the most direct link was via the courtyard. Jesus was taken from Annas to Caiaphas just as Peter was making his third denial, and it was then that he turned and looked at Peter.[149]

Peter has studiously avoided Jesus' name in any of the denials. Now Jesus himself stands before him. And Peter realizes that his attempts to talk his way out of his responsibility as a disciple, out of a direct, open involvement with the destiny of Jesus, have failed dismally. It would be easy to find excuses for his behaviour:

one might say that he had, after all, felt obliged to save his own life, as Jesus had predicted a future role for him; one might say that he only tried to get rid of the importunate servants who prevented him from quietly waiting for the outcome of the hearing. But in the aftermath of his failed attempt to defend the Lord with the sword in his hand, to begin the decisive, eschatological battle, he was in fact a dejected man without hope, still faithful enough to stick around and watch, but not sufficiently convinced to declare himself for the man whose Messiahship he was as yet unable to comprehend.

The cock crows, Jesus looks at him, and he breaks down and weeps bitterly (Mk. 14:72; Mt. 26:75; Lk. 22:62).[150] Not only has he failed his Rabbi and Lord whose prophecy has now been fulfilled; he has also given the lie to his bold statement of some hours before, that he would never disown him. The man who wanted to prove himself rock is shattered to pieces. He had to be broken by his own powerlessness before satanic temptation (Lk. 22:31), in order that he could be made whole (Lk. 22:32), and we may picture him, as so often in the history of art, crying with folded hands, in penitence, praying for forgiveness. And we can understand all the better why early Christian artists portrayed him with that pointed finger of guilt, and the cock at his feet. The keys were a symbol for the future, but the tell-tale signs of his betrayal demonstrated utter human frailty, against which the forgiveness of Christ would shine even brighter. If Peter could not only remain, but properly *become* the rock of the Christian community after such depths of faithlessness—how much greater was and is the hope for ordinary men and women, believers as well as not-yet-believers, that God will patiently forgive them their sins! Indeed Peter himself hints at this in his second letter, in a thought he gladly shares with Paul who had also experienced the Lord's forgiveness (Rom. 2:4): 'Bear in mind that our Lord's patience means salvation' (2 Pet. 3:15).

II

Peter was not at the cross. Where was he? We have no certain knowledge. His name is not mentioned again until after the Resurrection. After his denials and tearful prayers of remorse and penitence, he did not have the strength to face the crucified Jesus;

the only disciple who had a right and the courage to do so was the 'beloved disciple', who had walked a straight line, unshakenly neither fleeing nor disowning the Lord, and who joined some of the women, among them his own mother, Salome, and Jesus' mother, his aunt Mary, who was than placed in his care by Jesus (Jn. 19:25–27; cf. Mk. 15:40–41; Mt. 27:55–56; Lk. 23:27, 49).[151]

John says that the smaller group joined Jesus by the cross, at least for a while, whereas all the other followers watched the scene from a distance. This is made particularly vivid by Luke, who writes in 23:49, 'But all those who knew him, including the women who had followed him from Galilee, stood at a distance, watching these things.'

Recent archeological work has led to the re-discovery of the gate through which Jesus was taken on his way to Golgotha, the Gennath or Garden Gate, mentioned by Josephus (*War* 5, 4:2), and indirectly alluded to by John (19:41–42). This gate stood at the beginning of the so-called Second Wall, lying on a north-south axis, which is today known as Suk es-Zeit. It is on this wall, at the point opposite Golgotha, that the witnesses mentioned by Luke would have stood—at a safe distance, but close enough not to have missed anything.[152] It is reasonable to infer from Luke's description of 'all those who knew him', that at least the disciples, including Peter, were on that wall. There is no need to assume that Peter had been in hiding. No one would have singled him out for questioning up there, and the least he could do after his tearful breakdown was to watch for himself how his Lord would end his life.

Remarkably, outside the gospels it is only Peter who uses graphic, visual language to describe the actual crucifixion. In his speech before the Sanhedrin in Acts 5:29–32, he speaks of 'Jesus . . . whom you had killed by hanging him on a tree' (v. 30) and goes on to say, 'We are witnesses of these things' (v. 32); in his address at the house of Cornelius, Acts 10:34–43, he confirms that 'we were witnesses of everything he did in the country of the Jews and in Jerusalem. They killed him by hanging him on a tree' (v. 39); and in his first letter (1 Pet. 2:24), he says of Christ that he took up our sins in his body on the tree. Only Paul, who had obtained his information directly from Peter (Gal. 1:18–19), comes anywhere near this language: cf. Acts 13:29 and Gal. 3:13.[153]

The apocryphal 'Gospel of Peter', written at the beginning of the second century, offers a speculative conjecture: purporting to be written by Peter, it portrays him as an eyewitness of the crucifixion, as he himself does in the canonical NT writings, but then goes on to say that he hid himself with the others afterwards, since they were sought after as evildoers and as persons 'who wanted to set fire to the temple'.[154]

III

Paul, in his great exposition of the historicity of the Resurrection, 1 Cor. 15:1–11 (which he owes not least to Peter: cf. 1 Cor. 15:3 with Gal. 1:18), mentions Peter first in his list of witnesses to the Risen Christ. It is not surprising that he omits the women who had been the first to see him risen from the dead (Mt. 28:8–10, Jn. 20:14–18), as the testimony of women had no legal validity,[155] and the particular aim of his list is of course to convince his readers of the historical *and* legal trustworthiness of his witnesses. What is surprising, however, is the fact that our earliest gospel, Mark (the one written under Peter's personal influence), does not mention any appearance to Peter at all but ends instead with the scene at the empty tomb, in a beautiful Greek sentence which just melts in the mouth (and so it should, as Mark's gospel was probably initially meant to be read aloud at gatherings of the Roman Christians,[156]) with the two words *ephobounto gar*, 'for they were afraid' (Mk. 16:8).[157]

Peter plays an important role all the same; in 16:7 he is singled out most emphatically. 'But go, tell the disciples and Peter', says the young man in white. Not only does this underline the forgiveness for his denial, it also stresses the special position he has continued to hold. And if we assume, as manuscript evidence and internal considerations suggest (see p. 157 below), that the gospel was written during Peter's lifetime and in Rome, we can almost see him standing up after 16:8 has been read and, continuing the story himself from the point when the women found him and he then became the first of the disciples to see what really mattered: that Christ was risen indeed. For those who did not have Peter to sum it all up for them personally, the empty tomb itself and the message of the young man (v. 6) said it all, anyway. The holy fear of the women at the end made it unambiguously clear: God had been at work.[158]

Peter hears the women's story. Sceptically, like a (rabbinical) law-abiding man (see above, note 154), he doubts their report, which seemed like nonsense to him and the others (Lk. 24:11). But curiosity, and the dim hope that something extraordinary may have happened, gain the upper hand. He runs to the tomb. In John's account, the 'other disciple' runs with him (Jn. 20:3; cf. Lk. 24:24); both versions confirm that there was more to their action than 'perhaps we should give it a try'. They know, in their hearts, that the women are trustworthy, for they have been with them long enough. But whereas they had not wanted to accept such female 'nonsense', they put on a sprint once they are outside the house. One cannot help seeing a trace of wordly-wise humour in both accounts, with the evangelists discreetly taking sides with the women. This is made even more apparent by John, who turns the fact-finding expedition into a race between the two disciples (but in the event reserves his first report of a resurrection-appearance proper to a woman, 20:10f).

Peter arrives second at the tomb (Lk. 24:12),[159] but although the other disciple is the better sprinter, he acknowledges Peter's seniority and stays outside, after a first glance at the 'strips of linen' (Jn. 20:4–5). Peter examines the evidence. Luke does not specify whether Peter actually enters the tomb; his formulation, 'bending over' literally 'peering into', *parakuptō*, is however the same as is used for John's first glance before Peter and he enter the tomb, and for Mary when she looks into it (Jn. 20:5, 11). The usage of 1 Pet. 1:12b suggests that an intense, thorough inspection is meant. For Luke this was sufficient, so he breaks off at this point. John concludes his report with the detail of the next step, the entering of the tomb. From outside, both John (20:5) and Peter, before he enters it (Lk. 24:12), see the *othonia*, literally the 'linen burial cloths'.[160] The women were right, after all—the tomb was empty.

But the angels had left. Their precise number, one (Mk. 16:5; Mt. 28:5) or two (Lk. 24:4, and cf. Jn. 20:12) can be determined in favour of the latter, as Mark, followed by Matthew, applying a characteristic technique, mentions only the one who actually spoke. This is a technique used interestingly enough by John in the same context: he implies that several women were at the tomb (Jn. 20:2b), but mentions only the Magdalene in his report (20:1–2a). Luke does the same when he mentions only Peter (Lk. 24:12), but implies that another disciple was there with him (24:24).

So were the women also right about the message that Jesus had risen? Peter could not ask the angels any more, he had to make up his own mind. Was it this, after all that the Lord had tried to tell him so many times before? He goes away, 'wondering to himself what had happened' (Lk. 24:12 NIV).

Before he left, he had been inside, as John tells us, and the closer inspection of the contents of the tomb had confirmed the initial analysis. Not only were the burial cloths lying there; the head-cloth, the *soudarion*, was in its place, too: rolled together in a way suggesting that it had not been removed from the body and then folded up—but still in the original form, as it had been at the burial.[161] 'Only' the body was missing. John understands that this cannot have been the work of tomb-robbers. They would not have left the burial cloth folded up, and could not possibly have restored the head-cloth to the shape it had had on the head of Jesus.

'The other disciple', John writes, enters the tomb, 'sees and believes' (20:8). The 'believing' has no object; it could refer to the story told by the women (although in John's abbreviated account, no mention is made of the Resurrection), or it could quite simply mean that he believed something extraordinary had indeed happened; but it could also mean that he believed in the truth of what Jesus had predicted all along: that he would rise again from the dead (cf. the usage of Jn. 20:29). It is, as yet, only a first step towards full faith, as the following verse explains—'They (i.e. both John and Peter) did not understand *from Scripture* that Jesus *had* to rise from the dead.' (Jn. 20:9, NIV). The importance of this understanding is emphasized by Jesus (Lk. 24:25–26, 44–48), and Paul (1 Cor. 15:3–5); cf. also Peter's speeches, such as Acts 2:16–36, 3:17–26 (esp. 3:24), and 4:8–12. It is the initial insight, the first step of faith, that counts; what follows is secondary proof. John has made this step; but has Peter? The evangelist does not explicitly mention his reaction, but one may suppose that he shared this initial insight to a certain degree: this is, at any rate, implied by the plural of v. 9—and the Greek construction of v. 8, an enumeration with three 'ands', may even suggest that Peter 'saw and believed' first—*and then* John entered, *and* then he saw, *and* then he believed, *too!* John's account helps us to understand Lk. 24:12: Peter was not quite 'wondering to himself what had happened'—he was *marvelling* at it. (For this use of the Greek word *thaumazō*, see, e.g. 2 Thes. 1:10; Lk. 1:63; 2:18, 33; 11:14; 24:41).

It is noteworthy that John, unlike Peter, never meets the risen

Christ on his own; he shares in the appearances to the eleven. And it seems that he acts as something like Peter's circumspect aide. The preparation of the Passover meal, the question about the traitor and the admission to the high priest's courtyard are earlier examples; now, at the empty tomb, he is linked with the thought-provoking insight into the importance of the event; on Lake Tiberias (Jn. 21:7) it is he who sees the Lord first, whereupon Peter jumps into the water; and later, in Acts, we find him at Peter's right hand more than once. In all those instances, Peter's pre-eminence is never questioned once. But the events after the Resurrection point out that he is not isolated, and that the establishment of the early Christian communities depends upon teamwork from the start. The role given to the 'other disciple' in John's gospel is thus no attempt to belittle Peter; corroborated by Luke's Acts, and indeed by the other gospels where John is named as a member of the inner circle of the Three it merely goes to show that these two different disciples complemented each other purposefully. They must have been aware of this from the days when they had been partners in their fishing business in Capharnaum. Even though John wanted to make sure that he and his brother James would have positions of special privilege in the New Age (Mk. 10:37), during their joint earthly ministry he accepted Peter's authority which had, after all, not been Peter's own desire, but Jesus' decision.

IV

Peter is singled out to receive an individual appearance of the Lord (Lk. 24:34; 1 Cor. 15:5). According to the context of Lk. 24:34, it appears that this meeting took place prior to the one between Jesus and the two people on the road to Emmaus (Lk. 24:13–33). This seems to be corroborated by 1 Cor. 15:5, but as Paul does not mention Cleopas and his companion at all, we cannot be sure. The apparition on the road to Emmaus is peculiar in two respects: it mentions two people who, like the women mentioned earlier, were not disciples proper, but members of the larger circle of followers. This in itself is proof of its historicity; how else could Luke, assembling his sources (cf. Lk. 1:3) and obtaining this report, have given such pride of place to two otherwise unimportant followers of the 'second rank', in the ordering of this section? He even places it before the chronologically earlier appearance to Peter. The Emmaus incident also shows Jesus appearing without identifying himself. The two witnesses are meant to think for themselves, to draw their own conclusions from what they see and hear: his exposition of Old Testament prophecies and the breaking of the bread help them to overcome the spiritual blindness which had prevented them from recognizing Christ.[162] But as soon as they have recognized him, he disappears from their sight (24:31). In all other appearances that are told in any detail, Jesus sooner or later identifies himself with characteristic words (cf. Jn. 20:16–17; Mt. 28:9–10; Lk. 24:36–40; Jn. 20:19–21, 26–28). The only exception is the special scene, Jn. 21:4–7; but even here the action in v. 6 has the same evocative impact on John as the breaking of the bread had on Cleopas and his companion (see below); and unlike at Emmaus, Jesus does not disappear upon recognition, but stays on for a while. These peculiarities of the Emmaus apparition give it its lasting significance, but they may also explain why Paul omitted it from his list.

As striking as the Emmaus incident is the lack of detail in Luke's note about the appearance to Peter. It takes the form of a shared outburst of joy, coming from the disciples assembled in Jerusalem, in confirmation of the news from Emmaus: 'It is true! The Lord has risen and has appeared to Simon' (Lk. 24:34).

It is indeed remarkable that neither here, nor in the two additional endings of Mark, nor in fact in any other NT writing (including Peter's speeches in Acts and his own two letters) is there any description of what occurred between Christ and Peter. Peter does refer to his witness to the Resurrection in his speeches in Acts (see e.g. Acts 1:21–22; 3:15; 5:32; 10:40–41), but he stops short of relating the details. He was, this reticence seems to imply, under obligation from Jesus not to tell anyone. The mere fact of this appearance to him alone was all the other disciples had to know in order to understand that Peter was still the first among them as equals.

When Jesus later appears to the others, their initial reaction is one of (holy) fear, doubt and self-doubting (see Lk. 24:37–43; and cf. Mt. 28:17; Jn. 20:19, 24–25)—the Resurrection is simply not self-evident, as it were, and in the first days of his appearances, Christ was certainly not dealing with people who radiated *expectant* faith.[163] The one incident in which faith and forward-looking expectancy are present from the beginning is the last in

John's gospel, and it is the one where Peter is finally and fully reinstated as the leader of the community (Jn. 21:4–19).

The disciples are back in Galilee, and they know that Jesus will come to them there: his appearances in Jerusalem must have strengthened their trust in the command and promise recorded at Mk. 16:7 and Mt. 28:10. Seven of the old group (v. 2) have returned to their old business of fishing, the most natural thing for them to do.[164] It is perhaps only a minor touch, but nonetheless, characteristic, that the initiative to go out to fish is Peter's, and that the others follow him (v. 3). It is, as might be expected, an expedition at night, the most promising time for a big catch—they were, after all, professionals.

In the morning, on their way back with empty nets, they see standing on the shore a man whom they do not recognize (v. 4)— it is dawn, and they are still some way out. On finding that they have not caught anything, the stranger tells them what to do. His directions are quite specific, but completely different from what he had told them on that earlier occasion, Lk. 5:4. Then they had to go out into deep water, but now they must stay where they are and throw out the net on the right side. As before, the disciples follow his advice, and again the catch is enormous (although this time the net—and it is only one—holds). But by now, John has put two and two together. He remembers the first catch, and, as the morning light grows stronger, he recognizes the familiar posture of Jesus. His cry, 'It is the Lord!' (v. 7), alerts Peter. He stops pulling at the net, and, having worked in a loin-cloth, puts on his outer garment—a polite gesture towards Jesus, though not very practical prior to jumping into water: one realizes that even in a hurry, Peter is conscious of the reverence due to the Lord. The distance between Peter and Christ is mentioned by John with his customary love of detail, 'about two hundred cubits' (v. 8), roughly 90 metres. To try and reach Jesus faster than with the boat by swimming and wading such a distance fully clad, demonstrates Peter's completely restored eagerness of discipleship. And—this again is characteristic of his re-established inner strength—he wants to prove it to Jesus, unnecessary as the gesture as such may be from a practical point of view. There is indeed exuberance in his action, and in this he sets a positive example to the others. As he had left his work behind when he had followed Jesus the first time, he now leaves it behind to find out what the Lord has in store for him.

When Jesus asks them to bring some of the fish to supplement the meal he had already started preparing (vv. 9–10), it is again Peter who obliges and drags the net ashore—no mean feat and a hint at his physical strength, although technically this was easier than trying to haul the load into the boat out at sea, an attempt in which they had failed. John mentions the number of fish caught, 153—a factual record, typical of an experienced fisherman who knew that the catch had to be counted before it could be shared out between the members of the crew.[165]

Up to this point the narrative reads like an eye-witness record, and is, with its careful asides, a useful source of information about the life of Galilean fishermen. But as every historian knows, incidental details often serve to highlight the culmination of a sequence, and this is the case here, too. After a silent supper, with everyone expecting Jesus to talk about himself (v. 12), Jesus does finally begin the conversation, which turns out to be a dialogue with Peter about his final reinstatement. The importance and even formality of the occasion is made apparent by the introduction—John identifies him with both his names, 'Simon Peter', and Jesus addresses him formally as 'Simon, Son of John', as he had done at his first calling (Jn. 1:42; cf. Mt. 16:17 and note 49 above).[166] Peter can have had no doubt about what was at stake. Three times he had denied the Lord, but three times the Lord gives him the chance to reaffirm his love and commitment. The three questions and answers differ slightly, but the emphasis is clear: in the most solemn manner possible, the bond between Jesus and Peter had to be sealed.

'Simon, Son of John, do you truly love me more than these?' (v. 15). The Greek text leaves undecided what 'than these' is referring to—the question is deliberately all-encompassing, and Peter could have understood it as 'Do you love me more than you love these things' (i.e. your re-established business?) or as 'Do you love me more than you love your friends and partners?', or again, 'Do you love me more than any of these men love me?'. In view of Peter's earlier statement at Jn. 13:37 where he had boasted of a loving faithfulness superior to that shown by the others and had been unable to keep his word, the latter must be the decisive meaning behind the question: 'Do you really love me more than these men do, and do you know what this means?'

Peter's reply is matter-of-fact. 'Yes, Lord, you know that I love you.' And the first command is the reward: 'Feed my lambs.' This was clear enough for Peter—Jesus' teaching about the Good Shepherd in Jn. 10:1–18 would have come to mind, and he would have understood that the commission of the keys is now supplemented by the commission of shepherding. But Jesus asks again, 'Simon, Son of John, do you truly love me?', and receives an answer identical with the first one. The commission now is slightly different in its wording, 'Take care of my sheep.' The third repetition of the question again introduces slight changes: a different Greek word for loving and, in the final commission, a combination of the words used in the first two versions.[167]

Peter is sad (v. 17b, *elupēthē*); he knows why the question had to be put three times and does not like the memory at all. His answer is an appeal to the all-knowing forgiveness of Jesus: 'Lord, you know all things; you know that I love you.' What more can he say? If Jesus does not know that Peter's love is matured and genuine, what could his words do to convince him? And Jesus confirms his knowledge by a final, and binding, repetition of the task he has for Peter. In the presence of the other disciples, the message is clear: if there was symbolism in the catch of fish, it was meant to show that the unbroken net, pulled ashore by Peter, was like the vast numbers of coming converts to the faith, to be gathered in under Peter's stewardship, in a developed confirmation of Lk. 5:10. If there is symbolism in the feeding and tending of the sheep, it is to show that Peter's authority over and responsibility for the budding communities is restored and enhanced with no shade of blemish. Peter himself shows a clear understanding of this in his first letter: 'To the elders among you, I appeal as a fellow elder, a witness of Christ's sufferings and one who will also share in the glory to be revealed: Be shepherds of God's flock that is under your care, serving as overseers—not because you must, but because you are willing, as God wants you to be; not greedy for money, but eager to serve; not lording it over those entrusted to you, but being examples to the flock. And when the Chief Shepherd appears, you will receive the crown of glory that will never fade away' (1 Pet. 5:1–4). Peter, identifying himself as an eye-witness of the Passion of Christ (5:1), and addressing those in authority as one of their number (but still with higher authority—see 1:1), demonstrates that he is taking his authority seriously, and that he is a competent trustee of Jesus' commission. This sense of a stewardship coming directly from Christ and to be rewarded with an everlasting crown of glory at

the Second Coming, is precisely what distinguishes Peter's role
and the job description he transmits from similar or near-similar
imagery, as in Ps. 23, Is. 40:10–11 or Ps. 80:2, let alone the
mebaqquer or overseer in the Qumran documents, who is once
likened to a shepherd in charge of his flock (6QD 13:9; cf. also
1 Pet. 2:21–25). Paul in turn was influenced by Jesus and Peter, as
his farewell speech at Miletus shows (see Acts 20:28).

Christ's reinstatement of Peter is followed by a solemn
prophecy; 'I tell you the truth, when you were younger you
dressed yourself and went where you wanted; but when you are
old, you will stretch out your hands, and someone else will dress
you and lead you where you do not want to go' (Jn. 21:18). The
evangelist explains the metaphor to his readers: 'Jesus said this to
indicate the kind of death by which Peter would glorify God'.
That the saying refers to Peter's death is a straightforward
deduction from the shepherd analogy in Jn. 10:11; but the kind of
death is not apparent from the description. In other words, the
evangelist's explanation may well have been written *before* Peter's
death: John simply alludes to the way Peter would be led to his
death—i.e. as an old man, in the charge of others. The first
interpretation of this passage as referring to Peter's historical
crucifixion in Rome comes from Tertullian, in his *Scorpiace*, 15,
written at the end of the second century. What Tertullian implies,
however, is merely that Jesus' prophecy as such was fulfilled and
that the cryptic words of Jn. 21:18 with the 'outstretched hands'
must therefore symbolize the position of the hands on the
crossbeam. What he does not say is that the evangelist knew all
this when he wrote his generalised parenthesis.

Peter, at any rate, knew that he would follow in his Master's
steps by dying an unnatural death, at the hands of others. Jesus'
challenge, 'Follow me!' (v. 19), although much wider in scope,
hinted at this form of sacrificial discipleship.

Having been assured of his own future, Peter turns and sees
John, described here in v. 20 as the beloved disciple who had
leaned against Jesus and asked the question about the traitor.
Peter wants to know the future role of his friend and aide: 'Lord,
what about him?' Is this perhaps an attempt to show that he
already takes his role as caring shepherd seriously? Jesus does not
see it that way. Jesus' plan for John's life is of no concern to Peter:
'If I want him to remain alive until I return, what is that to you?
You must follow me.' This is no rebuke, merely a helpful

reminder: the task Peter will have to fulfil, right up to his martyrdom, must not be influenced or impeded by worrying about what God's will may be for the lives of his co-workers. Peter will need a one-track mind, focused on the commission Christ has entrusted to him. *each one has their own comis*

Soon afterwards, people began to misunderstand Jesus' pointed remark, concluding that John would not die. The evangelist clears the matter up; a timely decision some thirty-five years after the meeting on Lake Tiberias. It is not difficult to understand why Peter in his second letter puts such emphasis on the removal of misconceptions about the Parousia: too many people had already begun to cramp the statements about Christ's second coming within the straitjacket of their subjective hopes and desires.

Peter has his commission renewed; in addition, he shares in those given to the others (cf. Jn. 20:21–23; Mt. 28:18–20). As rock and shepherd, he will face a unique responsibility in the building of the Christian community among all nations. And there is no time for a lakeside holiday before it all begins: only a few days later, back in Jerusalem, in the aftermath of the Ascension, Peter starts to take the strain.

II

Peter in Acts and Paul's Letters

'Peter, filled with the Holy Spirit'

CHAPTER FIVE

Peter's First Speeches

I

Four documents of corroborative historical value have served as sources of partly sketchy, partly very detailed information about Peter's development from his early days in Capharnaum to his reinstatement at the same lake where it had all begun for him. One of these documents, Mark, is based on his own teaching and authority; another one, Luke, provides the link between the old ministry and the new one. Back in Jerusalem, the disciples witness the Ascension of Christ. Luke ends his gospel with a brief, incomplete sketch of this event, which he takes up and fills out at the beginning of Volume II of his historical writings, dedicated to the same Excellency Theophilus. From now on, this Volume II is our only source for most of the events concerning Peter; within the New Testament, only Paul comes up with some helpful details in 1 Corinthians and Galatians, and these three writings are supplemented by the two avowedly personal Petrine letters themselves.

Until Paul appears on the scene, there is only Luke's account of the development of the first community under Peter in Jerusalem. For the historian, who prefers several sources, preferably slightly conflicting (see above p. 83 and n. 145), this poses an important question: how reliable is this single source in its own right? Can we trust Luke's detailed renderings of Peter's seven speeches, the miracles he performs or has performed for him, the implicit reference to his whereabouts between his escape from prison and his reappearance at the Apostolic Council, and so forth? Only by analysing the passages concerned can we begin to answer these questions. There is, however, and has been for a long time, a general consensus among historians. It is based not least on careful comparison with secular historiography, its methods, scope and contents, and also with archaeology, medical and legal history, and other "complementary" sciences. This consensus can be summed up in the words of the classical philologist E. M. Blaiklock, 'Luke is a consummate historian, to be ranked in his own right with the great writers of the Greek.'[168]

Most New Testament critics would not (yet) dare to call Luke a 'consummate historian';[169] problems abound, and some of them are certainly not negligible. For our present purposes, the self-confessed striving for exactness (Lk. 1:3, *akribōs*) of the man who wrote the two longest New Testament texts, must stand, as it did in the case of the gospel, until conclusive evidence—not mere presuppositions—can be marshalled against it. Dates and data have a habit of speaking for themselves, and one must let them do so.

One example will suffice here: in the quest for the date of Acts, two vital items of information occur at the end, and both concern Paul. One is positive: Paul's arrival in Rome. The other one is negative: the lack of any reference to Paul's death (and to that of James, the Lord's brother, c. AD 63), well-attested by later, non-biblical sources.[170] Even though the exact year of his arrival (c. AD 60) is still debated—as is that of his death under Nero (after AD 64), the conclusion is obvious: c. AD 62 (cf. Acts 28:30) and the end of the Neronian persecution with the emperor's suicide on 9th June AD 68 determine the *maximum* period within which Acts was concluded. Not a single conclusive argument has ever been put forward against this basic observation; on the contrary, it is backed by a considerable number of complementary observations. For example, the Roman authorities are portrayed as neutral or even kindly disposed towards Paul (e.g. Acts 13:6–12, 18:12–17, 21:31–40, even 28:16); this attitude ended brutally with the fire of Rome in AD 64. The single most catastrophic event in contemporary Jewish history, of decisive influence on the future of the Christian community in Jerusalem, the destruction of the city with its temple by the Romans under Titus, is not so much as hinted at.

Arguments from silence are always problematic. But if they are there in force and corroborate internal evidence (e.g. the recording of the deaths of Stephen and James the brother of John, but not that of Paul and James, the brother of Jesus), the literary historian has no choice other than to accept the pretty conclusive case for a date prior to the Neronian persecution and the death of Paul.[171]

There is no need to be dogmatic about this: the case of the authenticity of the portrait of Peter in Acts does not stand or fall by the date of the work. It is, however, worth remembering that if there have to be presuppositions in historical—and by all means critical—analysis, they must always be in favour of the text, rather than the analyst. In other words, Peter's portrait in Acts, even if based on this solitary witness for the first twelve-and-a-half chapters, is *a priori* not questionable, but reliable. An investigation into the probable date of the work has to take the work itself into account. Those who say that Acts must be late(r), because Part One, the Gospel of Luke, uses Mark, which was written around 70, are therefore in for a surprise when their yardstick is adjusted into the fifties.[172] It is, one might dare to say, much less likely that Nero's fire of Rome will ever be redated into the eighties or nineties of the first century . . .

II

An unprecedented responsibility rests on Peter after the Ascension. His role as spokesman and figurehead of the disciples had been crowned by his confession of Jesus' Messiahship and the commission of the keys, but it had, before and afterwards, been marred by signs of weakness which had cast doubt on his claims to strength. Three major attempts to prove his faithfulness had failed (the walk on the water, the stroke of the sword, and the entry into the high priest's courtyard). The denial, more than anything else, had demonstrated his vulnerability. But out of dejection, he had come back. He had run to the tomb, hoping against hope; he had seen the sign of the Resurrection in the empty tomb and marvelled at it; he had been the first of the disciples to see the risen Lord, and if that had not been enough to demonstrate to himself and to the others that his discipleship had been fully restored, he had been reinstated and recommissioned as the leading representative of Christ at Lake Tiberias, the Sea of Galilee. Would the new Peter be the real one? Would he relapse under pressure, or would he justify the trust Jesus had placed in him? Would he, the ex-manager of a fishing business, be circumspect enough to manage the affairs of the budding church? His fellow-disciples must have been wondering about that. But they do not hesitate to follow his directions.

The framework is unambiguous; Jesus himself had given them instructions during the forty days prior to the Ascension (Acts 1:2), he had told them to wait in Jerusalem for the baptism with the Holy Spirit (1:5, 8), he had, once again, cautioned them against speculating about the coming of the kingdom (1:7), and he had renewed the 'great commission' of Mt. 28:19–20 (1:8). They are now his 'messengers' (*apostolos* = messenger) even more so than they had been before (cf. Lk. 6:13, 9:10, 11:49, 17:5, 22:14, 24:10; Mk. 3:14, 6:30; Mt. 10:2). Whereas their task during Jesus' earthly life had been to pass on his teaching as literally as possible, using his own words which they had memorized,[173] they now have to preach, to teach and to act independently, finding new words, drawing new conclusions, adapting themselves to changing situations. For Peter and the others, the promised power of the Holy Spirit (1:8) must have appeared like an umbilical cord, a lifeline that would sustain them in the daunting task that lay ahead. No longer to call them disciples, but apostles, is therefore a programmatic development of Luke's earlier usage of the term and justifies the title given to the book by its first 'publisher': 'Acts of Apostles'.[174]

After the Ascension, an event which the eyewitness Peter does not fail to mention later (Acts 1:22, 2:32–36; 1 Pet. 3:22), the Eleven reassemble at the house of Mark's family (see above n. 142) with Mary, the other woman, and Jesus' brothers, who now make their first appearance among his followers (contrast Jn. 7:5). It is noteworthy that Luke does not hint at any deliberations on future activities—the emphasis is on constant, unanimous prayer (1:14). Not long afterwards, this prayer meeting had grown into an assembly of some 120 followers (1:15), and Peter uses the first opportunity to carry out his duties. The suicide of Judas necessitated the election of a twelfth apostle, perhaps in order to complete a group which, according to Jesus, was to sit in judgment over the 'twelve tribes of Israel' after the Second Coming (see Lk. 22:29–30; and cf. Mt. 19:28, and p. 59 above). But Judas did not have to be replaced so much because he was dead, as because he had been a traitor: after the execution of James, the brother of John, some eleven years later (Acts 12:1–2), no 'by-election' is called for. The reason may be that by that time, Paul had established himself as the true supplementary apostle— but Luke calls him apostle only once, and even then only in connection with Barnabas (Acts 14:3–14). Nor did Paul fulfil the conditions set out by Peter in 1:21–22: he had not been an eyewitness of Jesus' baptism by John, nor of any of the other events up to the Ascension. Judas had to be replaced by someone with the same historical credentials, and that his treason was the real reason for the new election is made plain by Peter's remarkable election speech. The 'approximately 120' brethren[175] are immediately reminded of OT prophecy, predicting, in Peter's exegesis, the betrayal by Judas: Ps. 41:10 is adduced, and after a brief recollection of the events for the benefit of his audience (some of whom must have been very recent newcomers), two more psalms are referred to, Ps. 69:26 and Ps. 109:8 (1:20). Again Peter understands these two verses as prophecies, and their combination within one sentence leaves no doubt about the link between the betrayal and the necessity of finding a new eyewitness apostle: "'For,'" said Peter, "it is written in the book of Psalms: 'May his place be deserted, let there be no-one to dwell in it', and: 'May another take his place of leadership'. Therefore it is necessary to choose one of the men who have been with us all the time . . .'"! With quotations from three Davidic psalms (and the emphasis on comparison of Davidic elements with elements concerning the suffering—and glory—of the Messiah is typical of Peter; cf. e.g. Acts 2:25–36; 4:24–26), Peter makes out a good case for the choice of an unblemished successor to Judas.[176]

The middle section of his speech has puzzled many readers, as his account of Judas' death (1:18–19) seems to conflict with Matthew's (Mt. 27:5–8). This has been explained more than once as two compatible versions of the same event, which none of the disciples had witnessed so that variations due to hearsay evidence were to be expected. Already Augustine in his *Contra Felicem* (1:4) had read with deductive logic that Judas had hanged himself—Mt. 27:5 (*collum sibi alligavit*), that by inference after his death when the rope had broken he fell on his face, was torn asunder in the middle, and that all his bowels poured out onto the ground, as in Acts 1:18 (*deiectus in faciem diruptus est medius, et effusa sunt omnia viscera eius*). This interpretation was followed by Jerome in his Vulgate, the official Latin text: *et suspensus crepuit medius*, etc. ('and being hanged, he burst in the middle', etc). In addition it has been suggested that even if the field was bought by the priests (Mt. 27:7), the money legally still belonged to Judas, so that it was bought in his name (Acts 1:18); and it was the field thus purchased by the priests (Mt. 27:8–10) where Judas committed suicide (Acts 1:18–19), so that both etymologies of the name of the field make sense. Such exercises in harmonization are, however, not required. Luke would have checked his facts: if he did not 'correct' Peter's account editorially when he wrote it down, it either implies that he found Peter's to be the accurate one, or, more plausibly in view of the whole context around Judas' confusing and unwitnessed death, two similar but not entirely identical reports were making the rounds very soon after the event. What matters is that Peter's exegesis of OT prophecy is consistent with the known facts.

Much more interesting is an editorial aspect of this part of Peter's speech. Some editors of the Greek text and some modern translations (Westcott & Hort, 1881; Hodges & Farstadt, *The Greek New Testament According to the Majority Text*, 1982; RSV; NEB, NIV) place these two verses between dashes or in brackets. This is an editorial decision for which there is, needless to say, no basis in the original Greek text, as such punctuation does not exist in the manuscripts. The reason, however, is a comprehensible one: it is argued that verses 18–19 cannot be part of Peter's speech but must be Luke's explanation of the background for the benefit of his readers. Peter himself would not have had to tell his audience about Judas' death and the 'Field of Blood'. But v. 18 clearly is part of Peter's own speech: it is necessary as the peg on which he hangs the psalm reference in v. 20. And since *not everyone* in Jerusalem would have heard the story of Judas' death—let alone those who will have come from further away—there was no harm in both reminding those who had and telling those who had not how tragic the traitor's end had been. It is only v. 19 that is an obvious aside to Theophilus (and any other readers), where Luke speaks of the people in Jerusalem and their everyday language, i.e. Aramaic, in the third person plural.

requirement of 12th Apostle

Peter concludes his speech by stating the requirements the new twelfth apostle would have to fulfil: from the very beginning of Jesus' ministry to the Ascension he had to be an eyewitness in order to become an apostolic witness of the Resurrection. This is interesting since if we take the beginning as being literally the baptism of John, then it was not even, as far as we can tell from the sources, seen by all the eleven present at the election (Levi-Matthew, Lk. 5:27–28, is, according to Luke's own account, definitely a post-baptismal addition to the circle, and some of the others may have been, too: only Peter, Andrew, John, James and Philip are known by name or by inference—Jn. 1:35–44—as witnesses of the baptism of Jesus by John). Even if Peter merely wants to say that the beginning of the ministry of Jesus as such is the decisive 'starting-point', it puts a significant emphasis on the role of the Baptist as a forerunner of Jesus and also limits the number of candidates quite considerably. (It reminds us also of the fact, hinted at often enough in the gospels, that there were more than the twelve disciples who followed Jesus around).

Luke's accuracy is apparent in his recording the names of both candidates. He might have been content to mention the successful candidate only, but his sources included both names, and he uses them in order to point out to his readers that the early beginnings of the Christian community in Jerusalem are not shrouded in anonymity. It should be mentioned here in passing that Peter himself was most probably among Luke's informants for parts of his book. Whenever and wherever they may have met before, they can hardly have missed each other in Rome: Acts 28:14b, 16 tell us of Luke's arrival in Rome with Paul, and there can be no doubt about Peter's presence in the city at that time. (See below, p. 153f.) A beautiful little piece of historical embroidery affirms that Luke, Peter and Paul shared lodgings in Rome, at an address that still exists today: Via Lata, at the corner of Via del Corso—'Basement, please ring twice'.[177]

The names of the two candidates, Joseph Barsabbas called Justus, and Matthias, do not tell us much. Joseph is interesting in so far as he has two by-names. Barsabbas is Aramaic for 'Son of the Sabbath' (not an uncommon name: there is a second example of it in Acts 15:22). All it means is that he was born on the Sabbath. This does not rule out that he and the Judas of 15:22 were relatives. To distinguish him further, he has a Graeco-Roman epithet, 'Justus', the just one, as his third name. Here again, the NT mentions another person with this name: 'Jesus called Justus' in Col. 4:11. One can see to what lengths people went in order to prevent confusion (even so, the Codex Bezae Cantabrigiensis D 05, one minuscule, and a couple of ancient versions contrive to misname him 'Barnabas', identifying him with the Joseph of Acts 4:36). Even though he eventually lost the election, he must have been a man of some standing among the 'brothers', otherwise they would hardly have suggested him as one of only two. But we hear no more of him: even later legend-mongers were not that interested in him.

Matthias, the other candidate—and with one name only—remains equally obscure. With all his qualifications he never once reappears in the course of Acts. Not even his name contains illuminating information; it is merely an abbreviation of Mattithiah, the name of four people in the Old Testament (1 Ch. 9:31, 15:18, 21 etc; Ezr. 10:43; Ne. 8:14). On the strength of having become an apostle, he was naturally the true stuff of legend. He was supposed to have been at the Caspian Sea, and in Ethiopia. An apocryphal gospel was circulated under his name and was known to Origen and Eusebius (see *HE* 3, 25:6), and others. The apocryphal Acts of Andrew and Matthias link him with the 'land of the cannibals'. All this makes for fascinating bed-time reading, but even if Matthias must, after all, have been somewhere and done something, we know nothing about him for sure beyond the fact that he had been among the followers of Jesus from the first, that he may have been one of the 'Seventy' (Lk. 10:1, Eusebius, *HE* 1, 12:3), and that he may have influenced some ascetic teaching on the growth of the soul (*ibid.* 3, 29:4).

Peter, however, is not interested in whether or not the new apostle would later prove to be a great hero of the faith. Not future greatness is required, but witness, and in particular witness to the Resurrection. And the assembly makes doubly sure that human preferences cannot influence the decision between Joseph and Matthias. They pray to Christ for a decision (1:24–25), in a prayer which speaks of their common task as 'apostolic ministry', literally service (*diakonia*) and messengership (*apostolē*). Their ministry was to be one of service to Christ's glory, and of serving others in voluntary lowliness (cf. the use of the word in Lk. 10:40: see also Acts 6:4 for serving the word of God, and Acts 20:24 for serving Christ by preaching the gospel; for the use of the verb see in particular 1 Pet. 4:10–11). Their second safeguard against human influence on the outcome of the election is that they do not hold a proper election at all, but draw lots (1:26). This has appeared to some readers as a somewhat pagan procedure, but Peter certainly knew what he was doing: having prayed for the Lord's decision, and in the absence of the full powers of the Holy Spirit at a time before Pentecost, they followed traditional procedure: 'The lot is cast into the lap, but its every decision is from the Lord' (Pr. 16:33, cf. also Lv. 16:8 and 1 Sa. 14:41–42).

Peter's handling of this meeting is remarkable for three reasons. It shows his consciousness of tradition and the applicability of tradition, with a firm grasp of the Old Testament— that is, in this case, of the psalter for prophecy, the Pentateuch, 1 Samuel and Proverbs for precedent. It shows his precision in singling out the basic requirements for apostleship. And it shows his smooth authority over an assembly of some 120 people. Any of his fellow apostles who may have doubted his talents will have breathed a sigh of relief. If this was his way of running community affairs even before the outpouring of the Holy Spirit promised by Jesus, their future under Peter's leadership must indeed have looked bright.

III

In the above section, Peter's speech is taken seriously as a speech by Peter, i.e. not as a creation of the historian Luke. Even the non-specialist Bible reader cannot help wondering, however, how it is that we have a considerable number of speeches by such different people as Peter, Stephen, Gamaliel, James and Paul, all given verbatim. To put the question simply: since in most cases Luke does not claim to have been an eyewitness, did others record or memorize them—Peter himself or Mark, who was also in Rome with Paul and Luke (see Phmn. 24, etc)? Or did he make them up in some way, as a considerable number of critics still assume?[178]

The situation is, of course, easier as far as the gospels are concerned. Not only is the reliability of the oral transmission of Jesus' teaching, due not least to the painstaking memorization techniques demanded of the disciples and others at the time, safely established;[179] there is also increasing evidence for the use of written notes, abbreviated protocols or even shorthand notes, at least among the locally resident followers of Jesus.[180]

Neither Peter nor any of the other speakers in Acts could or did claim the teaching authority of Jesus. But the events after the Ascension, beginning with the momentous decision to elect a new twelfth apostle, were sufficiently important to suggest at least the possible preparation of rough notes from memory immediately afterwards. Mark, who was not only present in Jerusalem until Peter's first departure (Acts 12:17, 25), but also joined Barnabas and Paul on their journey to Antioch (Acts 12:24) until he left them in Perga (Acts 13:13, rejoining Paul at the time of Colossians (Col. 4:20, cf. 2 Tim. 4:11), would seem to be the most likely secretary until Luke himself took over on Paul's later travels.[181]

Whereas a convincing case can be made out along these lines for the sources behind Luke's rendering of the speeches, no one would want to claim that they are all that was said on those occasions. Paul, for example, certainly spoke for more than one and a half minutes on the Areopagus. We have the gist of their contents; but (and this is decisive) this 'gist' is, as far as one can see, true to character. Peter does not speak like Paul, nor does Stephen speak like either of them; and Peter's speeches in Acts are entirely consistent with his manner of arguing in his letters where they deal with related subjects and concepts.[182] They are also significantly faithful to the historical context in which they appear. Before the age of the tape recorder this is a remarkable state of affairs.

Some critics have offered a simplistic explanation. Luke, they say, did not record historical speeches, any more than classical historians did so (cf. n. 178). The favourite source for this claim is Thucydides, in his *History* 1:22, but to use the passage in this way shows a lack of perceptiveness on the part of those who apply it to Luke.[183] Polybius, in his *Histories*, is adamant that writers who *invent* discourses of historical personalities are despicable—much rather should even banal utterances be reported, if they were actually made.[184] The same attitude is shared by others, like Lucian in his *The Way To Write History*. With Lucian we are already in post-Lucan times, as we are, of course, with Josephus' *Jewish Antiquities* (published c. AD 93) which do offer some entertaining examples of invented speeches by the Patriarchs (e.g. *Ant.* 1, 13:3). But, as has been shown convincingly before, Josephus' elaborate rhetoric could not be farther removed from Luke's sober, concise recordings.[185] Regardless of whether or not classical historians always followed their high ideals, Luke is here perhaps not only their peer, but their superior.

IV

Matthias had been chosen, and Pentecost had come. The outpouring of the Holy Spirit affected the public behaviour of the apostles, and people took notice, 'utterly amazed' at such inexplicable multilingualism. As always with supernatural events, one wants to know what was going on, or, in the words of the onlookers, 'What does it mean?' (Acts 2:12). As always, there are people whose embarrassment about the supernatural leads them to mockery: 'They have had too much wine.' A similar self-protective evasive response can still be found among those who even today accuse the resurrection witnesses of hallucinations or wishful thinking.

Peter, however, rises to the occasion. By taking the critics seriously, he makes them look very silly indeed. It is only nine in the morning (Acts 2:15), and as traditionally wine was drunk only with the evening meal (i.e. not even at lunch time and not on its own), it was too early for drunkenness. Their detractors would have to try again, but, as you all know (Peter might have added), the true explanation, which every good Jew would understand, is in Scripture anyway.

The way Peter addresses the crowd and leads them to his lengthy scriptural quotation is instructive: 'Fellow-Jews and all of you who are in Jerusalem,' he says at the beginning (v. 14b), indicating that the motley crowd of people watching did not consist of Palestinian Jews and Jews from the Diaspora (including converts: v. 11) only, but also of non-Jews who happened to be in Jerusalem. Jews had lived in all the countries and cities mentioned in Luke's list (v. 9–11), not least in Rome, the capital of the empire, but Peter clearly wants to appeal to the Gentile bystanders, too; and this is further underlined by the context of the passage in Joel which he quotes. His fellow-apostles and fellow-Jews, at least, would have realized the change of emphasis at the beginning—whereas the original text in Joel 2:28 reads, '*And afterwards*, I will pour out my Spirit on all people', Peter rephrases it: '*In the last days*, God says, I will pour out my Spirit on all people'.[186] For Peter, the last days, the importance of which Jesus had explained to him on the Mount of Olives (Mk. 13:3–37 *par.*), have been initiated; and although he refrains, needless to say, from specifying their duration (cf. 2 Pet. 3:3–9), the mere choice of this passage with its application to all mankind (v. 17) leaves no doubt that Peter takes Jesus' command of a universal mission, which would have to precede his Second Coming, seriously from the very beginning.

It is certainly no accident that his first public speech in Jerusalem after the Ascension places his proclamation of Jesus as the true Messiah so firmly in the context of eschatological prophecy. It was a subject dear to his heart, and in his second letter he was to enlarge upon it once more (2 Pet. 3:7–13, see p. 64 above). One may in fact say that Peter's enlightened post-resurrection thinking and preaching show a considerable continuity over some thirty years: anyone reading Peter's use of Joel 2:30–31 in his Jerusalem speech and comparing it to his admonition in his second Roman letter, 2 Pet. 3:7, 12–13 must realize that the same mind is behind them: still very Jewish and non-hellenistic even in the second letter, but, while remaining true to his roots, unmistakably including all mankind, Jews and Gentiles alike:

> 'I will show wonders in the heaven above and signs on the earth below, blood and fire and billows of smoke' (Joel 2:30; Acts 2:19).
> 'By the same word the present heavens and earth are reserved for fire, being kept for the day of judgment and destruction of ungodly men' (2 Pet. 3:7).
> 'The sun will be turned to darkness and the moon to blood before the coming of the great and glorious day of the Lord' (Joel 2:31; Acts 2:20).
> 'That day will bring about the destructions of the heavens by fire, and the elements will melt in the heat' (2 Pet. 3:12b).
> 'And everyone who calls on the name of the Lord will be saved' (Joel 2:32).
> 'But in keeping with his promise we are looking forward to a new heaven and a new earth, the home of righteousness. So then, dear friends, since you are looking forward to this, make every effort to be found spotless, blameless and at peace with him' (2 Pet. 3:13–14).

As was said above, more OT prophecies than those found in Joel were in Peter's mind when he wrote the third chapter of his second letter. What matters here, however, is the astounding similarity between the speech in Acts and this passage in 2 Peter.

A good thirty years later, Peter saw the necessity to be more detailed—a letter, after all, is different from a public speech. But he is still the same man who drew upon Joel and who remembered Jesus' discourse on the Mount of Olives when the Holy Spirit moved him to speak up at Pentecost.

Peter continues his speech by addressing the 'men of Israel' (2:22–36). Simply and directly he lays before them the basic elements of Jesus' Messiahship—his real humanity (he was a man not from nowhere, but from Nazareth, 2:22); his undeniable miracles, wonders, and signs, as God's way of showing that the promised new age had begun (2:22b); his crucifixion, part of God's plan but carried out by them of their own accord (2:23); his resurrection from the dead, prophesied by David in Ps. 16:8–11 (2:24–32); and his exaltation to the right hand of God, again prophesied by David (Ps. 110:1), followed by the outpouring of the Holy Spirit (2:33–35); all leading to the inescapable conclusion: 'God has made this Jesus, whom you crucified, both Lord and Christ' (2:36).

Peter is proclaiming established history, not just a projection of faith: Jesus of Nazareth had been seen, his actions had been witnessed by (some of) the audience, he had been crucified publicly, but his tomb was empty, for all to see and to contrast with the tomb of David, still sealed with the body inside, decayed and not ascended to heaven (2:29–35). But the empty tomb was not alone; there also was the unanimous witness of Peter's people to the resurrection of 'this Jesus' (2:32).

Three times Peter addresses his hearers, and each time he intensifies his appeal to their reflective attention, pulling the net ever closer in his attempt to create a fellowship of converted followers: 'Fellow-Jews and all of you who are in Jerusalem', he began in 2:14; 'Fellow-Israelites' he says in 2:22; and in 2:29, they have become 'brothers'.[187] On the one hand, these three steps of familiarity are meant to draw in his Jewish audience; on the other hand, the non-Jews, who had momentarily been left out when he spoke about those responsible for bringing about the crucifixion,[188] are now back, as it were, among the 'brothers', all alike confronted by the compelling challenge of the Resurrection and Ascension.

Peter's appeal is successful. The people realize their danger: if Jesus is the Christ, the Messiah, then they have been his enemies, and his enemies, as David had said in his prophecy quoted by

Peter (Ps. 110:1), will be made a footstool for his feet by God. They are 'cut to the heart' (2:37) and, echoing Peter's note of fellowship, 'brothers', they want to know what to do. As before, Peter comes straight to the point. Two prerequisites, repentance and baptism in the name of Jesus Christ, will lead to the forgiveness of sins and the reception of the Holy Spirit. Again he emphasizes the universal validity of his promise: it applies not only to his audience and their descendants (2:39a), but also to 'all who are far off', to 'all' whom the Lord our God will call' (2:39b). One can hardly be more encompassing in a promise, without linking its fulfilment to human achievement: 'the Lord our God' will call men to himself.

The observant reader will notice that Peter places Jesus next to God five times in his exhortation: the 'Lord' from Joel 2:31, clearly signifying God when Joel wrote those words down, is shown to be one with Jesus in the middle of the speech ('The LORD said to my Lord', 2:34), at the end of the speech ('both Lord and Christ', 2:36), and by implication in the final attribution of authority ('whom the Lord our God will call', 2:39); and to these four occurrences of 'Lord' is added the fulfilled Davidic prophecy that Christ is sitting at the right hand of God the Father (2:33–34). Like the Father, he is now to be addressed by the elevated title, 'Lord', *kúrios*.[189] Like the English 'Sir' today, 'Lord' is an ambiguous appellation; when the disciples addressed Jesus in this way at the very beginning of his ministry, they could not see it as a messianic title. The applied interpretation is what counts; Peter's way of using Joel and the Psalms, over-specific as it may appear to those who are not acquainted with its basis in Jewish exegesis (see n. 186 above), did not antagonize his audience; far from accusing him of wilful playing with words, they see his point and realize that his exegesis is the right one. They may also have understood that this was not simply his own interpretation: Peter had alerted them to the fact that what they could 'now see and hear' was the direct result of Jesus' outpouring of the Holy Spirit (2:33). Now if Jesus could bring this about by fulfilling his promise, he was again shown to be the Messiah—here were no empty words, but explanation based on visible facts. Even those who had not seen the Risen One appear to them could now see the Risen One at work in his apostles.

But those who take Peter's speech to heart will also participate in this gift of the Holy Spirit (2:38–39). This was, of course, the decisive challenge: to test the promise for themselves. Some may have heard of or even seen John the Baptist and remembered his call to repentance and baptism (Mk. 1:4); even if they had not, Peter's statement is clear enough: unlike John's baptism, this is not an act of 'changing one's mind' and 'washing' for the remission of sins as such, it is an act of allegiance to Jesus, for they will be baptized in his name.[190] Once they are baptized in his name, he will be present in them and work in them through his Holy Spirit.

It is hard to overestimate the power behind Peter's words. One has read or heard them so often, that their radical newness—a newness, of course, which his first audience could relate to the solid basis of Scripture—can easily lose its impact on Christians today. Peter was no mere preacher of repentance like John the Baptist before him or so many others after him: He was a witness to the Resurrection, a witness to the Ascension and finally, on this day more than on any other, a witness to the reality of the Holy Spirit.

Luke records only excerpts from his speech: 'With many other words he warned them', he writes, 'and he pleaded with them, "Save yourselves from this corrupt generation".' (2:40). This last quotation from Peter's speech alludes to Jesus' own pronouncement about those who would not follow his words (cf. Lk. 9:41, 11:29), and it rounds the discourse off by coming full circle. For v. 40 takes up the prophecy from Joel in Acts 2:21: 'And everyone who calls on the name of the Lord will be saved.'

Not quite everyone, Luke implies, accepted Peter's message, but about three thousand did. At this time of the religious year, Jerusalem was full of pilgrims wanting to celebrate the 'Feast of Weeks' (cf. Ex. 23:16, 34:22; Lv. 23:15–22; Nu. 28:26–31; Dt. 16:9–12). If one assumes that the Pentecost speech took place near the temple, thousands would have been there and would have been prepared to listen to the Scriptures being explained.

For the second time after the Ascension, Peter has shown himself in command of a situation. If one compares his masterly handling of so large a crowd, a considerable advance on the 120 of his first assembly, with any practical experience he could have gathered during Jesus' ministry, only the Sermon on the Mount and the feeding of the five thousand come to mind. There it was Jesus, here it is Peter—but it is, of course, a Peter whose rock-like steadfastness is inspired by Jesus himself, and by the Holy Spirit.

V

There is no doubt that Peter's authority is safely established after these events, even for any who may still have wondered if he would be equal to the task. After such a glorious day of evangelizing, some may even have seen total triumph—and thus the Return of the Lord—within immediate reach. But the authorities had kept a low profile only during the one-day 'Feast of Weeks'; the next opportunity would see them strike back. Several days later (for the minimum period of time cf. 2:46) they did so.

The Christian community had been growing quietly; Luke points out that it was *the Lord* who added to their number (2:47b; cf. 1 Pet. 1:1b, 2 Pe. 1:1b). This is precisely what Peter had said before (2:39): the promise is for all those whom the Lord will call. Their selfless sharing and their adherence to traditional temple worship (2:46, 3:1) made them popular among the people (2:47a). As the response to Peter had already shown, plain speaking about repentance, about responsibility for the crucifixion and the need for forgiveness did not arouse antagonism as long as scriptural warrant and an appropriate lifestyle united to make their testimony trustworthy. Peter had already referred to the miracles of Jesus as witnesses to God's approval of him (2:22). Now the indisputable healing of a well-known invalid would demonstrate the presence of the Spirit of Jesus within the community, and provide evidence that his love and power were still at work. Not that this would be an end in itself, but it would form the starting point for more outreach to the people. On their way to afternoon prayer at the temple, Peter and his trusted fellow-apostle and aide John meet a cripple at the so-called Beautiful Gate.[191]

Peter heals him in the name of Jesus, in a scene vividly recorded by Luke. (We note the emphasis on their looking into each others' eyes, and the development from the beggar's abject humility to his walking and jumping into the temple courts, praising God. These details clearly indicate an eye-witness source, and are worlds away from the apocryphal, legendary miracle stories where vivid but sober recollection was to give way to fanciful embroidery). The people at the temple knew the cripple, as he had been there regularly (cf. 3:2); his healing was therefore beyond dispute, and thus provided the ideal starting point for Peter's next public address, on their way back from worship, at Solomon's Colonnade, where Jesus had preached before (Jn. 10:23), and where the first Christian community was to hold its public meetings (Acts 5:12).

Peter's speech displays confident authority. After his first success on the Day of Pentecost, he knew how to reach his hearers' minds and hearts. He comments on his hearers' astonishment and explains that it was neither his own nor John's power and godliness that produced the miracle, but God, 'the God of *our* fathers' (3:12–13). This introduction is noteworthy for two reasons. One is pretty obvious: Peter uses a traditional formula to speak of God—he is the God of Abraham, Isaac and Jacob (cf. Ex. 3:6, 15; Mk. 12:26; Lk. 20:37, etc.)—and he thus strikes a familiar chord at once. The other is less obvious: Peter's emphasis on god-given, as opposed to human 'power and godliness' recurs strikingly at the beginning of his second letter, 2 Pet. 1:3. 'Why do you stare at us if by our own power (*dunamis*) or godliness (*eusebeia*) we had made this man walk?' he asks in his speech; and he gives an answer to his readers in 2 Pet. 1:3: '*His divine power* (*dunamis*) has given us everthing we need for life and godliness (*eusebeia*) through our knowledge of him who called us by his own glory and goodness'. It is yet another example of Peter being consistent in his spiritual and exegetical thinking over a period of more than thirty years.

Peter orders his speech along tried and tested lines. He reminds his audience of their responsibility for Jesus' death and makes the accusation even more telling by pointing out that Pilate had decided to let him go (3:13); and that they had asked for the release of the murderer Barabbas when they had been given the choice (3:14). So they had killed the 'author of life'. To modern readers of the RSV and NIV translations this expression may suggest Jesus' role as Creator; but the AV ('Prince of Life') and NEB ('he who has led the way to life') are closer to what the Greek text actually says. The *archēgos tēs zōēs* is, first of all, the *source* of true life, and as the Greek also implies, the *leader* towards true life (cf. Acts 5:31 and Heb. 12:2, but also Heb. 2:10). There is a triple juxtaposition in Peter's sentence: the Jews killed him, but he was and is the source of life and was raised from the dead by God. This third step introduces the second element of Peter's speech: his witness and that of his fellow-apostles to the Resurrection (3:15b). As in his Pentecost address, he emphasizes that the

Resurrection initiated the outpouring of a new and special power: 'It is Jesus' name and the faith that comes through him that has given this complete healing to him, as you can all see' (3:16). Once more, the consequences of the Resurrection are not imaginary or metaphorical but plainly visible. Baptism in the name of Jesus and healing in the name of Jesus are closely linked in Peter's two consecutive speeches.[192] As at Pentecost, Peter begins his appeal for decision with the more personal appellation 'brothers' (3:17). First, he offers a moment of respite: 'I know that you acted in ignorance, as did your leaders'. Peter here recalls one of Jesus' words on the Cross: 'Father, forgive them, for they do not know what they are doing' (Lk. 23:34). The victim on the cross had indeed been the Suffering Messiah predicted by the prophets (Acts 3:18; cf. Isaiah 53; Ps. 22:69; see 1 Pet. 1:10–12; 2:21, etc.). Accepting this was the only hope for Peter's hearers. Rejecting it, however, they would lose their ignorance: as evil-doers conscious of their action, judgment would be theirs. Peter does not say this in so many words, but his call to repentance 'so that your sins may be wiped out' (3:19) is unambiguous enough.

Characteristically, Peter goes on to make a twofold promise. 'Times of refreshing' will come as a consequence of repentance, and God will send Christ for the second time (3:19–20). There is something comforting about the first promise: the word used in the Greek text, *anapsuxis*, is very rare in the Bible: it occurs only in Ex. 8:15, in the sense of 'relief', and here in Acts 3:20; even the related verb, though more common in the Greek Septuagint version of the Old Testament, makes only one NT appearance, in 2 Tim. 1:16, in the sense of 'refreshing'. In spite of its rarity, it is a well-attested term for a cooling, strengthening respite. Homer (*Iliad* 13:84) and Euripides (*Helena* 1094) had used it in this sense, and even if Peter could well have known it himself, Luke's interest in it may have been due to its medical background.[193]

For Peter's hearers and first Greek readers, both promises were probably closely interrelated: the future times of refreshment would come 'because of' (*apo*) the appearance (*prosōpon*) of the Lord. This helps us to understand the meaning of those refreshing times. The Israelites, i.e. the whole people of God, would, at an undisclosed future date ('*times* . . . may come') experience a soothing respite from the turmoils of the end times— which, as Peter's audience would have known and remembered, had already been initiated by Christ's Messiahship as such: cf. his first speech 2:16–21 etc. We may perhaps compare this 'respite' with the one experienced by the Egyptians, when Moses' fervent prayers ended the plague of the frogs, in the only Septuagint passage where the same word occurs.

In one sentence, Peter first prevents people from thinking that repentance and turning to Christ would bring his *immediate* Return, and also reminds them that the historical precedent where others (the Egyptians) had not used a promised and fulfilled respite could be repeated if the Israelites did not act decisively now. The Return of the Messiah brings rejoicing only for those who have repented in time. Peter even includes an unmistakable allusion to the Ascension he had witnessed. 'He must remain in heaven until the time comes for God to restore everything', he says of Jesus (3:21); yet another indication, too, of the incalculability of the Second Coming. God's promise made through his holy prophets will be fulfilled—but there are conditions which must be met, and the attitude of those who hear his message will play a part in this. Again we are reminded of a thought of Peter's some thirty years later; at the end of his second letter, he explains to his readers: 'The Lord is not slow in keeping his promise, as some understand slowness. He is patient with you, not wanting anyone to perish, but everyone to come to repentance' (2 Pet. 3:9).

Peter concludes by offering some examples of prophecy fulfilled—Moses prophesying the coming of Christ (Acts 3:22–23; cf. Dt. 18:15–16, 19), and God's own word to Abraham (Acts 3:25 Gen. 22:18, 26:4). Then he makes a final appeal: 'You are heirs of the prophets and of the covenant made with your fathers' (3:25). Would they understand? After all, and Peter ends on this strategic note, God had sent his servant Messiah into human history and to the Israelites first—theirs is the first opportunity to receive God's blessing by repenting. The stress falls significantly on the fact that it is a 'first', not an 'exclusive', offer. Peter well knew and made it quite clear that Christ had come for all people, Jews and Gentiles alike. What he had said in his first speech, he repeats here, and this time he appeals to God's word to Abraham: 'Through your offspring *all peoples on earth* will be blessed' (3:25).

Once again, Peter's speech meets with success. The number of believers grows to about five thousand. Luke mentions this figure only after his brief account of the arrest of Peter and John (4:4)—probably a conscious placing which seems to imply that this growth was not solely accounted for by the numbers of people present at Solomon's Colonnade when Peter spoke, but also by the passing on of their message by the other apostles and by converts. It is also likely that some time elapsed between the Pentecost speech and the speech at Solomon's Colonnade: see 2:46–47 and 3:1 for indications that despite their imprecision, suggest a considerable interval.[194] If the maximum estimate for the population of Jerusalem at that time, including all non-domiciled residents, is taken as a basis,[195] those c. 5000 converts would have formed a mere 5.3% of all people in the city—a remarkable figure in a way, but certainly not suspect, as some have thought.

Whatever the precise number may have been, the religious authorities disapproved. To them a crucified Messiah was a scandal, an impossibility, a contradiction in terms. What was more, they had been accused of having been guilty of his crucifixion, and had, directly or by implication, been called his enemies (3:18–19; cf. 2:35). But the greatest problem was the success of the apostolic preaching—the widespread appeal of the message of the resurrection of the dead in Jesus. This was a particularly sensitive point for the Sadducees who dominated the temple hierarchy and were opposed by the Pharisees. They were allies of the temple priests, and clung tenaciously to the letter of the Torah. For them, there was no such thing as a resurrection (cf. Lk. 20:27–40; Mk. 12:18–27; Mt. 22:23–33; Acts 23:7–10; Josephus, *Ant.* 18, 1:4, etc.). As the temple police had unquestioned authority within the temple precincts, an arrest was easy and ran no risk, initially at least, of causing unrest. Peter and John were put in jail overnight. There was to be no hastily convened night session of the Sanhedrin as was the case with Jesus, no premeditated sentence: public support for the apostles was evidently too great for a radical solution. They would have to discover calmly how best to deal with these men face to face.

Luke describes a plenary session of the Sanhedrin on the following day. The inquisitors had probably hoped to conduct a proper hearing, beginning with an analysis of the cripple's healing, a public event that could not be denied. But they had not reckoned with the inspiration of the Holy Spirit within Peter (4:8). Their leading question, 'By what power or what name did you do this?', is partly rhetorical: the whole hearing is, after all, based on the information that Peter and John had publicly healed the cripple in the name of Jesus and had preached about his power. Instead of inducing a guarded, self-protective reply, the question unleashes another of Peter's masterly speeches. It is very brief, very succinct and goes straight to the point. And since it is simply the answer to an initial question, there is here no need to assume that Luke gives only an edited summary. Peter follows his usual outline: he takes up the immediate cause and rephrases it with an overtone of accusation, 'If we are being taken to account for an act of kindness . . .' (4:9). He then answers the question more specifically, and the three points fall like blows in their unembellished brevity. First, the fact of Jesus Christ of Nazareth—the Messiahship is again part of his name (cf. 2:38, 3:6); Jesus is not just called the Messiah, he *is* the Messiah. Second, he was crucified by those who are conducting the present hearing—a condensed form of Peter's earlier accusation, but necessarily so: the Sanhedrin, and in particular Annas and Caiaphas, did not need a legally refined analysis—they were meant to feel the blow directly. Finally, God had raised him from the dead: the unabashed repetition of the testimony which had so angered the Sadducees. This, in brief—and what else should Peter have said? —was the power and the name behind the healing of the cripple.

Only one more thing was required: scriptural prophecy as proof that the new revelation was firmly based on the old. Peter this time refers to a passage he had not employed before, but which was among those the members of the Sanhedrin must have known by heart almost more than any other, as it was part of the Paschal Hallel psalms (cf. p. 73 above): Ps. 118:22, 'The stone you builders rejected has become the cornerstone.' Peter's addition of the 'you' will not have escaped the Sanhedrin's notice—it was a powerful example of his mastery in not only quoting Scripture but also applying it in the best rabbinical tradition. Small wonder that they were astonished (4:13). What the Sanhedrin did not know, of course, was that Peter was, once again, influenced directly by Jesus, who had himself used that verse from Psalm 118 in one of his parables (Mk. 12:10; Mt. 21:42; Lk. 20:17). Peter, realizing its illuminative potential, was later to apply it a second time, in his first letter (1 Pet. 2:4, 7).

He concludes with a challenge: 'Salvation is found in no-one else, for there is no other name under heaven given to man by which we must be saved' (4:12). Peter has turned a judicial hearing into an evangelistic proclamation.

The reaction of the Sanhedrin is interesting, as it points to the elitist educational and cultural thinking prevalent in Jewish society at the time. Since Peter and John were no scribes, no priests or rabbis, they were seen as 'unschooled' (AV 'unlearned', RSV 'uneducated', NEB 'untrained', *agrammatos*) and 'ordinary' (AV 'ignorant', RSV 'common', NEB 'laymen', *idiōtēs*). They would not believe that ordinary elementary education could lead to such powerful scriptural exposition and witnessing. Unwilling to accept that the Holy Spirit was inspiring Peter and John, they remembered ('took notice') that they had been with Jesus, who had not only been their teacher, but had shown himself a master of embarrassingly incisive public speaking.[196]

The Sanhedrin could see no way to act decisively against Peter and John. The evidence of the healed cripple was undeniable (4:14—the verse seems to imply that he had been asked in as a witness), and 'everybody living in Jerusalem' (4:16) was well-informed about this 'outstanding miracle'. Even if the physical facts could not be denied, the preaching behind it had to be stopped. After the judges had briefly consulted together (4:15–17), Peter and John were faced with the Sanhedrin's command 'not to speak or preach at all in the name of Jesus' (4:18). Their reply renders the Sanhedrin helpless—their only remaining weapon is threats (4:21). For the two apostles establish, in no uncertain terms, the superiority of God's command over that of the Sanhedrin—'judge for yourselves', they say—a subtle appeal to the self-professed intellectual and moral superiority of the members of the Sanhedrin. It is revealing that these men, who saw themselves as representatives, as trustees of God, offer no counter-arguments. Peter, the trustee appointed by Jesus, has won a spiritual and intellectual battle. This is by far more important for his flock than the fickle backing of 'all the people' (4:21) who are behind them for only so long as the impact of the miracle remains.[197]

VI

The thanksgiving prayer of the Christian community after the release of Peter and John (4:24–30) is not marked as Peter's (or John's) but as a joint utterance: 'They raised their voices together to God' (4:24). It is possible that the people present prayed alternately (this might account for some of the stylistic and grammatical problems of the text); or they may have followed a 'precentor', repeating his words a phrase at a time.[198] Either way, traces of Peter's voice are detectable: the rare form of address at the beginning of the prayer, 'Sovereign Lord', consists of only one word in the Greek text, the vocative *despotes* (literally our English 'despot'). Prior to this passage in Acts, it occurs only once as a title for God in the New Testament, in Simeon's song of adoration and prophecy, Lk. 2:29. Simeon uses it not because he wants to describe God as a despotic ruler, but because it underlines the contrast between God's omnipotence and his own lowliness: for himself, he uses the word *doulos*, servant or rather slave. This juxtaposition is maintained throughout the prayer in Acts 4; David is described as God's servant (4:25), and so is Jesus (4:27, 30). But whereas the servanthood of David and Jesus is described by the less lowly *pais* (a word that also implies a child-parent relationship), the apostles and believers use the slave-like *doulos* to describe their own position (4:29).

Peter preserves the same juxtaposition in his second letter: he calls himself *doulos* in the very first verse, 'Simon Peter, a servant and apostle of Jesus Christ', and goes on to speak of Christ as *despotēs* in 2 Pet. 2:1: 'They (he says of the false prophets and false teachers) will secretly introduce destructive heresies, even denying the Sovereign Lord who bought them, bringing swift destruction on themselves.' The tendency he had already hinted at in his Pentecost speech—applying a title of God (*Kurios*, Lord), to Jesus—has reached a more developed form in his second letter. While Simeon in his prayer of Luke 2, and Peter with his fellow-apostles in their prayer of Acts 4, are the 'slaves' of God, he is now, in 2 Pet. 1:1 (and also in his first letter, 1 Pet. 2:16) the slave of Christ. And the *despotēs*, the 'despot', the Sovereign Lord, clearly God for Simeon and the praying believers in Jerusalem, is equally clearly Jesus Christ in the second letter.[199] In 2 Pet. 2:1, the word has additional connotations which relate it to Peter's speeches in Jerusalem: Christ has *bought* his followers (his 'slaves,' therefore), Peter writes—and it follows he is technically their Lord and Master, their *despotēs*. And his readers will have understood the price which Jesus had paid for them: his life, in his death on the cross. For those among his followers who disown him, who disobey the Master by false teaching (2:1), his Lordship will be 'despotic' indeed: 'swift destruction' (2:1b) will be the result.[200]

The second Petrine link we find in the prayer of Acts 4:24–30 occurs in v. 28. 'They (the conspirators against Jesus) did what your power and will had decided beforehand should happen', the praying apostles say. In his Pentecost speech, Peter had said: 'This man was handed over to you by God's set purpose and foreknowledge' (Acts 2:23). In his first letter, Peter uses precisely the same terminology: 'We have been chosen according to the foreknowledge of God the Father' (1 Pet. 1:2), and 'He was chosen before the creation of the world, but was revealed in these last times for your sake' (1 Pet. 1:20; cf. also 1 Pet. 2:4–6 and Peter's speech in the house of Cornelius, Acts 10:42). The Greek words used here, *proorizō* (Acts 4:28), *prognōsis* (Acts 2:23; 1 Pet. 1:2), and *proginōskō* (1 Pet. 1:20; cf. 2 Pet. 3:17) all point to God's foreknowledge and the fore-ordained specifications of Christ's role and that of his followers. All these words are rare and related; in the case of *prognōsis*, the two instances in Peter's Pentecost speech and his first letter are the only ones in the whole New Testament. The continuity is striking; and thus even in a joint prayer, Peter's thinking and influence come to the fore.[201]

The prayer is answered by a renewed experience of the inspiration and power of the Holy Spirit (4:31). They had prayed for boldness in proclaiming God's word (4:29), and, as Luke notes in a matter-of-fact tone, they afterwards 'spoke the word of God boldly.' They had also prayed for a continuation of miraculous signs and wonders through the name of Jesus (4:30)—such signs had proved not ends in themselves, but ideal starting-points for attracting the attention of the populace and triggering Peter's evangelistic speeches.

VII

Against the background of these public appearances and the clash with the Sanhedrin, community life was beginning to take shape. Luke finds an impressive word for their togetherness: 'they were one in heart in mind' (4:32). His description of their sharing recalls the earlier days immediately after Pentecost (2:42–47). In fact the whole passage is meant to emphasize continuity: continuity in sharing the benefits of their possessions (4:32), continuity in powerful witnessing to the Resurrection (4:33a) continuity in the grace of God (4:33b), continuity in the selling of property for the benefit of the needy (4:34–35). We are not justified in assuming that the more wealthy members of the community were rushing out to dispose of their possessions in pursuit of some primitive 'communism'. Luke's account is quite specific in this respect: they did not all participate (Mark's mother is still the owner of her house in 12:12), nor was it all done at once (a comparison of 2:45 with 4:34 shows that it was a sporadic process—the NIV translation tries to express this by translating that they did it 'from time to time', v. 34); nor did those involved sell everything: Joseph Barnabas, singled out by Luke as a positive example (his by-name, as he does not fail to mention, means 'Son of Encouragement'), sells only a field he owned (4:37). Whatever they did, they did it voluntarily. Even so, the growing community would later need financial help from outside, and collections asked for by the Christians in Jerusalem and organized by Paul became necessary (cf. Acts 11:27–30; Rom. 15:26; 1 Cor. 16:1–4; Gal. 2:10.[202])

It is against this background that Luke sets Peter's clash with Ananias and his wife Sapphira over their contribution to the fund. The conflict is not about the handing over of only part of the proceeds from the sale—Peter even tells Ananias that he was free to deal with his property and his money both before and after the sale (5:4). The conflict is about lying, lying to the Holy Spirit under the influence of Satan (5:3, 4b)—Ananias, with his wife's full knowledge (5:1) *pretends* that he has given everything. Conceivably, the direct guidance of the Holy Spirit had been responsible for Peter's divining of the lie; it is equally possible that one of the others (for the plural note see vv. 2 and 5–6), who were present, had heard of the sale, had noticed the discrepancy between the price and the gift and had alerted Peter. The whole incident must have caused considerable upset among this close-knit community which had so far been able to live in mutual openness, indeed (as Luke has already stated, 4:32) as one in heart and mind. It is therefore significant that Peter, as the leader of the apostles, does not call for penal measures, nor pronounce judgment himself: his verdict is contained in his concluding sentence: 'You have not lied to men but to God!' (5:4). Ananias has thus brought 'swift destruction on himself', as Peter was to put it in his second letter (2 Pet. 2:1), writing about those introducing false teaching. (Predicting the *swiftness* of the destruction, he may well have remembered the swiftness of Ananias'

death). Medical explanations (a heart-failure or a fatal stroke) are therefore secondary to the fact that his death was a direct result of his lie to God and the Holy Spirit (seen as a unity: vv. 3, 4b).

Physical (not just spiritual) death as a result of sin is not as unusual as it may appear from the drastic directness of this passage: Paul refers to it in 1 Cor. 11:30; cf. 1 Cor. 5:5; 1 Jn. 5:16–17. And the Old Testament offers a number of examples: Gn. 38:7, 10 (cf. Dt. 32:39); see also a passage like Ps. 34:22 with the prayer in Ps. 139:19. Isaiah knows that God can kill the wicked (11:4c). And Hosea uses words that have clearly influenced the language used in the story in Acts when he describes God as killing through the mouth of his prophets (6:5).

When Sapphira appears on the scene, after the immediate burial of the sinner who had fallen under God's judgment, Peter gives her a chance to escape her husband's entanglement in death-bringing sin. But ignorant of his death she holds to their arrangement, not noticing the implications of Peter's question (why else would he have asked her if the donation was identical with the proceeds?). Confirming the lie, she has, unwittingly, brought swift destruction on herself as well. Again, Peter does not have to make a formal pronouncement. He expresses the unavoidable verdict as a question—'How could you agree to test the Spirit of the Lord?' (5:9). Like her husand, she has gone too far, and like her husband she will fall and die. 'Great fear seized the whole church and all who heard about these events', Luke adds (5:11). It is not irrational fear, but the fear of the holy, which we have met several times in the gospels. There were most probably no skeletons in the cupboards of other members of the community (Luke uses the word *ekklēsia* (cf. Mt. 16:18) here for the first time in Acts to denote the Christian community.[203]) Their fear is not that they might be found out: They realize how mighty God's Holy Spirit is, not only in sustaining the apostles as witnesses, but also in backing them in their role of sustaining an irreproachable common life.

It is not only the sudden use of *ekklēsia* which reminds one of Jesus commissioning Peter in Mt. 16:17–19. Here too is the first concrete example of the 'loosing' function. If we see the successful proselytizing by Peter and the others, together with the constant growth of the community, as evidence of the 'binding', then the pair of activities predicted by Jesus is now completed. Peter has 'loosed' Ananias and Sapphira. The probability that he (like the others: Mt. 18:18) would have remembered Jesus' pronouncement that their action would be valid in heaven may have contributed to the summary, even hasty carrying out of Ananias without any consideration for a devout family burial.

VIII

We are reminded of the almost superstitious craving for miracles present in society even today when we read about people bringing the sick into the streets and laying them on beds so that 'at least Peter's shadow might fall on some of them' as he passes by (5:15). Luke is not specific about Peter's attitude. In his account, the effect serves to illuminate a side-effect of the permanent growth of the community (5:14–15). When he says that 'all of them are healed' (5:16), the position of this statement makes it clear that it does not primarily (if at all) refer to those hoping for Peter's shadow, but to the crowds who gathered 'from the towns around Jerusalem, bringing their sick and those tormented by evil spirits' (5:16).[204]

In the eyes of the religious authorities, Peter's popularity as a healer and the blatant further use of Solomon's Colonnade as the meeting place of the Christians (5:12) were nothing short of provocation. 'Filled with jealousy' (5:17),[205] they arrest the apostles (no names or number given) and put them in the public jail overnight for the second time. The miracle that follows is the first of two similar ones concerning Peter (cf. p. 151 below on Acts 12:5–10). Luke describes it soberly and not without a touch of humour. His account is sparse, almost bare of incidental detail; in other words, all the characteristics of later literary legends are missing. The messenger of the Lord who appears during the night opens the doors, brings the apostles out (5:21) and locks everything behind him (implied by v. 23) so quietly that the poor guards do not notice a thing. And why not? Jesus himself had explicitly stated that he had angels at his disposal (Mk. 13:27; Mt. 13:41, 24:31; cf. Mk. 8:13; Mt. 4:11; Mk. 8:38; Mt. 16:27, 25:31; Lk. 9:26 etc.); and an angel of the Lord had rolled back the stone from his tomb (Mt. 28:2).

For the Sanhedrin, the message that the apostles are not in jail, but happily teaching in the temple courts (as the angel had told them to do) contained salutary lessons in humility and in realism, in view of the presence of the Lord and his Spirit with these men.

One of them in fact learnt the lesson, the Pharisee Gamaliel the Elder, 'a teacher of the law, who was honoured by all the people' (5:34). The temple police had arrested the apostles (note Luke's illuminating aside that they did not use force, 'because they feared that the people would stone them', 5:26—an indication of the apostles' popularity, but indirectly also of their definite disapproval of a popular revolt: Peter's sword had been cast aside in more than one sense). The high priest had reproached them for having disobeyed the Sanhedrin's explicit order and for accusing them of responsibility for Jesus' death (5:28). Peter had reiterated, if possible even more forcefully than at the first hearing, their utmost loyalty to God's command, to their witness to the Resurrection, to the Ascension to God's right hand, and to the presence of the Holy Spirit among his followers (5:29–32).[206] Gamaliel realizes that more is at stake than opposing expressions of religious zeal.

He may or may not have been present at the first hearing; but Peter's emphatic words, backed by his actions, his popularity even with those who had not yet been converted, and finally the miraculous rescue from prison, were arguments sufficiently strong for him to recommend caution and, indeed, the application of a Pharisaic principle. The Babylonian Talmud preserves the statement of Rabbi Yohanan (John) the Sandal-Maker, that 'every assembly which exists for the sake of heaven will in the end endure, but if it is not for the sake of heaven, it will not in the end endure' (Mishna *Awot* 4:14). Gamaliel expresses a very similar thought: 'If their purpose or activity is of human origin, it will fail. But if it is from God, you will not be able to stop these men; you will only find yourselves fighting against God' (5:38–39).[207]

Gamaliel, mentioned by his much less circumspect pupil, the ex-persecutor Saul/Paul (Acts 22:3), carried considerable authority with the Sanhedrin. After his death, he was remembered as one of the great men of the law: 'When Rabban Gamaliel the Elder had died, the glory of instruction ceased to exist, purity and separation died' (Mishna *Sota* 9:15). Even those whose religious zeal had led them to demand the death-sentence for Peter and the others (5:33) could hardly accuse Gamaliel of lack of principle. All the same, as a Pharisee he was a member of a minority group within the Sanhedrin, a group opposed to the Sadducees not least because they *did* believe in the resurrection of the dead. His success at the meeting was therefore all the more remarkable.

It seems that the Pharisees began cautiously to look more sympathetically at the Christians; some even became Christians themselves: (cf. Acts 15:5, 6:7. As for Paul, see Acts 23:6.) One may even assume that Peter had secret sympathizers other than Gamaliel among those who deliberated behind closed doors, here and after the first hearing.[208]

In this connection it is perhaps surprising that we hear nothing of Nicodemus and Joseph of Arimathaea, two members of the Sanhedrin who had been supportive of Jesus (Jn. 3:1–4; 7:25–44; 19:38–42; Mk. 15:43; Mt. 25:57–60, 27:57; Lk. 23:50–53). Later legend, in particular the *Legenda Aurea* (Golden Legend) of Jacobus de Voragine, the thirteenth century archbishop of Genoa, utilised material of unknown origin and substance to fill the 'gap'— Nicodemus and Joseph are both expelled from the Sanhedrin as followers of Jesus; Nicodemus is made a nephew of Gamaliel, Joseph is rescued from persecution by the risen Christ himself. Both also figure in the apocryphal *Gospel of Nicodemus* and the *Acts of Pilate*.[209]

Gamaliel cannot and probably does not want to prevent the standard punishment for offences against the law, in this case disobedience against orders of the administrators of the law, a fixed beating of 'forty strokes less one' (Paul confirms the ritual from personal experience in 2 Cor. 11:24). But even though this was anything but a pleasant experience, Peter and the others had known all along that it would happen sooner or later: Jesus had predicted it to them on the Mount of Olives (Mk. 13:9). Their reaction therefore is one of rejoicing 'because they had been counted worthy of suffering disgrace for the Name' (5:41). The thought is expressed in a form which recurs in Peter's first letter: 'If anyone suffers as a Christian, he should feel it no disgrace, but confess that name to the honour of God.' (1 Pet. 4:16, NEB).

The beating was meant as a severe warning ('they ordered them not to speak in the name of Jesus', 5:40), but as before, Peter and the other apostles disobey for the sake of the gospel. They continue proclaiming the good news that Jesus is the Christ, and they supplement their public teaching in the temple courts with door-to-door evangelism (5:42).

IX

Peter is not mentioned again until a considerable time later, when he goes to Samaria with John (8:14–25). The far-reaching events which took place between his release and the journey to Samaria had not happened without him, but they had not been shaped exclusively by him, either. In fact, after the initial, formative period, when Peter's role had been decisive, a certain process of 'democratization' seems to have set in—the first decision after the release is the election, by the whole community, of seven deputies responsible for administrative matters (6:1– 7),[210] and the decision which makes Peter reappear on the scene by name, the sending out of Peter and John to Samaria, is jointly made by all the apostles (8:14).

We do not know how Peter reacted to the arrest of Stephen, one of the Seven, 'a man full of faith and of the Holy Spirit' (6:5), 'a man full of God's grace and power' (6:8), nor to his theological manifesto (7:1–53) and his illegal execution in the presence of Saul/Paul (7:58–8:1a). It is however apparent from 8:1b that neither Peter nor any of the other apostles were directly afflicted by the persecution which followed on Stephen's death and in which Saul/Paul took such a cruel part (8:3): 'On that day a great persecution broke out against the church at Jerusalem, and all except the apostles were scattered throughout Judaea and Samaria . . . But Saul began to destroy the church. Going from house to house, he dragged off men and women and put them in prison.'

It is slightly puzzling that only the apostles were spared, but Luke clearly distinguishes between three groups, those that were scattered, those that were put in prison, and the apostles. Consequently, 'all were scattered' presumably means all those who were not in prison. The exclusion of the apostles from both groups may have been due to their continued popularity which had protected them twice before, and in addition, the wrath of the persecutors was directed against the adherents of Stephen's outspoken attack against the temple and the law, which the apostles themselves had not publicly supported.

Luke does not say when those in prison were eventually released, or when or if (some of) those who had been dispersed returned to Jerusalem. What he does say is that the apostles, far from going into hiding, were in constant contact with those in Samaria and had at least some freedom of movement (8:14). The most important consequence of this local persecution is the (involuntary?) beginning of the mission outside Jerusalem with

Philip and others (8:4–5). Those who persecuted the community in Jerusalem furthered the course of the gospel.[211]

The missionary activity undertaken by Philip had not been planned beforehand; it had, as it were, no direct apostolic authority behind it. What is more, its success occurred among the Samaritans of all people, who had indeed not always been popular with Jesus and the disciples. In Mt. 10:5, Jesus explicitly tells them not to enter any town of the Samaritans, and in Lk. 9:54, when they visit a Samaritan village *with him*, John and his brother James ask Jesus if they may call down fire from heaven to destroy its inhabitants.[212] Clearly the actions of Philip, who was not one of the apostles but one of the seven 'deputies', demanded apostolic, authoritative authentication at this very early stage of mission outside the walls of Jerusalem. Caution was appropriate, too, as evangelism had not been among the tasks allocated to the Seven (they had been selected to supervise and administer 'parish' matters, in particular the distribution of alms). When Stephen had exceeded his responsibilities the result had been confusion and persecution.

Such thoughts may have influenced the decision to send Peter and John to look at the situation for themselves. Peter's voice would be decisive as leader of the community; and John would be able to satisfy himself that not fire, but the Holy Spirit, should be called down from heaven. The unique situation in Acts, with the Samaritans not having received the Holy Spirit in spite of baptism in the name of Jesus (see 2:38; cf. 10:44–48, where the gift of the Spirit precedes baptism) may well be understood in view of these special circumstances. It needed Peter, the Rock of the Church, to vindicate this pioneering step of the expansion of the church and to pray for the gift of the Holy Spirit, which was granted immediately and effected through the laying on of hands by Peter and John.[213]

Peter's responsibility for the community in Samaria did not end with the mediation of the Holy Spirit. He had to deal with Simon who 'used sorcery' (AV; the Greek text uses the verb *mageuō* (v. 9) and the noun *mageia* (v. 11), both only here in the whole NT). Luke gives a brief portrait in the context of Philip's mission, i.e. before Peter is confronted with him. From this portrait, it appears that his popularity was due entirely to his magical art (which is not described in detail—we do not know, for example, if it extended to miracles of healing), and not to any particular teaching. His effectiveness depended on his ability to put on a show (8:11) and on his boasting (8:9b–10), two qualities that have always held a popular appeal. His claim to be 'someone great' had led to the popular belief that he was 'the divine power known as the Great Power' (8:10)—a characteristic way of describing a 'divine man' or *theios anēr*, a not uncommon phenomenon in hellenistic times.[214] It seems that Simon saw himself as such an emanation of God's will and power. At the time when Philip's mission overwhelmed him, he was, in spite of persistent critical opinion to the contrary,[215] no 'gnostic', but a somewhat boastful magician in a definable judaeo-hellenistic mould.[216]

When he realized that his followers were going over to Philip, he, too, 'believed and was baptized' and 'followed Philip everywhere, astonished by the great signs and miracles he saw' (8:13), impressed by the Christian's superior powers, and evidently trying to discover more about the secret behind it. Watching the laying on of hands by Peter and John and the subsequent reception of the Holy Spirit, he revealed his true character and offered Peter money for the ability to transmit the Holy Spirit (8:18–19). It is noteworthy that Simon had apparently not received the Holy Spirit through Peter or John himself when he made his wrong move; he was thus not a full member of the community, and all attempts to describe him in his later career as a Christian gnostic should take this into account.

Peter's reaction to Simon's approach is razor-sharp and uncompromising. 'May your money perish with you, because you thought you could buy the gift of God with money!', the NIV translation, is almost too harmless, too colloquial (cf. NEB: 'Your money go with you to *damnation*, because you thought God's gift was for sale.') The Greek word, *apōleia*, carries overtones of hell, of the loss of eternal life, as we may see from Peter's own later usage in his second letter (2 Pet. 2:1, 3; 3:7; 3:16). Indeed it seems as if 2 Pet. 2:3 looks back to the confrontation with Simon: 'In their greed for money they will trade on your credulity with sheer fabrications. But the judgment long decreed for them has not been idle; perdition waits for them with unsleeping eyes.' (NEB). The twofold use of the word occurs in 2 Pet. 2:1, the well-known passage where Peter talks about those who will bring destruction upon themselves (see pp. 123, 125 above).[217]

Peter tells Simon that he has no share in the word of God (8:21) and calls him to repentance. Yet he is not totally optimistic about

Simon's future—*perhaps* God will forgive him, he says—and 'I can see that you are doomed to taste the bitter fruit and wear the fetters of sin' (NEB).[218]

Simon in turn realizes that Peter's verdict is nothing short of devastating. His request, 'Pray for me so that nothing you have said may happen to me', may be sincere, if only because of his sincere shock, but it may also be empty words, appropriate to the man's character. Whatever his true motives, Peter does not react—or rather, Luke leaves Simon to pass into oblivion. It is only outside the New Testament that he reappears, first as the historical personality he was, then as a figure of legend.[219]

Having for the first time demonstrated his authority outside Jerusalem, and in two separate instances, Peter returns to the city with John, 'preaching the gospel in many Samaritan villages' (8:25). His rejection of Simon had shown the community how to cope with threats from outside mainstream Judaism. In the initial stages of spreading the gospel outside Jerusalem it was an issue of utmost importance.

CHAPTER SIX

Peter, Paul and the Gentile Mission

I

Luke proceeds to tell the story of Paul's conversion. At its end, we hear of the apostles' first contact with Paul (9:26–30). Although Luke does not say so—he leaves the length of the interval completely open, although he does hint at one (9:23)—more than two years[220] have passed when Paul is forced to leave Damascus. All sorts of rumours may have reached the apostles in the meantime. One assumes they had received a report from Ananias and the others in Damascus; but Paul himself had been far away. 'Arabia', he says himself in Gal. 1:17, though without any information about what he actually did there—was it a desert retreat to converse with God, was it mission among the nomadic Gentiles, or both? In any case, his failure to contact the leader(s) of the church must have appeared somewhat discourteous or even suspicious. Could Paul, the arch-persecutor, really be trusted? When he finally condescends to pay a visit, the community in Jerusalem is not particularly welcoming: 'He tried to join the disciples, but they were all afraid of him, not believing that he really was a disciple' (9:26).

Barnabas, however, has independent information about Paul's

conversion. He reminds them of what they have (most probably) already heard from Damascus and confirms it with the trustworthiness of one who had set a positive example himself (4:36–37) and he introduces the dubious newcomer to the leadership of the Jerusalem community (9:27).

Luke does not mention Peter in his account. It goes without saying that he was one of the apostles of 9:27, but Luke gives no names at this point. That he reserves for the strategically decisive 'Apostolic Council' of chapter 15. Paul, on the other hand, in his brief reference to his first visit to Jerusalem after his conversion (Gal. 1:18–19), says nothing about Barnabas or the fear of the apostles. He concentrates rather on what for him was the reason of the exercise, as we may infer from the way Luke underlines his 'staying with them', (9:28). Luke's generalized 'apostles' of 9:27 were in fact Peter and James,[221] and it was Peter in particular whom Paul had wanted to meet: 'I went up to Jerusalem to get acquainted with Peter and stayed with him fifteen days. I saw none of the other apostles—only James, the Lord's brother' (Gal. 1:18–19).

The NIV translation elegantly glosses over two peculiarities of the text. One is the true meaning of 'getting acquainted with' (AV 'see', RSV 'visit', NEB 'get to know'). The other is Peter's name (AV 'Peter', RSV and NEB 'Cephas'). It is in fact *Kēphas*, not *Petros*, in the Greek text—and as one knows from Jn. 1:42 at least, Kēphas is the Graecized form of the Aramaic for *Petros*, Peter, Rock. Paul's use of the form throughout (cf. 1 Cor. 1:12; 3:22; 9:5; 15:5; Gal. 1:18; 2:9; 2:11; 2:14; for the only exception, Gal. 2:7, see below) documents his awareness of the origins of the name in Jesus' Aramaic-speaking ministry. He thus shows a remarkably rigid adherence to his sources which encourages us to trust such received accounts as the list of resurrection witnesses in 1 Cor. 15. As for the 'getting acquainted'—the Greek verb, certainly not accidentally employed here by Paul, is one of those iridescent words of the Greek language: *historeō*, etymologically present in the English 'history' and its relatives. In hellenistic, *post*-Pauline literature (e.g. Plutarch, *Pompey* 40, *Lucullus* 2, etc; instances also in Josephus and Epictetus) it was to acquire the meaning given to it in the NEB translation of Gal. 1:18, 'to get to know someone', 'to make someone's acquaintance'. Originally, however, it meant 'to investigate something', 'to enquire into', and Paul—the only New Testament author to use the word—conveys with a single word the complexity behind his visit. Certainly he wanted to get acquainted at long last with the Rock of the Church, but he also realized that his Christ-given task of Gentile mission demanded a solid historical basis in the history of Christ's own ministry. For this purpose, Peter, the first among the apostles, trustee of the keys and foremost of the witnesses to the Resurrection, was the ideal source of authentic information. With his fifteen-day investigation concluded, Paul was fully qualified to begin his missionary journeys. Whenever Paul's independence is emphasized (not least by himself, for good reasons), one should not forget that his independence as a missionary rested on two solid foundations: Christ's command, and Peter's supply of basic facts during those two weeks in Jerusalem. 1 Cor. 15:3–11 is not the only testimony to Paul's indebtedness (even if it is the most elegant).

Paul does not say much more about his stay in Jerusalem. The singling out of James alongside Peter is certainly due to the fact that he did not want to ignore the Lord's brother, whose influence on community matters must by then have become apparent—beyond that, there was no need to consult anyone else. Luke adds the information that Paul used his stay to evangelize publicly and to contact the Hellenistic Jews in particular (9:29). In that, he was no more successful than Stephen before him: 'They tried to kill him.' Both the Jerusalem Christians and Paul knew the signs of danger from Stephen's martyrdom, and thus he made a hasty retreat (the second one after his escape from Damascus) with their help. 'They *took* him down to Caesarea and *sent* him to Tarsus' (9:30b), and Luke's choice of words may be significant: Paul is not escaping on his own accord and to a place of his own choice, but he is sent off (*exapostellō*) by the 'brothers'. Here we can recognize Peter's confirmation and validation of Paul's role. Coming to Jerusalem had been Paul's (somewhat delayed) personal decision; but when he leaves, he goes as someone who is sent. And his destination is well-chosen: from Caesarea, a hellenized city, he moves to Tarsus, his home-town, whose privileged status had made him a Roman citizen. Where better to begin the mission among the Gentiles?

II

As if to drive home to his readers that Paul, at this stage of church history, is not yet Peter's equal in matters missionary (Paul's claim to this effect would have to wait for another fourteen years: see Gal. 2:1, 7), Luke relates two events which again show Peter as the trustee of the keys. Paul has been sent off to Tarsus, and Peter resumes his own travels, which take him to Lydda, where a Christian community already existed—probably due to Philip's earlier evangelization in this area (8:40). Lydda, some 40 km. northwest of Jerusalem, gained fame and importance only much later, both in history as a medieval bishopric, and in legend as the place of the martyrdom of St. George, the soldier-saint and dragon-slayer. In New Testament times, it was 'in size no smaller than a city' (Josephus, *Ant.* 20, 6:2). The whole plain of Sharon (9:35) was in fact partly hellenized, and thus we see Peter moving consciously to an integration of the Gentiles which will find its culmination in Acts in his conversion of Cornelius. The name of the paralytic, Aeneas, points to the same hellenizing influence present in Bethsaida and Capharnaum, where some of the first disciples had distinctly Greek names—Philip, Peter's brother Andrew, and of course, Peter himself with the root of his original name Simon (see p. 21 above). Like these three, Aeneas, in spite of his Greek name, was probably a Jew, not a Gentile, though this is not certain. His name is certainly evocative of Graeco-Roman literature: in Homer's *Iliad*, he was a hero equalling Hector (5:467), recipient of highest honours (11:58), and a protégé of Poseidon (20:307), and Vergil made him the protagonist of his large-scale epic about the origins of Rome's greatness, the *Aeneid*. The parents of the bedridden man of Acts 9:33 apparently had rather high ideals for their son. A well-educated reader such as Theophilus will not have missed the irony of the glory of the man's name and his years of suffering.[222]

Peter cures him with the simple words 'Jesus Christ heals you', (9:34), acting as Jesus' representative, and acknowledging that the real power is not his, but Christ's. The subsequent command, 'Get up and tidy up your mat', is Peter's way of saying that the days of illness are over for good. He may have remembered the similar healing Jesus had performed in Peter's house in Capharnaum (Lk. 5:18–25; Mk. 2:3–12), when the paralytic demonstrated his complete healing to everyone by leaving with his mat under his arm, as Jesus had told him to (see p. 24 above).[223]

As so often before, the miracle has an instant effect on those who see Aeneas healed; they all 'turn to the Lord' (9:35). And the news spreads to Joppa, some 19 km. away, a thoroughly-hellenized seaport and trading-centre (modern Jaffa has preserved the international flavour of New Testament times). Luke maintains his historian's interest in recording names, and as 'Tabitha' did not evoke instant connotations in the same way as 'Aeneas', he translates the name into Greek—*Dorcas*, gazelle. If the paralytic's name had the potential to arouse literary-cultural associations in readers like Theophilus, the gazelle-like name of the dead girl-disciple could arouse special sympathy for an attractive woman 'who was always doing good and helping the poor' (9:36). (The fact that Luke records her Aramaic name first and then translates it, while leaving the Aeneas association to his Graeco-Roman readers' level of education demonstrates that he does not invent them.)

The trust of Tabitha's friends in Peter's powers was so great that they did not bury her. Luke's consecutive ordering of events gives the impression that they sent for Peter only after her laying-out in the upper room, when the news of Peter's presence in the vicinity had reached them, but this is most probably not what Luke implies. There is no need to assume that they did not bury her because they believed that Christians would not die before the return of the Lord: witness the widows of 9:39b. The case of Tabitha is a special one.

Tabitha's effectiveness as a helper is emphasized as the wailing women show Peter the clothing she has made for them, but Peter, very much the efficient man of action, sends them out of the room. A similar attitude to noisy distraction had been shown by Jesus when he had sent out everyone except the closest circle before raising Jairus' daughter (Mk. 5:40; Mt. 9:25; Lk. 8:51).

By praying, Peter once again commits the person to Christ. Only then does he address the dead woman, and he uses a word he must have remembered from Jesus' raising the daughter of Jairus: *anastēthi*—'arise', or, in the Aramaic used by Jesus in Mk. 5:41, *cum(i)*. If Peter spoke those words in Aramaic, the resemblance to his Lord's own triumph over the death of Jairus' daughter cannot have escaped his notice: *Tabitha, cum(i)* is all but identical with *Talitha* (meaning 'little girl') *cum(i)*. This parallel, for Peter another sign of his Christ-given stewardship even over life and death, is however not evident from Luke's text alone. He does not use the Aramaic word, and the Greek word he assigns to Peter (provided that Peter, perhaps speaking Greek on this

occasion, did not use it himself), *anistēmi*, is not even the same as
the one in the Greek translation of *talitha koum* in Mk. 5:41, viz.
egeirō, which Luke follows in his gospel account at 8:54 (cf. Lk.
7:14).[224]

Tabitha comes to life and sees Peter, but it is only when she sits
up by herself that he takes her by the hand and helps her to her
feet (9:41, contrast Jesus in Lk. 8:54; Mk. 5:41; Mt. 9:25). As with
the earlier healing of Aeneas, news of Peter's action spreads fast,
and the community grows as a result. We may infer from 9:43a,
'Peter stayed in Joppa for some time', that he followed up his
miracles with preaching and teaching. But in a passage which
puts such emphasis on names, the information in 9:43b is
particularly illuminating: the man Peter was staying with was
'Simon the tanner'. The significant fact is not that Peter and the
tanner are namesakes, but the profession of the man. As a tanner,
he had chosen an occupation to which ceremonial uncleanliness
had been attached, and his house was therefore outside the town
('by the sea', 10:6). Luke records his name, profession and the
location of the house in a dispassionate manner; when the angel
tells the Roman centurion Cornelius to send for 'Simon who is
called Peter' and who is 'staying with Simon the tanner, whose
house is by the sea' (10:5–6), it seems more the provision of a
sketch-map than the identification of someone professionally
unclean. On the other hand, Cornelius was not quite clean in
Jewish eyes himself, and as a 'Godfearer', a non-circumcised
adherent of the Jewish faith,[225] he knew precisely the bounds and
limitations set by a religiously-structured society. To detect, from
Peter's address in Joppa, that the man he was going to see had no
inhibitions about associating with 'outsiders', must have been
highly reassuring. Peter's choice of Simon the tanner as his host
was a tactical move of strategic consequence for his future
missionary career.

III

A modern reader of the story of Peter's contact with Cornelius
may not be unduly surprised at the role of angels and visions.
These, after all, are common occurrences for anyone who has
followed Peter's career so far. What may seem more remarkable is
the involvement of a Roman officer, a representative of the

occupying power, first with Judaism, the faith of the occupied people, and then with Christianity, the faith of those who believed in someone the Romans themselves had helped to put to death by their most common and most degrading form of execution. However, Jewish monotheism had begun to exert a certain attraction on Romans of all strata of society. Seneca's admiration for Jewish basic education (see note 16, p. 22) is only one example. Nero's wife Poppaea moved in Jewish circles and may even have been a 'Godfearer' herself (see Josephus, *Ant.* 20, 8:11); Juvenal, in his *Satires,* some fifty years later, shows himself well-informed about a tendency that was apparently sufficiently widespread to be satirized: while the fathers obey Mosaic law, he writes, but avoid circumcision, the sons will have their circumcision soon enough: *mox et praeputia ponunt* (14:96). But even before Seneca, Poppaea and Juvenal, Judaism had been given official status among the many religions of the Roman Empire; the synagogues and the observance of the sabbath were protected by law. Even three expulsions of Jews from Rome (139 BC, AD 19, and AD 49—the last one featuring in Acts 18:2, and, although far from exhaustive, including Judaeo-Christians for good measure) did not prevent Romans from becoming "Godfearers", or occasionally circumcised proselytes. Although anti-semitism was also real enough, a Roman officer like Cornelius, serving in Palestine, who saw fit to turn to the one God of the Jews, was certainly not an outcast. His colleagues would have accepted his devout faith (Acts 10:2) as one among many other possible options. His eventual choice of Christianity, the religion of an executed trouble-maker, was much more courageous and potentially dangerous.

Luke's information that Cornelius was an officer of the Italian cohort is one of his characteristically precise details, which secular historians often did not bother to record—indeed, if it were not for Luke, our knowledge of Roman troop movements in Judaea would be even scantier than it is. Between AD 41 and 44, i.e. during the reign of Herod Agrippa I, troops stationed at Caesarea consisted mainly of local recruits. (Josephus mentions the squadron of cavalry composed of men from Caesarea and Sebaste, *Ant.* 19, 9:2). The first archaeological evidence for the Italian cohort dates from AD 69 and points to the presence of this cohort as an auxiliary unit in Syria.[226] This has led to the assumption that Luke was mistaken in his dates and facts,[227] but quite apart from the obvious mobility of this cohort and its members (the AD 69 inscription was found in Austria), Roman auxiliary contingents are known to have been stationed in Judaea before AD 41, when Herod Agrippa I became king and cultivated a certain independence from the Roman military. However, even during his reign, the Roman cohorts were never far away: the same passage from Josephus' *Ant.* 19, 9:2 mentions five cohorts, and whilst he points out that the cavalry consisted of local people, he does not say the same of the cohorts which the prefect Cuspius Fadus had at his disposal in Caesarea. One of them could have been Luke's Italian cohort with Cornelius. There remains, of course, the possibility that the event of Acts 10 took place before the accession of Herod Agrippa I. Not only does the time sequence in Acts make this probable but it is almost certain if one dates the execution of James, the brother of John (Acts 12:2), ordered by Herod Agrippa I, in AD 42 or even in the spring of AD 41.[228]

Cornelius, at any rate, fits in very well with what we know about the Roman army at the time. Luke's brief portrait of him in 10:1–2 shows a man who has settled down, with an established household sharing his religious attitude. One could almost see him as a veteran, enjoying a leisurely lifestyle and freedom of movement.[229] It is a fact of some importance that the first two Gentiles whose conversion stories are related in Acts, the Ethiopian Chancellor of the Exchequer (8:26–39) and the Roman centurion, are both men of influence and standing in their respective environments. The traditional view that the mission outside Jerusalem (particularly later in Rome) began among the lower strata of society, is not borne out by the facts. Even if we do ignore later stories from outside the New Testament concerning Peter's contacts at Rome with senators and their families, these two conversions, and the fact that Luke's two books are dedicated to a high-ranking Roman official, give a completely different picture.

Luke leaves no doubt that God's hand is in the meeting between Peter and Cornelius as much as it had been when Philip met the Ethiopian (see 8:26). While Cornelius is prepared for his encounter by a messenger of God through a vision at prayer-time (3 pm, the second set prayer-time of the day), Peter in turn is prepared by another vision in his own prayer-time at noon. This was not an official, but a private time for prayers, as indicated by

Ps. 55:18, and was observed by many Jews who followed Daniel's example. Peter's choice of the roof indicates that he had sought privacy. His vision discloses the sense of humour that God betrays occasionally in his dealings with his servants. Now, when Peter feels the first pangs of hunger, God confronts him with an assortment of unclean animals. The heavenly command, 'Get up, Peter, kill and eat!' (10:13), is provocative. Staying with a tanner is one thing—but even a *tanner would not normally eat* unclean food. Peter duly protests, and he addresses the voice in the vision with 'Lord' (*Kurie*), which means that he accepts the message as coming from God or Jesus, rather than a temptation to sin. At this stage in the development of the community, neither Peter nor any of the other apostles or disciples had needed to think about the traditional dietary laws. They were accepted without question. Philip's meeting with the Ethiopian ended with Philip's sudden disappearance after the latter's baptism—there was no need to consider Ethiopian eating habits over against Jewish ones, and since the Ethiopian went back to his homeland immediately, the question of joint meals did not arise. The command given to Peter in his vision was new for the Jews who had turned Christian without giving up temple worship and the traditional customs attached to Jewish culture. The reply of the voice to Peter's protest is therefore both a reminder and the allocation of a new task: a reminder, because Jesus had already explained to Peter that it was not food that was unclean or that made a man unclean (Mk. 7:1–19; Mt. 15:10–20, the version where Peter is mentioned explicitly, see p. 31 above), and a new task, because what may have sounded like theoretical teaching before was now to be put into practice.

The instruction given by the heavenly voice is repeated three times (10:16), and Peter is set 'wondering about the meaning of the vision' (10:17). This is not to insinuate, of course, that he does not understand its content; what he does not quite see then and there is its applicability to a concrete situation. Why should it happen just then? A few minutes later, he has the answer. Indeed, we find a reflection of this in Mark's gospel, where as a parenthesis after Jesus' teaching about the clean and the unclean (Mk. 7:14–19a), Mark adds the explanation: 'In saying this, Jesus declared all foods clean'. This is surely Peter's voice speaking through Mark. After the vision at Joppa, Peter knew precisely what Jesus had meant—better and more fully than before. In

Mark's comment, we see the reflection of Peter's thinking and his interpretation of the events which had made him initiate the official mission to the Gentiles.

The three messengers from Cornelius[230] arrive the very moment when the Holy Spirit tells Peter that they are downstairs and that he should not hesitate to go with them, as they are sent by the Spirit.[231] Such a warning was certainly appropriate: the three men, one of them an armed soldier, had probably come the 50 km. from Caesarea on horseback,[232] and they must have been a somewhat surprising, if not a frightening sight outside the tanner's house.

The explanation given by the three confirms the Spirit's words and allays whatever fear or uncertainty may have lingered in Peter's mind. He courteously asks them in, and the two Simons (the tanner's consent as the host is implicit) offer them hospitality overnight (10:23), thus avoiding a late departure with an inconvenient arrival back in Caesarea in the middle of the night. Peter's companionship with the Gentiles is thus furthered step by step: before he is the guest of a Gentile household himself, he has already given hospitality to Gentiles.

When the group leaves the following morning, Peter takes an escort of his own with him, 'some of the brothers', six to be precise (see 11:12). They take their time and are considerably slower than the messengers the day before. It may be that the six Christians from Joppa did not have horses, or that Peter made use of the journey for a couple of visits on the way. When they arrive on the second day, i.e. on the fourth day after Cornelius' initial vision (cf. 10:30), everything is prepared for their arrival (10:24)—which suggests not only that one of the servants or the soldier had ridden ahead to inform Cornelius, but also how seriously he takes Peter's visit. One may assume that he had used the intervening days to obtain further information about Peter—which cannot have been too difficult for a man in his position—so that he knew the qualifications of this 'man named Simon who is called Peter' (10:5) before he arrived. Accordingly, Cornelius falls on his feet in reverent welcome (10:25). Peter's reaction is illuminating: he refuses the homage, but the words he uses, 'I am only a man myself', have a twofold meaning. Being 'only a man', he rejects a gesture reserved for a master, or, in Peter's experience, for Jesus (see Mt. 8:2; 9:18; 15:25; 20:20; Lk. 24:52; Jn. 9:38; Mk. 5:6; cf. Lk. 4:8; Jn. 4:22, 24; Acts 8:27; 24:11; cf. also Mt. 18:26), but by stressing that he is 'a man himself', i.e. a man like Cornelius, he also establishes his equal standing with the Roman officer.

The level of Luke's elaborate and detailed introduction to the meeting is maintained throughout the narrative. When Peter explains to 'the large gathering of people' inside, the 'relatives and close friends' of Cornelius (10:27 with 25) that it is against the law for a Jew to associate with a Gentile or to visit him, but that God has shown him that he should not call any man impure or unclean (10:28), he demonstrates publicly that he has fully grasped the meaning of his vision. Peter overstates the case slightly, perhaps in order to emphasize the absolutely revolutionary importance of his step. Strictly speaking, contacts with Gentiles 'only' made a Jew ceremonially unclean (as Simon's profession as a tanner was ceremonially unclean), but that was purifiable under certain conditions.[233] An orthodox Jew would however do everything to avoid entering a Gentile house (cf. Jn. 18:28).

Cornelius explains why he had sent for Peter[234] and ends by expressing his belief that God is present among them (cf. Mt. 18:20) and that Peter's word will not be of his own making, but will be what the Lord commands (10:33; cf. Mt. 28:20; Lk. 17:10). It is obvious that Cornelius had spent the days between the vision and Peter's arrival thinking and praying extensively about the significance of the meeting.

Peter's speech, 10:34–43, is primarily a repetition of his familiar evangelistic message. We note the recapitulation of Jesus' ministry (10:37–39a), the crucifixion with the characteristic 'tree' for the cross (v. 39b), the resurrection (v. 40), the emphasis on the appearances to witnesses chosen by God (v. 41), and the fulfilment of OT prophecy with the added stress on the forgiveness of sins, through the name of Christ (v. 43, cf. Je. 31:34; Dn. 9:24). Even more than in his previous speeches, he underlines the historicity of these events, beginning even with a reminder that his hearers know some of it already.[235]

The most important additional detail occurs in v. 42, after Peter's insistence that he and the other witnesses had not only seen the risen Christ, but had eaten and drunk with him: 'He commanded us to preach to the people and to testify that he is the one whom God appointed as judge of the living and the dead.'[236] The Greek word for 'people', *laos*, is almost exclusively used for the people of Israel in the Septuagint and the NT, while *ethnos* is used both for the Jewish people, and, in the plural, for Gentile peoples and nations (for the contrast see Acts 26:17, 23; Rom. 15:10–11). This has led to the assumption that Peter is applying Jesus' command to the Jewish people.[237] It seems, however, that this is not Peter's way of thinking. The introduction to his speech points the way: he states that God does not show favouritism (10:34) but accepts men from every nation (*ethnoi*, 10:35). Jesus did appear to the people of Israel (literally 'the sons of Israel') so that they were naturally the first recipients of the message (10:36); but the inclusion of both Jews and Gentiles is already established by v. 34. The shift of emphasis in the meaning of *laos* becomes finally apparent in v. 40, when Peter says that the risen Christ 'was not seen by all the people but by witnesses whom God had already chosen.' *Laos* is no longer a word for the Jewish people only, but for the community of potential followers of Christ, regardless of nationality. (Peter's very first public speech, at Pentecost, had already attracted some non-Jewish hearers.) When Peter relates Jesus' command 'to preach to the people' in v. 42, race or nationality have disappeared from the term. He makes this unambiguously clear on two later occasions: in his address at the Apostolic Council, 15:7–11, he vigorously maintains that there is no distinction between Jews and Gentiles before God, and he is understood by James, who, in his own address, even uses the very word *laos*, saying that 'Simon has described to us how God at first showed his concern by taking from the Gentiles a people for himself' (15:14). Finally, in his first letter, Peter restates the point that all believers are the people, the *laos*, of God: 'But you are a chosen people (*genos*), a royal priesthood, a holy nation (*ethnos*), a people (*laos*) belonging to God . . . . Once you were not a people (*laos*), but now you are the people (*laos*) of God; once you had not received mercy, but now you have received mercy' (1 Pet. 2:9–10).[238] The Lord's own voice later confirms this usage to Paul (18:10), who feels free to use it in the same sense in Tit. 2:14.

This speech, then, is a turning point in the history of the church. Indeed it is possibly the single most important speech in the entire book of Acts. It is the fullest summary of the gospel message: all later exposition, as indeed all later NT theology, is inherent in Peter's speeches with this one as their peak. It opens the door to the Gentiles, to 'all nations', as commanded by Jesus (Mk. 13:10; Mt. 28:19). And it prepares the way for a comprehensive redefinition of the people of God. If one had to choose a single example for the fulfilment of Jesus' prophecy that Peter would be the rock of the church, this speech and its consequences would surely be the one. It is no exaggeration to state that 'Peter is certainly the first in his preaching. Others will join him and the words of Peter will develop in their words. But they will never exceed Peter in the gloriousness of his witness concerning Jesus Christ.'[239]

Luke seems to have treasured this speech so much that he did not alter any of the formal characteristics preserved by his source: it is clearly the speech of someone thinking in Aramaic but speaking Greek as Peter would have done on this occasion.[240] And Luke's fidelity to the grammatical and stylistic idiosyncrasies of Peter's speech is only consequential in view of the Holy Spirit's fidelity to Peter himself and to the promise of his words ('While Peter was still speaking these words, the Holy Spirit came on all who heard the message,' 10:44). It is, for everyone present, the solemn and final confirmation of Peter's authority in admitting the Gentiles into the church, and it is more conclusive evidence, that throughout this episode Peter had been the vehicle of God, indeed the trustee of the keys. The radical rethinking demanded by Peter's action is amply demonstrated by the reaction of his six Jewish-Christian companions (10:45–46): they are amazed at this pouring out of the Holy Spirit on those uncircumcised Godfearers who begin to speak in tongues, praising God. It is the first time since Pentecost that any act of speaking in tongues is recorded (although there have been several instances of the gift of the Spirit). As a seal under special circumstances it occurs only once more in Acts (19:6), and one may even assume that Paul's companions had not experienced it themselves. There is thus no doubt, as Peter explains to them with his rhetorical question of 10:47, that these Gentiles are demonstrably as much in possession of the Spirit as circumcised Jews.

Peter orders their baptism in order to complete their acceptance into the church (10:48). Neither he nor any of his companions so much as even hints that circumcision is necessary. Since they are still uncircumcised when Peter explains his action to the community in Jerusalem (11:3), we may conclude that they never were.

Cornelius and his household ask Peter to stay with them for a few days; they need, and desire, further instruction. Peter's compliance casts a light on the priorities of an apostle and servant of Christ. Unlike many ecclesiastical leaders of the 1980s, the head of the young church is not ruled by his diary. His people back in

Jerusalem may wait impatiently for his report, but they will have to wait. Explaining his revolutionary action to a group of doubting inquirers is one thing; the action itself and the following through of its immediate consequences is another. Peter knows what he wants and where his duties lie.

IV

News of the beginning of the mission to the Gentiles spread quickly, 'throughout Judaea' (11:1). Back in Jerusalem, Peter was immediately faced with anxious questions. Although Luke does not say who or how many 'criticized' Peter for his fellowship with uncircumcised men, the problem was a very real one for all of them, and we may imagine the group of questioners as fairly large and representative. The word rendered 'criticize' by NIV and RSV (AV 'contend', NEB 'raise the question') shows their sincere concern. *Diakrinō*, as it is used here, implies doubt and hesitancy rather than open, negative criticism (cf. Mt. 21:21; Mk. 11:23; Acts 10:20; Jas. 1:6; Rom. 4:20; 14:23; Jude 22). Of these instances, Acts 10:20 and Rom. 14:23 are particularly interesting, as the former occurs when the Spirit commands Peter not to hesitate in meeting the Gentile messengers, and the latter occurs precisely in the context of Paul's own attempt to come to terms with those who have doubts about eating supposedly 'unclean' food.

As so often with rumours, what had reached the community in Jerusalem was probably only half of the story, and out of that they quite naturally filtered what concerned them most directly in their own daily lives—not the baptism of the first Roman officer, but the sudden break with their hitherto unquestioned way of life as Jews in Christ. Their situation was precarious enough anyway. They had rebuilt their community after Stephen's death and the ensuing persecution and dispersion; anything likely to antagonize the priests, the Sadducees, perhaps even all the Jews in Jerusalem, again or even further, was bound to make living, let alone preaching and evangelizing among their fellow-Jews in Jerusalem and Judaea, very difficult if not downright impossible. How could Peter do it?

Peter's explanation is anything but an apology. Luke's narrative is sober and concise as Peter tells them the whole story, from the vision which authorized his action to the outpouring of the Holy

Spirit. There are obvious variations in detail, as parts of the story are now told for the third time, but for the first time by Peter himself (v. 14, for example, is an extension of the angel's message to Cornelius as given in 10:4–6 and 31–32, but was already implied by 10:22, 33). A characteristically personal touch appears in 11:15: 'As I began to speak, the Holy Spirit came on them as he had come on us at the beginning.' In other words, Peter's exposition in 10:34–43, which was interrupted in v. 44, was for him only the beginning of what he had intended to teach Cornelius—but nothing more was needed there and then, and the acceptance of it by his hearers was sufficiently complete for the Holy Spirit to come on them. There is thus no need for any prolonged teaching and initiation of the Gentiles before they can join the church. Detailed instruction was of course necessary—and Peter did stay with Cornelius for a few days—but as an adjunct, not a prerequisite.

Peter likens the outpouring of the Holy Spirit on this occasion to the first one at Pentecost. This interpretation safeguards equality of the Gentiles with the Jewish believers both before God and also within the church. The promise of Jesus to his apostles that they will be baptized not merely with water, but with the Holy Spirit (11:16 with 1:5) is thus extended to include non-Jews. And the customary baptism with water which was continued by the church had thus, by definition, to be granted to the Gentiles as well. Finally Peter re-emphasizes the vital point that he was carrying out the Lord's explicitly stated wish, not his own wishful thinking: 'Then how could I possibly stand in God's way?' (11:17, NEB).

The combined authority of Peter's position and the manifest confirmation by the Holy Spirit leave no room for further doubt. Instead, all present praise God, agreeing to Peter's action. They accept that God has given the Gentiles the chance to repent and win eternal life (11:18). The way in which their reaction is put, however, is somewhat ambiguous. They recognize that Peter has been vindicated, but they see no obligation to turn to the Gentiles with any special vigour. 'So then, God has even granted the Gentiles repentance unto life'—that is good to know, but the very special courage needed to implement this in Jerusalem, under the shadow of the temple, was a different matter. The delicate situation of the Jerusalem community, intent on reaching their fellow-Jews more than any other audience, was not eased by the new perspective. Conflicting interests would flare up soon enough, and they would show, to Peter as much as to Paul and the other missionary apostles, that local interests are often much smaller than God's will. Peter's acceptance of Cornelius has spearheaded a development that must put an end to the parochial stage of church growth. It is certainly not without significance that Cornelius was a centurion not in Jerusalem or its immediate vicinity, but in the heartland of hellenized, Gentile Palestine. The double name of Caesarea indicated its links with the Roman world; Caesarea Sebaste, (*Sebastos* = *Augustus* in Latin), built by Herod the Great and dedicated to the Emperor Augustus.[241]

V

The precedent set by Peter has immediate repercussions farther away. Some of the scattered members of the original Jerusalem community had gone to Antioch, the capital of the Roman province of Syria and, with some 500,000 inhabitants the third largest city of the ancient world at that time after Rome and Alexandria.[242] Here they had begun to preach to "the Greeks', i.e. to the whole Greek-speaking population of Antioch, including the Gentiles.[243] Communications between Jerusalem, Caesarea and Antioch were fast (cf. 11:1, 22) and when the Christians in Antioch, who had risked preaching to the Gentiles, heard of Peter's action they must have felt encouraged to proceed. We may assume that the 'turning to the Lord' of the 'great number of people' in Antioch (11:21) was thus followed, sooner or later, by baptism and official acceptance into the church; this last step may have coincided with the arrival of Barnabas, who was perhaps sent to Antioch for this very purpose (11:22–24). Of such importance was this development in Antioch that Peter himself would later go and see it for himself, at least once (see Gal. 2:1f.), perhaps even twice.[244] Paul was called from Tarsus to assist Barnabas (11:25), and Luke notes, without any further embellishment, that 'the disciples were first called Christians (*Christianoi*, those belonging to Christ), at Antioch' (11:26). It is not without interest that the only NT writer apart from Luke (also in 26:28, in the mouth of Herod Agrippa at Caesarea) who uses the term is Peter himself, in his first letter: 1 Pet. 4:16.

While these and other developments (11:27–30) were taking place at Antioch (but before the event of 11:30; cf. 12:25), those who remained in Jerusalem again became the target of persecution. Luke does not say why;[245] he merely records that James, the brother of John, was beheaded on Herod Agrippa's orders, and that this execution pleased 'the Jews' (12:1–3), whereupon Herod proceeded to arrest Peter during the Feast of Unleavened Bread. The pattern is obvious: the execution of one of the apostles was a test case—would the people react violently, or would they acquiesce? If the latter— and that is what happened according to Luke's sparse account—he could attack and eliminate the leader of the church himself. Luke proceeds to tell the story of Peter's arrest and miraculous rescue in a tone of vivid recollection which suggests a direct source—either Peter himself or one of those to whom he told the story including, of course, Mark (12:17). It is Peter's second rescue from prison, and Luke again shows his skill as a writer of history by shifting the narrator's viewpoint. The first rescue was told from two perspectives—briefly as the apostles had experienced it, and more vigorously *via* the reaction of the temple police. The second rescue, with its attention to detail, is told entirely through Peter's eyes, though of course in the third person singular. Even Herod's orders in 12:4 shed some light on this: when Luke writes that Herod put Peter in prison, 'handing him over to be guarded by four squads of four soldiers each', one can almost see Herod explaining to Peter his elaborate precautions and warning him against any attempt to escape again.

The community, of course, was praying for Peter (12:5), but after the execution of James, hopes cannot have been very high. Luke reiterates the care taken in the guarding of Peter and the fact that it was the last possible night for a rescue (12:6), before describing the sudden appearance of an angel of the Lord accompanied by light—not an unusual concomitant (cf. Lk. 2:9). Even so, the angel has to wake Peter up, whereas the soldiers remain asleep—and the chains fall off Peter's wrists before any sudden movement could wake them up.[246]

Peter obeys the angel's instructions to dress fully (12:8) and follows him through the doors and gates of the prison, past the two other soldiers. The iron gate leading to the city opens by itself (cf. 5:19 and 16:26, and also Josephus, *War*, 6, 5:3), or so it seemed to Peter, who was admittedly still half asleep ('he had no idea that what the angel was doing was really happening; he thought he was seeing a vision' 12:9). He comes to himself as soon as the angel has left him (again a precise detail, 'when they had walked the length of one street', 12:10), and realizes that he is indeed free. His statement, 'Now I *know without a doubt* that the Lord sent his angel . . .' (12:11), is particularly emphatic in the Greek, as the adverb *alēthōs* ('truly', 'with certainty') is used only here in Acts, and only three times in Luke's gospel (9:27; 12:44; 21:3), where Jesus employs it to underline solemn declarations. Peter's statement, in direct speech, both to himself and by implication to Luke's readers, marks the event as the solemn confirmation of God's acting in history.

The conclusion of the story is equally rich in detailed memories. Peter goes to the house of John Mark's mother, where they were praying for him; the house is described as having an outer door (12:13), i.e. it possessed a corridor, hall or court. The servant-girl is still remembered by name (*Rhoda*, 'Rose'). She may not have been too bright—overjoyed, she forgets to open the door and runs back to the others instead. However, while she at least believed that it *was* Peter whose voice she had heard, the others first accuse her of stupidity and then assume that it must be Peter's angel (12:15), which is a somewhat enigmatic statement. Do they think that he is a human messenger—so that *angelos* would here be 'neutral', as in Jas. 2:25 and, in a way, Mt. 11:10,—not an angel, but someone with a last message from Peter, granted by Herod prior to the trial? Do they think it is his guardian angel (cf. Mt. 18:10; Heb. 1:14; Dn. 3:28; 6:22)—but why would he come to them without Peter? Do they perhaps believe it is Peter's angelic counterpart who has assumed his voice—but why should he?[247] The least unsatisfactory explanation seems to be that they are thinking of some kind of messenger with news from or about Peter.

Peter insists; his knocking finally makes them open the door, and they are of course astonished (the word Luke uses here, *existēmi*, is employed by him to describe states of utter amazement: cf. Acts 2:7, 12; 8:13; 9:21; 10:45). He tells them the story as we know it, asking them to keep quiet for a moment (12:17). Having finished, he instructs them to 'tell James and the brothers about this.' Two pieces of information follow from this command. The other apostles[248] and James were not in Mark's house, but—most likely—in hiding, as the persecution that had killed James the son of Zebedee and imprisoned Peter was obviously directed against the leaders of the church. (Other members of the community, like those assembled in the house, did not necessarily have to seek safety.) In addition, James, the brother of the Lord, is here singled out for the first time as a person of importance among the leaders.

In Acts, the Apostolic Council confirms this position (15:13f, cf. 21:18f). Paul does the same (Gal. 1:19; 2:9, 12) and his rank is further underlined by his own canonical letter and the reference to him in the introduction of Jude's letter. It was to be expected that a brother of Jesus would have natural and, so to speak, inherited, authority provided he was a believer—and James appears among the first post-Ascension Christians (Acts 1:14), besides receiving an individual resurrection appearance (1 Cor. 15:7).

With 12:17, Peter shows that he sees James as his successor. It is in fact quite probable that he had appointed James at the time of his arrest, when he must have been expecting certain death. James, at such a moment of danger to the community, had one additional qualification: he was, as we know from Gal. 2:12, scarcely a champion of the Gentile mission. Since it was the beginnings of this very Gentile mission that had caused this persecution, James must have appeared as the guarantor of the survival of the Jerusalem Church.

As an enemy of the authorities, Peter has no choice but to flee Jerusalem. As a fugitive, he would not have been safe for another day in the city. The same night he leaves 'for another place'. He may not have been unduly sad—he had established evangelization and community life in Jerusalem, but the church of which he was the appointed rock had a scope reaching beyond that city. For him, there was more to be done now outside Herod Agrippa's territory than within it. The divine intervention which had released him from prison prompted a move that had become necessary—or so he must have thought that night in the house of John Mark's mother. But where did Peter go? Where was the 'other place', the *heteros topos* of 12:17?

VI

Luke is a careful historian. If he does not even hint at Peter's whereabouts until he reappears in time for the Apostolic Council of Acts 15, he must have had good reasons. The assumption that he lost interest in Peter's further career because he wanted to promote Paul is too facile, and is contradicted anyway by the strategically important role he plays in Acts 15. It is understandable that Luke should not name the place(s) where Peter went.

His reason is the one that prompted the omission of Peter's name in the account of the cutting off of the servant's ear at Golgotha by Luke and Mark (followed by Matthew; see p. 78 above). Writing during Peter's lifetime and to a high-ranking Roman official, Luke wants to avoid anything that might compromise the activities of Peter, legally a fugitive from state authority, within the Roman empire. Luke knew where Peter went and where he was at the time of writing, but he remained silent. Even Peter himself keeps a low profile in this respect, when he sends his first letter from Rome using the topographical pseudonym 'Babylon' for Rome (1 Pet. 5:13). And it is this very use of 'Babylon' that gives us a clue as to the identity of Luke's 'other place'.

Even if we cannot determine when Babylon was *first* used as a cryptogram for Rome, the identification as such is indisputable.[249] The choice of Babylon—instead of, say, Sodom or Gomorrah—lay ready at hand, as it signified both the epitome of power and evil, of arrogance and corruption which would be overcome by the Lord (cf. Is. 13:1–14:23), and the 'exile' of the Christian church in the centre of paganism. But whatever the full array of reasons for Peter's choice, his readers would have been well aware of scriptural references to Babylon. There are many of these, but one is particularly illuminating: Ez. 12:1–13. It is about going into 'exile', about fleeing from Jerusalem in the middle of the night (12:7b), and it is about Babylon (12:13). While all these elements are present in this text (which has in itself, of course, a wider and much more complex oracular meaning), yet another verse offers the key to Luke's 'riddle'. 'Set out and go from where you are to another place', says 12:3. The Septuagint has *eis heteron topon*, the identical expression used by Luke for Peter's destination. 'The other place' is Babylon, and Babylon is Rome.

The time was ripe, it seems, for the symbolical use of 'Babylon' for Rome among Christians living or staying in the capital of the Empire in the late fifties and early sixties, and the reigns of Claudius and Nero offered enough illustrative material.[250]

Internal evidence thus clearly points to Rome as Peter's destination. Further confirmation comes from church history, in an intriguing detail preserved by Eusebius and Jerome. Peter arrived in Rome during the reign of Claudius, more precisely during his second year, i.e. in AD 42 (Eusebius, *HE* 2, 14:6, with *Chronicon ad loc*, and Jerome, *On famous men* 1, where he is the 'overseer' or *episkopos* for twenty-five years, i.e. until his death under Nero.[251]) This is confirmed by the fourth century *Catalogus Liberianus*, a list of popes from the beginnings of the Roman bishopric to Pope Liberius (352–66), and by the *Liber Pontificalis*, published (in its extant form) in the sixth century (mostly relying on the *Catalogus Liberianus*, but with some independent information and variations of detail).[252]

It is noteworthy that these sources date from the time when the church became interested in cataloguing, as it were, its history—there had been no apparent reason to do so before it gained official authority and security under Constantine.[253] But it is equally noteworthy that these historical sources nowhere run counter to New Testament evidence or indeed historical plausibility. Even if a certain vagueness about supplementary detail is perhaps unavoidable, the outline and succession of dates and data makes perfect sense.

Peter left Jerusalem immediately after his escape from prison in AD 41 or AD 42. (The latter date also would 'fit' a strange slightly implausible apocryphal command by Jesus that the disciples should not leave Jerusalem for twelve years: *Act. Pet.* 2:5; Clement of Alexandria, *Strom.* 6, 5:43—quoting the lost *Kerygma Petrou* ('Preaching of Peter'); Eusebius, *HE* 5, 18:14, traces the statement back to Apollonius, an anti-Montanist writer (*HE* 5, 18:1), but qualifies it by adding the wry comment *hōs ek paradoseōs*, "as if from tradition".) Peter then heads for Rome, but not directly. He may have visited Antioch (see above), and perhaps several towns in Asia Minor (cf. 1 Pet. 1:1; Eusebius, *HE* 3, 1:2), perhaps Corinth (cf. 1 Cor. 1:12,14; 9:5—possibly a trace of Peter's presence in Corinth with his wife, who makes no further direct appearance in the NT—(cf. Mk. 1:29–31) and dies a martyr's death before Peter according to Clement of Alexandria, *Strom.* 7, 63:3, and Eusebius, *HE* 3, 30:2). During the winter of AD 42, he reaches Rome. He was possibly not the first evangelist in the city (the Romans mentioned in Acts 2:10 may have spread the good news before him), but he was the first apostle to authenticate and establish the church officially. His arrival and the beginning of his work is the starting-point of his 'episcopate', which, like the one at Antioch, continues even during his absence, when he remains the titular head or the official 'overseer'.

The importance of Peter's foundation work in Rome is recognized even by Paul, who postponed his visit to Rome until he could include it as a stopover on his way to Spain, because he did not want to 'build on another man's foundation' (Rom. 15:20, 23–24). What Paul quite literally says is that the 'foundation stone' was laid by and belonged to someone else. It was not a faceless community, but an individual who had laid that stone. The Romans knew who he was: there was no need for Paul to mention his name in this context;[254] and Paul had every reason to acknowledge Peter's Roman pre-eminence: his own claim to priority centred in the mission to the Gentiles (cf. Gal. 1:16; 2:7–9), and his 'target community' in Rome was decidedly Jewish, even if it was predominantly Greek-speaking.

It was, in fact, the ideal 'hunting-ground' for a man with Peter's background, rather than Paul's. Through his revolutionary work in Caesarea, Peter had been prepared for contacts with Romans (Cornelius may even have reciprocated Peter's teaching by informing him about the situation in Rome and the Roman mentality), but his experience so far had been with Jews and pro-Jewish, 'God-fearing' Gentiles—precisely the kind of people he would meet and who might welcome him upon his arrival in Rome. With a Jewish population of some 50,000,[255] including God-fearers and Gentile proselytes, there was plenty of work to do. Even at the time of Paul's letter to the Romans, AD 57, when the communities had restructured themselves after the death of Claudius and the definite end of the expulsion, the Judaeo-Christian element was still stronger and more important than the strictly Gentile Christian one (cf. Rom. 1:16; 2:9–10; 7:1; 11:13–21). The mere fact, however, that there *was* a considerable group of Gentiles (cf. Rom. 1:13–15) points once again to Peter's policy of advocating Gentile mission also.

Peter was not alone in Rome. Mark either went with him straight from his mother's house or joined him not much later: as far as the chronology of Acts is concerned, Mark's presence in Jerusalem is not required again until Paul and Barnabas take him with them to Antioch (12:25) in AD 46, after the 'famine visit'. By contrast, we hear of him as Peter's interpreter (Papias, see note 1 above)—and if Peter, bilingual from his youth, ever needed an interpreter in order to spare the more sensitive Roman ears the onslaught of his uncouth everyday Greek which came complete with that daunting Galilean accent, it was at the beginning of his first stay, rather than towards the end of the second.[256] Eusebius (*HE* 6, 14:6, quoting Clement of Alexandria's lost *Hypotyposeis*) notes that Mark had followed Peter for a long time—an allusion to a lasting relationship between the two, of which 1 Pet. 5:13, where Peter calls Mark his son, is not the beginning, but the culmination. Whereas none of these sources states in so many words that Mark was with Peter in Rome from AD 42 onwards, the cumulative evidence suggests this solution more than any other.[257]

Mark's return to Jerusalem by AD 46 ties in with another datum: the writing of his gospel. We have seen from papyrological evidence (see pp. 18f. and note 3 above) that the gospel should be dated before AD 50—a result also advocated by independent non-papyrological arguments.[258] The most plausible date, taking this into consideration, would be between Peter's departure from Rome (soon after Herod Agrippa's death in AD 44, when a return to Palestine could be safely contemplated; Eusebius' chronicle sees him on his way back via Antioch in 44) and Mark's arrival in Jerusalem in AD 46 at the latest. This correspondence of papyrological and historical evidence has the added advantage of being corroborated by otherwise difficult comments in the Fathers.

Irenaeus, who knew Papias' note, is the first after Papias to comment on the Gospel. He begins with what appears to be the erroneous statement that both Peter and Paul founded the Roman community (unless one reads the verb he uses for 'founding', *themelioō*, as it is used in 1 Pet. 5:10, where it means 'to strengthen', 'to put on a solid basis'. In this sense, Irenaeus' statement is of course true both for Peter and for Paul).

Referring to a time when Matthew was writing his gospel 'among the Hebrews' 'in their own language', he states that Mark, Peter's disciple and interpreter, committed his preaching to paper after their (Peter and Paul's) deaths (*Haer.* 3, 1:1). Most commentators have understood this to be Irenaeus' meaning. However, the translation 'after their death' for *meta de tēn toutōn exodon* is very problematic and certainly not warranted by Papias' earlier statement. Papias merely says that Mark had written all things accurately as he remembered them (*hosa emnēmoneusen akribōs egrapsen*). But remembering someone's teaching most certainly does not presuppose that person's death—his departure would suffice, and that is precisely what Irenaeus seems to say. *Exodos* can of course mean death (as in the NT: Lk. 9:31; 2 Pet. 1:15). First of all, however, the Greek word bears the simple meaning 'departure', from the Greek tragedians to the Greek OT where it is applied to the departure of the Israelites from Egypt in the second book of the Pentateuch (cf. Ps. 104:38, 113:1, Heb. 11:22 *et al*). The meaning 'death' is an acquired one of high symbolical value (cf. p. 48 above), but its use in this sense must be obvious from the immediate context (a requirement clearly fulfilled by Lk. 9:31 but not quite so unambiguously by 2 Pet. 1:15). And since Irenaeus' source(s) do not demand or presuppose Peter's death, we should not read it into his text.[259] Peter has departed from Rome by the time Mark writes his gospel—that is all he says.

This is entirely compatible with the comments of Origen and Clement of Alexandria. Origen says that Mark wrote as Peter had instructed or taught him (*hōs Petros hyphēgēsato autō*—*Commentary on the Gospel of Matthew*, quoted in Eusebius, *HE* 6, 25:5). That is to say, he followed the example set by Peter's method and contents of preaching. Finally, Clement records that Mark, who had been Peter's companion for a long time, was urged by (Roman) Christians to write down what Peter had said, and did so. Peter's reaction was neutral: 'He neither hindered nor encouraged it' (*mēte kōlusai mēte protrepsasthai: Hypotyposeis*, in: Eusebius, *HE* 6, 14:7).

Elsewhere, paraphrasing Clement's report, Eusebius ends on a different note. Peter was pleased, he writes, and ratified the work for prayerful study in the churches (*HE* 2, 15:2). These two statements, are, of course, not mutually exclusive: they show a progress from careful beginnings at a time when Peter was still preaching to a time when the work had reached its final form. 2 Pet. 1:15 could reflect the latter stage, the ratification and recommendation of the gospel.[260]

All these accounts and sources serve to confirm the conclusion that Mark's gospel was written in Rome, not just during Peter's lifetime, but immediately after his first departure from the city, between AD 44 and AD 46.

VII

Peter made his way back to Jerusalem soon after Herod Agrippa's death. As he had done on his way to Rome, so now he interrupts his journey for stopovers, one of which, Antioch, seems indicated by Eusebius' *Chronicle* (see above). We do not know when exactly he reached Jerusalem—the Apostolic Council of AD 48 is the *terminus ante quem*, but there may be an indirect hint in Mark's strange behaviour on his first journey with Barnabas and Paul.

It is intrinsically probable that it was Mark himself who had informed Peter of the problem caused among the more conservative wing of the Judaean communities by Barnabas' and Paul's methods and the success of their uncompromising evangelism in Antioch and elsewhere. As soon as he heard that Peter was on his way back or had actually reached Jerusalem, he leaves his companions in Paphos (13:13) and returns to Peter in Jerusalem. Luke merely records Mark's return at this juncture, but in 15:37–38, after the Apostolic Council, he tells of the conflict between Barnabas and Paul about Mark—Barnabas wants him again as a travelling companion, Paul does not. Barnabas, Mark's cousin (Col. 4:10), who appreciates Peter's style and sides with him when it matters (cf. Gal. 2:13), would have had no problem understanding Mark's previous return to Jerusalem if it had happened for Peter's sake. Paul, who, by the time of Acts 15:38 saw himself more than ever as Peter's equal in missionary matters, could not have condoned Mark's leaving him for Peter and did not want to risk any further conflict for Mark's loyalty. It is only later that a reconciliation takes place, probably in Rome, when Mark, knowing the community and being accepted in his own right as the author of the gospel, takes his place at the side of Paul and Peter alike (Phmn. 24; Col. 4:10; 1 Pet. 5:13; cf. 2 Tim. 4:11).

The Apostolic Council had been convened in Jerusalem by the leaders of the church (15:2) in order to settle, once for all, the question of the Gentile believers—would they have to be circumcized, would they have to obey Mosaic law, or not? For Peter, Paul, Barnabas and some others, the question had been settled, but those who had remained behind in Judaea and Jerusalem could see matters differently; a full debate was certainly appropriate. Luke records the triumphal journey of Paul, Barnabas and their companions through Phoenicia and Samaria, giving an impression of general rejoicing about the success of the Gentile mission, with only a vociferous minority opposing the way Paul and Barnabas had handled it.

Paul himself, in a very personal account of his conversations at the Council (Gal. 2:1–10), underlines God's guidance even in his undertaking the journey: 'I went up because it had been revealed by God that I should do so' (Gal. 2:2, NEB).

Luke narrates the events at the Council in his usual sober, reflective manner. (Paul, as we shall see in a moment, is much more involved, even agitated, and for good personal reasons, of course.) The main item on the agenda is brought up succinctly by some of the believers who belonged to the party of the Pharisees (i.e. those who had formerly been Pharisees and who had preserved their strict adherence to Mosaic food-regulations more than any other group (cf. 21:20): 'The Gentiles must be circumcised and required to obey the law of Moses' (15:5).

We then see the apostles and elders meeting to discuss the question. As they are already together in one meeting (v. 4), this implies the formation of committees and/or sub-committees, probably to sift all the arguments once again. One such committee may well have been headed by Peter, representing the traditionally more pro-Gentile group, and another one by James as the leader of the traditionally more conservative, pro-Mosaic group, so that their respective speeches would be the two chairmen's reports. (Paul's remark that he met the men of repute separately (*Kat' idian de tois dokousin*, Gal. 2:2) could well refer to his representations before these committees, later summed up in front of the whole assembly—Acts 15:12.)

In 15:7, 'after much discussion', they are all together again, and Peter begins with a speech which reiterates his own experiences and the conclusions drawn from them. It is of the utmost importance that Peter underlines his choice by God as an apostle to the Gentiles (15:7)—he emphasizes this point for the sake of the argument, but of course does not want to suppress the fact that he was continuing to preach to the (Grecian) Jews also. We find the reverse emphasis in Paul, when he writes that he had been 'given the task of preaching the gospel to the Gentiles, just as Peter had been given the task of preaching the gospel to the Jews' (Gal. 2:7)—this juxtaposition is no falsification, but a simplification for the sake of argument in the context of his letter.

Peter's summary includes the known facts—God's Holy Spirit had sealed the acceptance of the Gentiles (15:8), he made no distinction between the Jews and the Gentiles—their hearts have been purified by faith through the working of the Spirit. It is *this* purification that counts (15:9)—indeed, insisting on anything else, such as the necessity to observe Mosaic regulations like food laws and circumcision, was tantamount to testing, provoking God and the Spirit, all the more so as the Jews themselves had never been able to fulfil all the obligations of the Law (15:10).[261] Finally, Peter insists that the law of Moses was not a prerequisite for salvation. 'We believe it is through the grace of our Lord Jesus that we are saved, just as they are' (15:11). Those who want to continue obeying the old laws may do so; but neither Jews nor Gentiles may use them as a substitute for or an indispensable ingredient of salvation.

Having spoken with the authority of his position and experience, Peter gives Barnabas and Paul the chance to corroborate his speech by telling the whole assembly what they had told him before, and this they do (15:12). It looks almost as though the two are speaking as Peter's witnesses, emphasizing the miraculous assistance of God's presence (cf. 14:3). But James has come to the same conclusion himself. He has not been involved in Gentile evangelism, though he has listened to their detailed account before, he has heard Peter's speech, has witnessed its impact and the effect on the assembly of the report delivered by Paul and Barnabas. He sees his task as that of stressing the way in which their position is confirmed by the Old Testament prophets—a decisive argument for those among the assembly who insisted on the Old Covenant. He begins by agreeing with Peter, whom he calls 'Simeon' (the more literal transcription of the Aramaic form, over against the Greek form 'Simon'—interestingly enough, only Peter himself uses this traditional form of his name elsewhere in the New Testament, in 2 Pet. 1:1). 'God at first showed his concern by taking from the Gentiles a people for himself', he states (15:14),[262] and goes on to quote from the minor prophets to back up his stance (Am. 9:11–12; Zc. 2:11 may have been in his mind, too).

James's use of Amos implies that he sees the church as replacing the temple (15:16), so that the Gentiles will join it as the community of the saved (15:17)—and that he regards this as having always been God's intention (15:18). Consequently, James adds, life should not be made difficult for the Gentiles (15:19).

What follows now seems to be the ideal compromise solution. James backs the Gentile mission: he advocates renouncing the demand for circumcision, but he placates the Mosaic group, whose acting chairman during the assembly he appears to have been, by recommending the dispatch of a letter to the Gentiles concerned, urging compliance with some daily observances. These are: (1) abstention from food used by pagans in their temple worship and then sold on the market (15:20a, cf. 1 Cor. 8:1–13). (2) abstention from all forms of sexual immorality (*porneia*, cf. 1 Cor. 6:12–20), and (3) abstention from the meat of strangled animals and from blood (cf. Rom. 14:13–15:2). Although these instructions were firmly grounded in Mosaic law and traditional Jewish custom,[263] their ethical value made them appear an acceptable working solution; neither Peter, nor Paul, nor anyone else saw reason to differ. Indeed, Paul must have seen a certain common sense behind these instructions—they were not alien to his own thinking, as we have seen above (cf. also Rom. 3:31), particularly in view of his policy of avoiding everything that could become a stumbling block to fellow believers (cf. 1 Cor. 8:9–13; Rom. 14:13–16).

As committee decisions go, the Apostolic Council was certainly a great step forward for everyone concerned. Paul felt encouraged (Gal. 2:9), he knew that the future was his. Only later did it transpire that some people interpreted the agreed procedure in a much narrower sense than others (Gal. 2:11–14)—an all-too-human weakness to this very day.

The letter, then, is drafted and dispatched; Barnabas and Paul even get an escort in Judas Barsabbas and Silas/Silvanus, who was to become an indispensable helper to both Paul and Peter. Luke records the full text of the letter, a fact that underlines its importance as the official findings of the Council. It sums up the situation and authenticates the messengers (15:24–27), emphasizes the Holy Spirit's role in the result of the council's deliberations (15:28), whereas those who had caused the disturbance had had neither apostolic nor spiritual backing (v. 24), and concludes with the instruction we know from 15:20, only in a slightly altered order—which is interesting in that it demonstrates an interval of careful 'composition' between James's speech and the assembly's ratification of the document.

'You will do well', i.e. you will prosper, by avoiding those things (*eu praxete*; cf. the synonymous *kalōs poieite* in Jas. 2:8 and 2 Pet. 1:19!). This is the final, friendly admonition in a letter that is quite conscious of *burdening* its readers—even if with a light load (*baros*, 15:28).

The whole letter is structured carefully,[264] complete with greeting and farewell in the customary epistolary forms. (Cf. Jas. 1:1 for the greetings at the beginning, and Acts 23:30 for the 'farewell' formula, *errōsthe*, or *errōso* in the singular, which is the traditional Greek complimentary close).

We may note one remarkable fact about the addressees of the letter. It mentions Gentile believers in Antioch (where Paul and

Barnabas were going to stay—15:35), Syria and Cilicia, but *Galatia* is not included. We should therefore not be surprised that Paul does not refer to this apostolic circular in his letter to the Galatians: most of them did not know it (cf. Acts 16:4–6), and he had no conceivable reason to tell them about it later.[265]

This last observation leads us directly to Paul's own report on the Apostolic Council in Gal. 2:1–10. In the discussion of Acts 15:1–29 above, it has been tacitly taken for granted that Gal. 2:1–10 refers to the same visit, and the parallels drawn have in fact substantiated this assumption. This is not to say that the considerable body of opinion to the contrary[266] should be summarily discarded; but there is equally no reason to construct incompatibilities where there are none.

Some sixty-two years ago, a leading classical historian, looking back at a history of attempts to claim that Galatians 2 and Acts 15 refer to two different events, and that Galatians should be dated before the Apostolic Council, wrote: 'This is certainly completely untenable and has, it seems, been abandoned by now.'[267] It has not, and the quotation serves as a reminder that circular motion is motion nonetheless.

The case for identifying Gal. 2:1–10 with the account in Acts 15:1–29 is in fact satisfactory even beyond the points already listed. The undeniable differences in detail are not only natural, given the different perspectives and readerships, they are also not any more remarkable than those between Acts 9:23–30 and Paul's own version of his first Jerusalem visit, Gal. 1:18–24, where there is a general consensus as to their identity.[268] Attempts to equate Gal. 2:1–10 with the so-called famine visit of Acts 11:30 are unconvincing, as there are only superficial similarities, but manifest incompatibilities. Even the ostensible insistence of Paul that Gal. 2:1f. is his *second* visit to Jerusalem must not be used to yield an argument in favour of the famine visit: he merely uses the Greek word *palin*, which means 'again', 'once more'—theoretically, he could be speaking of his umpteenth visit, on the strength of this word. Even the introduction to his sentence, *epeita*, 'then', does not, of course, demand uninterrupted succession.[269] It is no more puzzling that Paul, on this evidence, does not mention the famine visit at all in Galatians—there simply was no occasion and no need to mention it. Galatians is not concerned with a complete record of his journeys to Jerusalem.[270]

What, then, does Paul say in his account? He sheds additional light on the procedure of the meeting (see above, *ad loc*; uses Titus as an example (he was not compelled to be circumcised, even though he was a Greek, 2:3); mentions the 'false brothers' who had tried to force Paul and Barnabas off course (and who had been thoroughly discredited by the Apostolic Council: Gal. 2:4–5; Acts 15:1–2, 14); makes clear that he is a missionary authority in his own right who does not see himself as inferior to the apostles, even if they had once been companions of Jesus, and even if others rank them so much higher than himself (2:6); emphasizes that his role as missionary to the Gentiles did not depend on *their* approbation, but on God's direct appointment of him on an equal footing with that given to Peter (2:7–8); and highlights his passionate defence with the triumphant note that the supposedly superior pillars of the community, James, Peter and John (for the last time in the NT, John, the aide, is here placed next to Peter) recognized God's grace given to Paul (and Barnabas!) and acknowledged them as their equals (2:9 with Acts 15:7–11, 13–18, 25). So eager is he in his almost breathless account,[271] that he stylizes into exclusiveness what was in practice a 'both/and', as he knew, of course, only too well (cf. in particular his own attitude in his letter to the Romans). He ends on a conciliatory note: all the apostles had asked him to do, he says, was to remember the poor—a request for prayer as well as for material aid[272]—and, needless to say, he was eager to do precisely this, anyway. (He implies that he had done so before, an indirect allusion perhaps to the earlier famine visit, but also an undertaking he was to implement enthusiastically in the years to come (cf. 1 Cor. 16:1–4; 2 Cor. 8:1–9, 15; Rom. 15:25–28). Behind all the tense stylization of the situation at the Apostolic Council, we can discern a spirit of mutual trust and profound understanding—it could have been the basis for a peaceful future, he seems to imply. Yet the following year was to bring that bitter clash with Barnabas and Peter.

VIII

With the end of the Apostolic Council, Peter disappears from Acts. The stage is set for the conquest of the Gentiles, and Luke, as the much debated 'we' passages disclose, joins Paul on more than one occasion until they reach Rome together. Peter, on the other hand, who had only returned to Jerusalem in time to prepare and to influence the Council, would naturally leave the city again and attend to his own sphere of interest. With his intervention at the Council—the decisive words on which James, his successor in Jerusalem, had based his recommendation—he had once more proved his solidity as the rock of the church. But as such, he was now needed elsewhere.

Antioch, the city where Jews, Godfearers, proselytes and Gentiles formed the nucleus of the Christian community, was common ground for Peter and Paul. It is no surprise therefore to see them come together in Syria's old capital not long after the Council. Paul tells the story himself. He is still in his vigorous, polemical, self-protective mood, and we find ourselves wanting to hear Peter's version of the story so that a complete picture might emerge as it does from the two parallel accounts of the Jerusalem Council. Even so, the situation is sufficiently clear. What had begun with a handshake in Jerusalem (Gal. 2:9), has deteriorated into open conflict.

Paul, from Acts 11:26 onwards, had seen Antioch as the centre of his activities, as his own missionary stronghold. Peter may have been there, too, in the early days of the community; but after the decision of the Apostolic Council as Paul understood it, Antioch, the place which had established him as the missionary to the Gentiles, was his. When Peter appeared on the scene again, Paul may thus have been slightly disconcerted; he will at least have watched Peter's activities carefully and perhaps apprehensively. Peter, at any rate, acted on the basic assumption that a clear definition of priorities did not constitute the granting of exclusive rights. As much as Paul continued preaching and writing to Jews or Judaeo-Christians (cf. also Acts 18:6; 19:8; 28:17) Peter felt entitled, if not even obliged, to continue his previous work which took the Gentiles into consideration. Indeed, his first letter demonstrates this attitude perfectly: it is addressed to a *mixed* readership which includes communities visited or even established by Paul.[273] Paul had been put in charge of the Gentile mission (with Barnabas), but there was nothing to prevent their circles from overlapping.

At first, Peter's behaviour gave no cause for concern to Paul: 'before certain men came from James, he used to eat with the Gentiles' (2:12), i.e. he shared the food they ate, as he had done at Caesarea. Paul does not say whether or how far Peter had begun to implement the instructions of the 'Apostolic Decree', concerning the food regulations.[274] But in any case, this was not the point. On the contrary, the instructions devised in Jerusalem were meant for a situation where Jews and Gentiles mixed company for their meals (and for communion), whereas the situation in Antioch was that they still ate separately, perhaps even in separate house-churches, as 2:12 implies. Apparently Peter was at this stage more interested in Gentile mission than in Jewish mission: at table, he stays with the Gentiles, living the spirit of the Apostolic Council, fully and publicly accepting these Gentiles as equals before God: a significant demonstration for the Jewish members of the Antiochene community.

But then the 'circumcision group', committed Jewish Christians, arrived—'certain men from James';[275] and Peter begins 'to draw back and separate himself from the Gentiles because he was afraid' (2:12). Back in Jerusalem, they had heard of what they must have seen as Peter's neglect of his supposed duties. Was he not to look after the Jews first of all and to bring the Gentiles into the fold by implementing the Decree? For Peter, the situation he was in had not been ripe for this—he was plainly not among those who wanted to force things. But he could see that James and his delegates had a point, particularly with respect to caring for the 'law-abiding', conservative members of the Judaeo-Christian community. Consequently, he acts diplomatically and shows them that they have not been forgotten nor become second-rate: he, together with those 'liberal' Jewish Christians who had shared meals with the Gentiles, accommodates the conservatives and eats with them (again), for the time being. It is significant that Barnabas, an old hand in diplomacy (cf. Acts 9:27; 11:22–24), joins Peter without reserve (2:13).

Paul finds all this difficult to stomach. He even assumes that Peter and the others acted out of fear. But what kind of fear was this?[276] Even if we allow for Paul's exaggeration in his choice of words throughout Galatians, it is understandable that Peter felt a certain apprehension: the people from Jerusalem could, by misinterpreting the situation, spoil his carefully conceived approach; he (and the others) may well have feared that the influence of the visitors among the conservative Jewish-Christians of Antioch was strong enough to cause a rift instead of allowing the gradual growing together of the whole church. Visible conciliatory action was therefore essential.

Paul, however, does not understand—or does not want to

understand—Peter's display of flexible leadership. He can only see it as 'hypocrisy' (2:14), and he is of course, from his personal point of view, from his unflinching position as the Gentile missionary, not entirely wrong. One can see why he reacted as he did: to him, Peter's action left the Gentile Christians in the lurch. He even goes so far as to claim that Peter forced the Gentiles to follow Jewish customs (2:14). Paul, with all his partisanship, does *not* imply that Peter actually forced them physically—he thinks that Peter's example obliged them to follow him if they wanted to remain equals in the church. It is clearly Paul who is afraid—afraid of losing his influence on the Gentile Christians. After all, not even Paul can have wanted to make his readers believe that men like Peter and Barnabas simply got up from table, saying in effect: 'Well, that's it; join the Jewish Christians at once or we have seen the last of you', leaving the room forthwith. Peter and Barnabas will have explained the situation to them as to intelligent people, and some of the Gentile Christians may have followed them at once, adapting themselves to the peculiarities of the situation. Paul's problem was that they followed Peter's flexibility, not his own clear-cut, uncompromising stance. For him, they were not 'on the right road towards the truth of the gospel',[277] but making a detour or even retreating.

What emerges from this analysis, and indeed from the consequences Paul himself drew from the controversy, is Paul's defeat.[278] Soon afterwards, he quits his base in Antioch, and returns there only once more, for a stopover on his journey to the Galatian region (Acts 18:22). Peter's style of leadership had proved acceptable to the Christians of Antioch as well as to the other Christian leaders.[279] But Paul did learn his lesson—and this of course is in turn the mark of his own greatness. In 1 Cor. 9:20–22, written perhaps some seven years after the incident at Antioch, he can claim that he has become 'all things to all men so that by all possible means I might save some'.[280]

III

Peter's Last Years in his Letters and in Church History

'Simon Peter, a servant and apostle of Jesus Christ'

CHAPTER SEVEN

Return to Rome

I

All our earliest extant sources which comment on Peter's death agree that it happened in Rome. It is less certain when and how exactly he returned from Antioch. He may have stayed in Antioch for a while (see n. 279), as he, unlike Paul, had no reason to leave the city. But whenever he departed for Rome, it is unlikely that he would have gone there directly: he was never one to miss an opportunity for evangelizing. Corinth may have been on his route again, and the possibility cannot be ruled out that some of the events which led Paul to allude cryptically to Peter's influence on the Corinthians (see p. 155 above) happened on such a (second) visit.[281]

The earliest date for his arrival is late AD 57. When Paul sends his letter to the Romans earlier that year, Peter's name is conspicuous by its absence from the long list of recipients of Paul's greetings in 16:3–16.[282] This list does, however, shed some light on the composition of the Christian community in Rome. We find two old acquaintances, Priscilla and Aquila (cf. Acts 18:2, 18, 26; 1 Cor. 16:19; 2 Tim. 4:19) who may well have worked with

Peter, before they left Rome in AD 49 as victims of Claudius' expulsion. Several things about them invite comment. According to Romans 16:3–4, they had a community in their own house, a kind of 'house-church'—Paul actually uses the term *ekklēsia* in v. 4—which points to an organisational form not unlike the one in Antioch, or (cf. Acts 12:12, 17) in Jerusalem: several smaller groups formed the church as a whole; and Jewish Christians did not necessarily share either meeting-places or meals with Gentile Christians. The latter fact is underlined by what we can infer about the groups and individuals mentioned, if we regard them as being leaders of house-groups much in the same sense as Priscilla and Aquila.

Andronicus and Junias are Jewish Christians (Paul calls them 'my kinsmen' Rom. 16:7). So are Mary (16:6), Apelles (16:10), and Herodion (16:11). On the other hand, we find Romans or Gentiles—Amplias (16:8), Urbanus and Stachys (16:9), Tryphena, Tryphosa and Persis (16:12), Rufus (16:13), Asyncritus, Phlegon, Hermes, Patrobas, Hermas (16:14), Philologus and Julia, Nereus and Olympas (16:15). If at least the couples are leaders of household groups,[283] Jewish Christians and Gentile Christian house-groups are definitely distinct. (It is interesting that Paul, although he is formally welcomed by two Christian delegations at Forum Appii and Tres Tabernae three (?) years later (Acts 28:15), does not show any interest in the (Gentile) Christian community; he is plainly concerned with the Jews (Acts 28:17–28). It is probably a consequence of Luke's way of compressing his historical narrative that the Christians have disappeared completely from Paul's view after 28:16. This does not mean that he operated independently throughout his two years of house arrest, ignoring the existing church. Neither should we assume from the silence of 28:30–31 that Peter was necessarily absent from Rome at this time, or that he and Paul did not meet.)

Aquila and Priscilla (or Prisca, as Paul usually calls her), were wealthy owners of an international tent-making business with branches in Rome, Corinth and Ephesus, and former employers of Paul (Acts 18:2–4). If we may judge by their place at the head of Paul's list, they may well have been the most important Roman Christians in Peter's absence. Paul, as we know from Acts and 1 Corinthians, had met them in Corinth and was later with them in Ephesus, where they once again established a house-church. But Paul excludes them from the list of those he had baptized himself (1 Cor. 1:14–16). They will therefore have been baptized in Rome before their expulsion; we may assume that it was Peter who had baptized them and instructed them in leading groups on their travels and in his absence. Like Mark, they are thus among Peter's links with Paul.[284]

II

Two visible results of Peter's second stay in Rome remain to this day: his two letters. To take them for granted as written by Peter is perhaps (at least as far as the second one is concerned) even more risky than examining the Pudens legend with serious historical interest. While the first letter has not only an excellent early attestation on its side,[285] but also carefully reasoned support from recent textual analysis,[286] the second letter has had a much more chequered career in church history[287] and is almost totally rejected by modern research.[288]

Within our survey of Peter's career from Galilee to Rome, there is no place for a recapitulation of this well-trodden field. Throughout this book, we have treated both letters as Peter's in accordance with the (literary) historian's approach of taking a literary source *a priori* seriously on its own claim *until* the contrary can be or has been proved conclusively. The implicit result has been, that time and again during the analysis of the gospels and Acts, we have found that Peter's experiences and thinking are clearly reflected in both letters. Indeed, it could be said that the most natural conclusion from the references to 1 and 2 Peter adduced in the previous chapters is that they stem from the same person who accompanied Jesus, was appointed his trustee, saw the risen Christ and received the renewed commission.

But this, of course, is only one side of the coin. In the context of the second Roman stay, we cannot avoid asking if those references fit the historical situation, or, in other words, if what we currently know about the years between AD 57 and the aftermath of the fire of Rome in AD 64 tallies with the general outlook of the two letters. On the basis of such an analysis, it is obviously inappropriate to ask whether the self-description of both letters as Peter's can be *proved*. The method of the textual critic, if he does not accept what a text says about itself, must be to substantiate his doubts. For the critic who starts off, as he should, by taking the text seriously, the challenge is therefore not to prove that it *must* be so, but merely to make plausible what the text claims anyway.[289] To put it differently: what he must scrutinise is not the self-identification of the text but rather the validity of the arguments brought forward against it. This approach demands a distinct openness on all sides, and the recent, animated debate,[290] whether or not one wants to subscribe to the results engendered by it so far, is certainly a step in the right direction. As far as this book is concerned no more is required than a survey of the compatibility of the two letters with Peter's Roman situation.[291]

As we have seen above (p. 154), 1 Peter is written in Rome. We also know to whom it is addressed: 'to God's elect, strangers in the world, scattered throughout Pontus, Galatia, Cappadocia, Asia and Bythinia' (1:1, cf. p. 155 above). That it is addressed to *eklektois parepidēmois diasporas*, i.e. 'the chosen, temporary residents in the Diaspora, the dispersion', indicates at first sight, a Jewish-Christian readership. 'Diaspora' was a term applied traditionally to the situation of Jews living outside Palestine, and in this sense it is used in the New Testament by John (Jn. 7:35). But since Peter does not write to Jews—whatever their background, they now are Christians—the term has obviously acquired a wider meaning: Christians are now temporarily dispersed in the world, they are strangers on earth (cf. Jas. 1:1; Eph. 2:19; Heb. 11:13; 1 Pet. 1:17; 2:11). This does not justify our making the converse assumption that Peter's readers are (exclusively) Gentile Christians. Indeed, we do not know of a single New Testament community that consisted of Gentile Christians only. Even the communities founded by Paul (and some of those reached by 1 Peter were perhaps among them) were often built on a foundation of Jews from the synagogues—cf. Acts 19:8, etc. The most natural assumption therefore is a mixed readership, like the one Peter would have known from Antioch, and of course, from Rome itself. Although it is not easy to detect direct allusions to either the Gentile or the Jewish Christians among the recipients of the letter, passages like 1:17–19; 1:24; 2:6–10 (with Acts 4:8–12); 3:6; 3:19–21, seem to appeal directly to readers with a Jewish background. (One might add 5:8, which is unexplained, but would have been clear to Jewish-Christian readers familiar, of old, with Ps. 22:14 and Ez. 22:25, as a reapplication of perennially valid prophecies). By comparison, 4:3 could, *not exclusively*, but mainly, appeal to Gentile Christian readers. With or without such tentative identifications, the point remains that it is written to all Christians in the areas concerned—and that conclusion, of course, is unaffected by how one might wish to define these areas in political or geographical terms.

The letter offers two further pieces of vital information: it was written with the assistance of Silvanus (5:12), and in the presence of Mark (5:13). Silvanus was a man of some importance; the Apostolic Council sends him out as one of two companions for Barnabas and Paul (Acts 15:22), he accompanies Paul later on Acts 15:40; 18:5) and even acquires the rank of a preacher in his own right (2 Cor. 1:19.[292]) Furthermore, he helps Paul to write two of his letters (1 and 2 Thessalonians, cf. the introductory greetings). Peter may have known him from early days in Jerusalem (Acts 15:22 does not specify when he became a Christian, whether before or after Peter's first departure in AD 42). At the present stage, he was a useful man to have around in Rome, as he—like Paul—was a Roman citizen by right (Acts 16:37). Peter praises both Silvanus and Mark, Silvanus as the 'faithful brother' (and Peter adds *hōs logizomai*, 'in my judgment', an added evaluation which carries the full weight of his authority; 'faithful brother' is not just a polite address, but a distinction). Mark, likewise returned to him from Paul, is even called 'my son' by Peter, a term of endearment which underlines the trust he puts in his 'interpreter', the author of the gospel. Peter can draw on the help of two experienced helpers, Silvanus, the preacher and co-author of two Pauline letters, and Mark, the 'interpreter' and author of the gospel: if anything, this demonstrates the increased importance of Peter's work in Rome. He now calls upon two experts who supplement his own gifts perfectly—not simply secretaries or assistants, like for example, the Tertius of Romans 16:22.

Silvanus proves his worth by the role he plays in drafting and finalizing Peter's first letter. Peter uses an equivocal word; he says that he wrote the letter 'by' (*dia*) Silvanus. There are several early Christian examples of its use to mean 'send by', or 'dispatch by' (cf. Acts 15:23(?), or, in Ignatius' letters, *Rom.* 10:1; *Phil.* 11:2, etc.). We might therefore be led to assume that Silvanus was sent off with the letter, and that his eulogy in 5:12 was meant to introduce and recommend him to the recipients; but Peter's letter leaves the matter open, for it includes no verb denoting the sending or receiving of a messenger (as in Acts 15:22: *pempsai*, or in Ignatius,

Phil. 11:2, *pemphthentos;* or in another of his letters, *Smy.* 12:1, *hon apesteilate met emou*).

One is therefore justified in understanding *dia*, 'by', as signifying the *drafter* of the letter; and it is of course quite possible that even the passage at Acts 15:22 designates him as one of the two who drafted that letter[293] and then took it to the Gentile communities where they distributed it (which means they would have copied it before) and/or read it out publicly (15:27, 30, 16:4).[294] And if the evidence from Acts already allows both possibilities, or even demands them, the passages from Ignatius' letters, as later documents, have to be seen as inconclusive arguments against Silvanus' hand in the drafting of 1 Peter—all the more so since he is already established as a man experienced in this field (1 Thes. 1:1; 2 Thes. 1:1)—they are one later possible use of the term.[295]

In addition, we may question whether Peter, fluent in spoken Greek as he obviously was, would have written such remarkably polished Greek as that of 1 Peter. Why indeed, one might ask, did he have two such experienced writers at his side, if he did not intend to use them? We should not forget that it took up to one hour to write a 'page' (or the equivalent of a page) of a papyrus codex and scroll at the time, as the writing material (reed pen and rough papyrus surface) did not allow speed. Peter had other things to occupy him than spending hour after hour over the written composition of his letter; a trusted amanuensis (like a 'faithful brother', 1 Pet. 5:12) would do it for him, using oral and/or written notes and/or instructions which would, as far as the contents and key terms were concerned, be quite specific if not absolutely binding (cf. the numerous similarities between 1 Peter and Peter's speeches in Acts in this respect), but which would leave the stylistic and general formal elaboration to the actual writer, who therefore had considerable responsibility, such as no simple secretary would be entrusted with.[296]

Even if the actual extent of Silvanus' contribution must remain undecided, we may assume that he was in fact both the trusted amanuensis and the messenger, as he probably had already been in Acts 15:22–16:4. The undeniable fact that there are some considerable formal and stylistic differences between 1 and 2 Peter is thus alleviated: Silvanus had left Rome and was somewhere in Asia Minor when Peter felt compelled to write his second letter.

At what stage during his second Roman stay did Peter write the first letter? The indications that can be derived from its contents are, like almost everything else concerning the two letters, hotly disputed, but a certain degree of probability can be attained nonetheless.

Obviously, the manifold allusions to sufferings and persecution are decisive. Could these allusions be identified as those under Nero, in the aftermath of the fire of Rome, one would immediately have a probable date: c. AD 65. This, or any other—later or earlier —state persecution is however ruled out straightaway by the surprisingly positive reference to the authorities in 2:13–14 where the state is clearly expected not only 'to punish those who do wrong', but also 'to commend those who do right', and by the corroborative verse 3:13, 'Who is going to harm you if you are eager to do good?'' The letter does not reflect any recent or immediate mortal danger either for Peter or for his readers. Even the death of James, the brother of Jesus, in c. AD 62 must from this point of view lie in the future,[297] especially if one keeps in mind that James was commonly called 'the Just'.[298] To write verses like 2:13–14 and 3:13 after the death of 'the Just' would have been quite impossible. It is therefore safe to assume that 1 Peter was written after AD 57 and before AD 62. The 'Babylon'-cryptogram is equally independent of actual persecutions, as we have seen (see p. 154 above), and the other references to persecutions are of the kind readers 'in the dispersion', in an anti-Christian environment, would understand as a general warning about hostilities and an encouragement to persevere in spite of them (cf. in particular 1 Pet. 1:6 and 4:13–19 with Mt. 5:11–12).

Not only are predictions of sufferings for the disciples a continuous feature of Jesus' teaching, as every reader of the gospels knows, persecution had already begun in the very first days of the budding church. In the immediate context of 1 Peter, Silvanus himself knew precisely what it meant to suffer physically for the faith (see 1 Thes. 2:2 with Acts 16:19–22). As for Peter, he knew long before Nero's accession what persecution and fear of death felt like—his very first journey to Rome had in fact been the result of such an experience. Nor was it only the apostles and their trusted companions who had endured such experiences; as 1 Thes. 2:14; 3:3; 2 Thes. 1:4–8 show,[299] the Christian communities knew only too well the insecurity of being harassed outsiders, 'aliens and strangers in the world' (1 Pet. 2:11). It was not something that had happened only in Jerusalem, to reappear under Nero and some of his successors.

Peter has a dual message for his readers. Be prepared, but do not despair—the Lord is with you and against the evil ones (1 Pet. 3:12; 4:19). Take courage and live your life under God. Do not sit back complacently, but go out and act positively. You will receive and enjoy the grace of God (2:20b; 3:17) and you will follow, as true Christians (4:16, the only occurrence of the term outside Acts) in the steps of Christ (2:21). Acting positively and being forward-looking, they will set a positive example which may influence others (2:15–17; 3:8–13, 15–16). This should be their attitude both within the community and outside it. A Christian lifestyle is to be an example, not only for brothers but also for pagan onlookers.[300]

Peter is writing from a 'Babylonian' Rome that had seen the depravity of public life under Caligula and Claudius; he is the overseer of a community which had experienced expulsion some ten years before; he is a witness of the worsening excesses of Nero's self-deification. Yet this is not a man given over to despair and gloom. His letter carries the weight of rock-like authority, unshakeable in its certainty that the faith will triumph in the face of all kinds of adversity. Given a choice within the period between AD 57 and AD 62, any year would probably be as good as another. One possibility, no more than a conjecture, would be late AD 59. When, in 4:15, Peter enumerates the sinful deeds which the Christians must avoid ('If you suffer, it should not be as a murderer or thief or malefactor, or as someone interfering with other people's business'—*allotriepiskopos*), that surprising word 'murderer' introduces a list that resembles the crimes alleged against Nero with the outrageous murder of his mother Agrippina, which provoked some public and political disquiet[301] in AD 59.[302] The 'malefactors' or 'sorcerers' (NEB 'sorcery', Greek *kakopoios*) also gain in clarity if put in the context of Agrippina's murder in AD 59: *kakopoios* is rendered as 'maleficus' by Tertullian, *Scorpiace* 12:3, and Cyprianus, *Testament* 3:37.[303] This term has been understood by several Fathers as meaning 'magician', or 'sorcerer' (Lactantius, *Institutions* 2, 16:4; Jerome, *on Daniel* 2:2; *Cod. Theodosius* 9, 16:4, hence the NEB 'sorcery').

If this is the sense (and 2 Tim. 3:13, *goēs*, magician/charlatan, *could* justify such an assumption), Nero comes back into the picture. According to Suetonius (*Life of the Caesars* 6, 34:4) he had called (Babylonian) *magi* to his side in order to make sacrificial offerings so that the dead spirit of his mother would no longer torment him. Rumours of such happenings spread over Rome; and Peter could easily have heard them from someone like Stachys (Rom. 16:9), Patrobas (Rom. 16:14) or Philologus (Rom. 16:15—cf. p. 172 above) who may be connected with Nero's household.

Finally, the strange compound *allotriepiskopos* (NIV 'meddler', NEB someone 'infringing the rights of others', RSV 'mischiefmaker', AV 'busybody in other men's matters') occurs only here in Greek literature.[304] It looks like a word coined by Peter and/or Silvanus for Nero: more than anyone else, Nero used his influence and position to infringe the rights of others, to meddle with and influence other people's lives and affairs, to 'make mischief' in public as well as in private. The existence of Nero's self-deifying statue (see n. 250) was, perhaps, the most obvious, visible reason for calling him *allotriepiskopos,* using the term in a religious sense: Nero had assumed a role that was not his, he had meddled with God's affairs. The catalogue of sins in 1 Pet. 4:15 could thus easily have been stimulated by the image of Nero's career, culminating in the murder of his mother Agrippina in AD 59—a deterrent mirror to be held before the readers of his first letter.

Peter's second letter offers fewer pointers than the first. Even those it appears to offer may be deceptive. In 3:1, Peter says, 'This is now my second letter to you. I have written both of them as reminders to stimulate you to wholesome thinking.' The apparently presupposed identity of both readerships has been questioned extensively, if for different reasons and with different results.[305] But it has also had its defenders, again for reasons often diametrically opposed.[306] The arguments against identifying the two groups have been based mainly on the assumption that one can define the readership of 1 Peter as (exclusively) Gentile Christians in a situation of actual persecution—which, as we have already seen above, is not the case. By contrast, the readers of 2 Peter have been regarded as (exclusively) Jewish Christians facing specific heretical dangers. This view seems to be ruled out straightaway by the fact that they knew at least one, and perhaps several letters of Paul (3:16)—a letter-writer who will scarcely have written to Jews exclusively.

In fact, the roots of those heretical dangers had already been identified by Paul: cf. 1 Cor. 6:12–20 with 2 Pet. 2:1–3, 9–22; 3:17 on libertinism; 1 Cor. 15:23–32 with 2 Pet. 1:16–21 etc. for the denial of future eschatology; 1 Cor. 6:12, 8:9 with 2 Pet. 2:19 (cf. 1 Pet. 2:16!) on the misuse of freedom; 1 Cor. 11:21 with 2 Pet. 2:13 on the misuse of the common (communion) meals; 1 Cor. 11:18–19 with 2 Pet. 2:2 on the danger of splits within the community.

There is absolutely no need to construct a late, gnostic context on the basis of the admonitions in 2 Peter. On the contrary, Paul's letter to a mixed, if not predominantly Gentile Christian community shows unmistakably that such problems arose at a very early stage. Even the contempt for the angelic powers could be a trait shared by the early heretics of 1 Corinthians and those of 2 Peter: cf. 1 Cor. 11:10 with 2 Pet. 2:11.[307] This point is particularly noteworthy, as the concept of angels as guardians over the purity of worship existed also at Qumran;[308] if we find this idea both in 1 Corinthians and 2 Peter also, we are not justified in assuming an exclusively Jewish-Christian readership for 2 Peter, but a mixed readership which was endangered by a very early type of heretical teaching under Essene influence which spread soon and widely.[309] The role of the angels, the possible allusions to Enoch, found also at Qumran,[310] and the role of the false prophets (2 Pet. 2:1, 15)[311] may also point to Essene influence on the heretics confronting Peter (and Paul). Indeed there are several indications, direct and indirect, that this may have been the case.[312] If the admittedly precarious and tentative identification of a fragment found in Qumran Cave 7 as 2 Pet. 1:15 could be substantiated,[313] one might even be inclined to think that a copy of the letter was used by ex-Essene Christians, who had settled near Qumran, in their debates with the community during the mid-sixties. However far one wants to take these points, the result is unambiguous: the heresies alluded to in 2 Peter are as early as any faced by the Christian communities after AD 30, and they could have sprung up sooner rather than later all over the mixed Judaeo-Gentile regions reached by the apostolic message. Nor is there any reason to think that 2 Peter could not have been sent to readers who knew 1 Peter; communities affected by the problems discussed in 2 Peter certainly existed in areas of the very same Asia Minor to which the first letter had been despatched.[314]

One aspect of 2 Peter is particularly striking. While he acknowledges that these heretical teachings offer a real threat (2 Pet. 2:10–22 etc.), Peter, unlike Paul, speaks of them as reaching *his* readers in the (immediate/foreseeable) *future* (2 Pet.

2:1–3; 3:3, 17). In 2 Pet. 2:1, the much-debated parallels with Jude's letter begin. But whereas Peter warns, Jude clearly presupposes something that has already happened (Jude 4, 17–19).[315] Jude is impelled to add his own apostolic authority to Peter's emphatic warning; the danger has become so overwhelmingly real (cf. v. 3) that he must take the matter up himself. In spite of the similarities, he adds his own very personal colouring both in the language and in the form of his letter, which he concludes with a beautiful and original section in praise of the Lord, a glowing document of faith and hope and jubilation (Jude 24–25). In no sense therefore is Jude a minor dependant of the great Peter: he, too, knows exactly what he is doing and why.

Jude, whose apostolic authenticity can be regarded as safely established,[316] must have written before the death of his brother, James the Just (Jude 1;[317] cf. p. 177 above on the date of 1 Peter) i.e. in AD 62 at the latest. We thus gain a possible date for 2 Peter. It must have been written long enough before Jude to allow the situation of the later letter to develop, and it must have been written after 1 Peter. A date between late AD 59 and AD 60 seems therefore the most plausible option, with AD 60 probably the safest choice.

This matches the situation in Rome, as we can tentatively reconstruct it. Silvanus has left with the first letter, when, some time later, news arrives from Asia Minor of the arrival of heretical teachers, perhaps from Corinth. As yet, they have hardly begun their work, but one knows what to expect. Peter remembers 1 Corinthians, a letter he knows (cf. 2 Pet. 3:16) and decides to act at once. Silvanus is not at hand, so he uses the messengers (or one of them) and dictates, more or less definitively, the second letter. The scribe is a man from Asia, of course—his style shines through in certain passages.[318] But Peter's own hand is even more obvious now than it had been in the first letter—the messenger from Asia is not of Silvanus' calibre. Consequently we have not only the lovingly conceived reminiscence of the events on the Mountain of Transfiguration (see pp. 51f. above), but an appealing personal touch like the self-description as 'Simeon Peter' in the address, which combines his old Jewish birth-name in its original form with his Greek title-name, Peter. And two further ingredients make this serious, hastily and urgently devised letter a very personal document.

First, there is 2 Pet. 1:12–15: 'I think it is right to refresh your

memory as long as I live in the tent of this body, because I know
that I will soon put it aside, as our Lord Jesus Christ has made
clear to me.' Peter, by now probably in his mid-sixties, realizes
that he, too, is getting older, and he remembers the prophecy
Jesus had given to him thirty years ago on the shores of Lake
Tiberias (Jn. 21:18–19, see p. 96 above). His death could come
soon, or rather, to translate the Greek *tachinē* appropriately,
'suddenly'. It is a touching personal note; there is no hint of an
imminent, violent death by a persecution already in progress, but
Peter feels, naturally and humanly, that the prophecy would be
fulfilled sooner rather than later. At any rate, he knows that this is
only a short letter and that his readers need more to keep them
going, a permanent reminder of Christ's teaching and the life
they are expected to lead as they follow him. So he is taking steps
to ensure that they will 'at all times' remember these things after
his death[319] when he can no longer communicate with them
personally (1:15). He is going to have Mark's gospel copied and
sent to them as soon as possible.[320]

The second personal touch comes in 3:15–16: 'Bear in mind that
our Lord's patience means salvation, just as our dear brother Paul
also wrote you with the wisdom that God gave him. He writes the
same way in all his letters, speaking in them of these matters. His
letters contain some things that are hard to understand, which
ignorant and unstable people distort, as they do the other
scriptures, to their own destruction.' This is both a touching proof
of the esteem in which Peter holds Paul as a brother in Christ, in
spite of the occasional tactical differences they had, and also a
diplomatic, backhanded compliment. Paul's letters (those at least
which Peter knew—there is no talk here of a completed collection
of Paul's letters) contain some things that are hard to understand
—and who would disagree? After all, to this day a whole
exegetical industry is thriving on these difficult passages. Even
so, Peter grants them special status; as Paul himself had already
expected his letters to be read, just like OT Scripture, in the
churches (cf. Col. 4:16; 1 Thes. 5:27), so Peter can describe them
by the word normally reserved for OT Scripture—*graphas*. The
writings (to translate *graphai* literally) are first of all the OT
prophecies (2 Pet. 1:19–21), and the apostles have become their
heirs (3:1), an idea already expressed in Peter's first letter (cf. 1 Pet.
1:11–12, 4:11).[321] Peter, who reserves for himself some criticism of
Paul's occasional obscurity, is, in his assessment of the high value

of Paul's letters (and by implication those of other apostolic writers, like himself), still theological worlds away from a mid-second century writer like Polycarp. Polycarp, who wrote a letter to the Philippians,[322] has a much less balanced opinion: he speaks of the 'blessed and glorious Paul' (3:2) and is the first Christian author to actually identify one of his letters, Ephesians 4:26, literally as *Holy* Scripture next to an Old Testament writing, Psalm 4:5 (12:1).

As Peter had been speaking of imminent or future dangers, so his warning that 'ignorant and unstable people' will distort Paul's letters is not a statement about something already taking place, but a weary warning: unlike our modern translations, we should read the future tense in the verb translated by 'distort', *strebloō*.[323] This further underlines the fact that Peter is not analyzing heretical misuse of a collection of Paul's letters from a post-apostolic (i.e. post-Petrine), vantage-point, but that the real Peter of AD 60 is fully aware of what will or could happen once he and Paul are no longer around to look after things for themselves.

Peter's second letter is a document of undeniable apostolic authority. The apostles, he says, are the reliable interpreters of prophecy of the Old Testament, they are the safeguard against the false teachers. They, the eyewitnesses (2 Pet. 1:16), refute, by their mere authority, the cleverly devised myths put up by others. The readers are encouraged to lead a life worthy of the Lord's calling 'by his own glory and goodness' (1:3), a life described in a list of rare beauty and appeal (1:5–8). Peter even finds a word of particular importance to the Gentile Christians among his readers, 'virtue' (*aretē*)—a term not unknown in hellenistic philosophy, and used effectively also by Paul (Phil. 4:8; cf. 1 Pet. 2:9, 2 Pet. 1:3). And he concludes his letter by re-emphasizing the reality of the heavenly powers and the final triumph of the second coming, the Parousia of Christ.

We do not know what happened to the letter when it reached its readers. Jude, at any rate, when he received it, felt almost instantaneously impelled to change plans and reiterate forcefully what Peter had written (Jude 3–4), as events had taken an even more serious turn in the meantime. It somehow happened therefore that Jude almost took over in the public eye,[324] with the older letter patiently waiting for the day when Origen would call 1 *and* 2 Peter the 'apostle's trumpets'.[325]

With all the differences of style, grammar and vocabulary due to different scribes,[326] and the occasional variations in applied theology due to the entirely different situations that had to be tackled,[327] the remarkable fact is, as we have seen throughout the chapters on the gospels and Acts, that Peter's character and mind, his authoritative personality, can be clearly detected behind both letters.

CHAPTER EIGHT

Death and Burial

I

When, why and how did Peter die? Our earliest source gives us a clue. It is the first letter of Clement of Rome, a man of the early second generation of converts, about whom we know a good deal. He began as a member of the church 'administration' (see *Shepherd of Hermas*, Vision 2, 4:2–3) and held this office until the mid-eighties.[328] During the later eighties or early nineties, he became Bishop of Rome, as one who had been a close disciple of Peter and Paul (Irenaeus, *Haer.* 3, 3:3; Eusebius, *HE* 5, 6:1–5; cf. Tertullian, *De praesc.* 32). It has even been asserted that he is identical with the Clement of Philippians 4:3 (Origen, *Commentary on John* 6:54; Eusebius, *HE* 3, 4:9). At some stage, he wrote his letter, on behalf of the Roman church, to the Corinthians (Dionysius of Corinth, in Eusebius, *HE* 4, 23:11; Hegesippus, in Eusebius, *HE* 4, 22:1–2, *et al.*) The date of the letter has been widely fixed as c. AD 96, but conclusive arguments have been raised against such a late date, particularly as a fully established church administration does not yet exist (1 Clement 42:4; 44:1–4; 54:2; 57:1) and as the 'calamities' (1:1) of the letter do not fit the persecution under Domitian, but rather the chaotic situation in

Rome in AD 69, as independently described by Philostratus, *Life of Apollonius of Tyana* 5:13.[329] For this and other reasons, and in view of the difficulties associated with all arguments for a later date, AD 70 has been suggested with some force.[330] But whatever the precise date, Clement writes as one for whom the Neronian persecution is still a vivid memory (5:1–6:2). And what he writes about Peter's (and Paul's) death is illuminating.

> 'Because of jealousy and envy, the greatest and justest pillars were persecuted and contended unto death. Let us set before our eyes the good [upright] apostles: Peter, who because of unjustified jealousy suffered not one or two, but many afflictions, and, having given witness (*kai houtō marturēsas*— martyrdom literally as a form of witnessing), he went to the place of glory which was his due. Because of jealousy and strife Paul displayed the prize of patient endurance (*hupomonē*) . . .'

Clement uses the term 'jealousy' several times in his letter (6:1, on the sufferings and martyrdom of Christian men and especially women, and 9:1); one could almost see the passages from ch. 3 to 6 as a section entitled 'Concerning the Results of Jealousy'.[331] But as we have seen in the analysis of Acts 5:17 (cf. p. 127 above), 'jealousy', *zēlos*, in such contexts, means also '(religious) zeal', and this is what lies behind Clement's passage as well. The Roman Church had grown considerably since the late fifties. It was a seed bed for a traditional Jewish Christianity and an independent-minded, indigenous Gentile Christianity. Both were entirely capable of Christian brotherhood, but as Paul's letter to the Romans already demonstrated (cf. p. 172 above), in Rome as in Antioch, the Christians had not yet developed a united, mixed church. Radical wings on both sides would have nurtured the traditional distinctions; and a man like Peter, whose long-term aim it had always been to bring Gentiles and Jews together in *one* Church, would have had his problems as much as Paul, the victim of Jewish law-abiding zeal (Acts 21:20–30; Rom. 2:17–29; 13:1–7, 13) with strong political undertones (Phil. 3:2, 5, 19–20).

It is not improbable that Peter returned to Rome in late AD 57 or 58 precisely because he had heard news of the expansion of the 'zealotist', law-abiding, Jewish Christians. The same people who had caused the problems in Antioch may now have appeared in Rome, an obvious eventual choice, when they wanted to advance from the third-largest city of the Empire to its capital. The reality of the conflict is highlighted by Paul's letter to the Philippians, 1:15–17; there were indeed Christians who 'stirred up trouble' for him during his imprisonment. While Paul was somewhat defenceless in such a situation, Peter could still try to act as a conciliator, but even he cannot have been too sure if he would live long enough to see his task completed (cf. 2 Pet. 1:13–14). With Mark's gospel written, copied, and sent to different destinations, he knew that his preaching and teaching of Christ, and with it the future of the church, were secured within the limits of what human endeavour could achieve; and since he also knew that the conflict between Jewish and Gentile Christians was totally opposed to God's will, he was able to persevere patiently in his daily community work without either undue optimism or despair.

His work will have been hindered by the contempt in which the Christians were held both by Roman public opinion and by the orthodox Jews. Paul's attempts to convert the Jewish establishment in Rome (Acts 28:17–28) had been only moderately successful (28:24); the hardened leaders of the Jewish community would have been antagonised rather than appeased, and the Christians, with all their internal problems, were thus surrounded by latent Gentile and Jewish enmity which could break out at the next opportunity. The Jews, in particular, would resist being expelled (as in AD 49) or even persecuted on account of a situation that ought to be attributed to the Christians. They, more than the rather nonchalant Roman authorities of the early sixties, would watch the Christians and their activities very carefully. Caution was in any case appropriate, since the Jewish zealots themselves had caused considerable tension under Claudius and Nero, and one could never be too sure what kind of disturbances would recur if both these zealots and the Christian 'social reformers'[332] were perceived as operating against the state. Who better than Paul to understand this way of thinking? His letter to the Romans, after all, deals with this aspect of Christian public life (Rom. 12:14–21; 13:1–14; 16:17–20) as vigorously and emphatically as the later letter to the Philippians (1:15–17; 3:2–20). Peter, too, was fully aware of the problematic nature of premature social action that would be regarded as *anti*-social by the authorities (1 Pet. 2:11–17, 3:13–17; 2 Pet. 3:14). He knew also that public opinion had always been quick to attack the Christians (1 Pet. 2:11–12; 3:16).

The precarious 'cold war' with minor skirmishes (1 Clement 1:4, Phil. 1:17) lasted for several years, until fire broke out at the

Circus Maximus, probably accidentally, in the small hours of the 19th July 64, destroyed ten out of fourteen districts of the city of Rome, and indirectly initiated the horrors of the Neronian persecution. Nero first showed himself as an able administrator. Hastily returning from Antium, he opened his own gardens at the Vatican hill and the Campus Martius for the tens, if not hundreds of thousands, who had been made homeless by the fire; he immediately began to rebuild the city, devised a forward-looking housing programme and provided grain and other food at greatly reduced prices. (Cf. Tacitus, *Annals,* 15:38–41, and (polemically) Suetonius, *Life of the Caesars* 6, 38:1–3.)

We have to imagine the situation in a place like Nero's Vatican gardens. At first the homeless were herded together regardless of rank or religion. Desperate citizens who had lost their prized possessions were camping next to Christians, who looked unmoved or perhaps with visible pleasure at the way in which divine punishment had fallen on the depraved city. The fire, predicted since time immemorial as an indicator of the Last Days, had finally come. Peter (and Paul) may well have tried to quell such rumours but the damage was swiftly done. Ordinary Romans would have seen the Christians as enemies of the state, of the city, perhaps even having themselves started the fire they longed to see. It may even have been the 'zealous' Jewish-Christians, who were (unlike their Gentile brothers) immersed in apocalyptic thinking, who began to provoke the others (Christian and non-Christian alike) with their talk about God's judgment. Any who may have known Peter's second letter would have pointed out to him that he himself had predicted it all (3:7,10–12). Peter, retorting that this was most certainly not the event he had had in mind, would have become the declared enemy of such 'zealots'—precisely as Clement implies in his letter (1 Clement 5:4).

These developments took some time. Tacitus, who reports how neither Nero's programme of rebuilding Rome nor the public amusements, nor prayers to the gods could quench the rumours that the fire had started on orders from above (*Annals* 15:44), implies a considerable interval between the fire and the eventual decision to make use of the Christians as scapegoats. Indeed, it is remarkable that none of the earliest Christian sources mentions the fire at all in direct connection with the persecution.[333] So important were the actual sufferings, the glories of martyrdom themselves, that they became detached from the secular event of the fire that had preceded them and that had indirectly helped to bring them about. Even the circumspect rhetorician and thinker Lactantius, writing as the tutor of Crispus, the son of the Emperor Constantine, in c. AD 317, passes over the fire in his emphatic account of Nero's persecution—at a time when Tacitus' history was public knowledge and readily available to him in the imperial archives (*On the kinds of death of the Persecutors* 2:5–6). And two other devotees of archive material, Eusebius and Jerome, also chose to omit references to the fire. Whatever apocalyptic ideas the Roman Christians of AD 64 may have had, from Clement onwards Christian historians made sure that their readers would not be confounded.

Yet Tacitus himself indirectly corroborates Clement's account. Not only does he record the public contempt for the Christians, whose faith he calls a superstition (*superstitio*) and a disease (*malum*), he also mentions that many Christians were convicted because of denunciation (*indicium*) by those who had been arrested first. This seems to substantiate, from a different point of view, Clement's allusion to 'jealousy/zeal' as the reason behind the mass persecution he describes in 6:1–2. Indeed, Clement's description in itself, with its allusion to the debasing costume games that were played with the Christians in the Circus or in Nero's gardens on the Vatican, reminds one of Tacitus' account. And there is yet another pointer which should not be overlooked: Tacitus states that the Christians were convicted 'not so much because of the crime of arson, but rather because of their hatred for humankind' (*odio humani generis*). Tacitus, a (perhaps) slightly younger contemporary of Clement's, provides here a good reason why the church fathers omitted mentioning the fire altogether in their accounts.

Peter would have realized that yet another prediction of Jesus was being fulfilled. When he had provided Mark with the material for his gospel, he had included his account of Jesus' discourse on the Mount of Olives (Mk. 13:3–37). Now, with denunciations, tortures and executions going on around him, 13:12–13 would have sprung to mind again: 'Brother will betray brother to death, and a father his child. Children will rebel against their parents and have them put to death. All men will hate you because of me, but he who stands firm to the end will be saved.'

Whatever Peter did while he still had freedom to act, one thing follows with certainty from this passage, and from its last verse in particular. He would not have behaved as the beautifully narrated legend in the *Acts of Peter* 35(5) has it. The story tells how he fled Rome in disguise, only to be met by Jesus, whom he asks, 'Where are you going?' (*Quo vadis?*) Whereupon the Lord tells him that he has to go to Rome to be crucified again—and Peter, realizing what has happened, turns back to be crucified himself. Whoever invented this (mildly edifying) story had forgotten that Peter after the Ascension was no longer the sometimes weak and vacillating Peter of yore, and that the mature Rock, so vividly reminded of Jesus' prediction in Mk. 13:14, would never have left his flock behind.

Clement, our earliest source, does not specify *when* Peter and Paul died. On the contrary his chronology is remarkably vague—and this is entirely in keeping with the content of the whole passage, which is not about the analysis of an historical event, but about its 'moral' for Christian readers. Other early sources confirming the deaths of Peter (and Paul) as occurring during the reign of Nero are no more specific than that. They simply mention Nero's reign, which ended on the 9th June 68 with his suicide.[334] But we have trustworthy indications of the way in which he died, by crucifixion. Those who mention the manner of his death are unanimous on this point. Lactantius (*On the kinds of deaths of the Persecutors* 2:6), sums it up neatly: 'He (Nero) crucified Peter and slew Paul.'[335] Origen records that Peter was 'crucified head downwards, for this is how he had demanded to suffer' (*Commentary on Genesis*, Bk. 3, in Eusebius, *HE* 3, 1:2). Suspicion may attach to this tradition, as it is also narrated in the legend-happy *Acts of Peter* 37(8)–39(10), which precede Origen by some thirty years. The quite un-Petrine speeches attributed to Peter on this occasion, the longest of them delivered head downwards, are, however, not so much hinted at by Origen). There is nothing intrinsically impossible about the tradition as such; crucifixions were common in the context of the Neronian persecution (cf. Tacitus, *Annals* 15:44), and such a variation in the procedure would have been in line with the desire for novelty among the Roman henchmen (cf. Tacitus again), let alone with the likelihood of Peter seeking a death even lowlier than that of his Christ. But the report cannot be evaluated decisively either way. The crucifixion as such is undisputed.

It is Eusebius, in Jerome's extant Latin version of his *Chronicle*, who provides a date for the event. If we accept his chronology, which is based on the years of Nero's emperorship (i.e. 1–14), his indication that both Peter and Paul died (not necessarily on the same day or in the same month) during Nero's fourteenth year points to the period between the 13th October 67 and the 9th June 68.[336] This appears to be somewhat precarious if one sees the Neronian persecution as an intensive but short-lived one which would have ended when Nero left Rome for Greece on the 25th September 66, only to return in January 68.

One does not have to enter into the perennial discussion about the existence or non-existence of Neronian *laws* against the Christians, the so-called *Institutum Neronianum*, presupposed by Tertullian (*Adv. Nat.* 1, 7:9).[337] What both Suetonius (*Life of the Caesars* 6, 16)[338] and Tertullian[339] clearly imply is the unlimited, or at least not suddenly ended, duration of the persecution once it had been officially sanctioned. There is no trace, either in the secular historian Suetonius or in the Christian apologist Tertullian, of a sudden end to such procedures simply because Nero himself had decided to leave the scene. Only his virtual death could offer an official reprieve. Whether or not there was a written law, now lost, the persecution had a lasting, sanctioned impact on the Christians.[340]

As far as the existing evidence is concerned, the death of Peter during Nero's fourteenth year cannot be ruled out, but neither, in the nature of the case, can it be proved beyond doubt. Those who see no compelling reasons to doubt the tradition that Peter was the (titular) overseer of the Roman Church for twenty-five years (see p. 154 above) will readily subscribe to the plausibility of Eusebius' dating. If Peter first arrived in AD 42, his death in AD 67 would follow, and this reasoning works in reverse of course: if Peter died during the last year of Nero's reign, he would have arrived in Rome for the first time in AD 42 or in early AD 43.

II

About AD 200 a Roman called Gaius wrote attacking Proclus, the leader of the so-called Montanists. He claims that he can point out 'the trophies (*tropaia*) of the apostles', for 'if you go to the Vatican or to the Ostian Road, you will find the trophies of those who founded the church' (Eusebius, *HE* 2, 25:7). Although the precise meaning of the term 'trophy'/*tropaion* has engendered some debate,[341] it clearly means burial-place here. Gaius is pointing out to Proclus that he knows where the apostles are buried, as a clinching argument against the Montanist who had previously referred to the tombs of Philip and his daughters as the basis of the Montanist claim to authority (Eusebius, *HE* 3, 31:4, 5, 14–18). Whereas excavations underneath the basilica of San Paolo fuori le Mura on the 'Ostian Road' (today's Via Ostiense) are far from completion,[342] the Vatican has been widely excavated, and the Petrine trophy mentioned by Gaius has been re-discovered.[343] The precise dates of the memorial and its surroundings are still being debated with varying degrees of passion. We have some clues, however.

Near the Vatican Gardens of Nero, where Nero had first sheltered the victims of the fire and then begun to execute the Christians (Tacitus, *Annals* 15:44), a first-century pagan necropolis existed—tombs from that period have been identified and dated.[344] It was a pagan graveyard, but excavations taking us into the third and fourth century have demonstrated that Christians were occasionally buried there, possibly because they had pagan relatives or perhaps for other, special reasons. In the early stages, when the necropolis was beginning to be established, tombs embellished with mosaics, frescos and stone-carvings were rare. The area was not yet clearly defined (we still do not know the exact measurements of the Vatican Gardens and graveyard). Peter, an executed criminal in the eyes of Roman law, would have fallen under the legal provision whereby his body could be released to friends or relatives for burial.[345] A New Testament parallel has been adduced more than once: Joseph of Arimathea had to ask Pilate officially for the body of Jesus before he could bury him. As this was a legal prerogative, the person(s) asking for the body, whoever they were, would not necessarily have endangered their own lives by coming into the open. The body of Peter, then, was taken[346] to a place just outside the gardens and in the area that had had been reserved for burials. No one at that time would have thought of erecting a glorious monument— official Christian glorification of martyrs and their bodies began only in the mid-second century, with the death of Polycarp as our earliest detailed literary source.[347] Peter, it is true, was the leader of the Roman Church and burial in itself was the minimum—and probably also the maximum—that his followers could do for him in the dire and dangerous circumstances. They simply buried

Peter's body in a shallow grave (a type of tomb rediscovered also in a necropolis at the Isola Sacra near Ostia Antica), on a southward-facing slope at the Vatican Hill. It would have been covered by tiles and earth.[348]

When Constantine began to build the church which over the centuries was to develop into what we know as St Peter's, in about AD 315, the tradition of Peter's tomb and its memory was so secure that he not only built the church on top of the memorial (which by then had become the simple but purpose-built *tropaion*) but actually re-structured parts of the Vatican Hill, on the southern slope of which the 'trophy' stood, so that a church could stand there. Constantine had decided to cling tenaciously to the historical site. So had previous generations of Christians who had been compelled to build the *tropaion* of Gaius in AD 160 (archaeological date) asymmetrically over the original tomb because a pagan construction of the same period, the so-called "red wall', had already encroached on the space required for a symmetrical construction.[349] Their determination to build here and not elsewhere witnesses to the conviction of these second-century Christians that this was the authentic site of Peter's burial. The red wall barred the Christians from reaching the tomb site from the south, the most convenient approach. But they used the red wall for graffiti instead: a mid-second century fish-symbol and (perhaps) the Greek words *Petros eni*—'Peter is in here'[350] demonstrate its use between AD 160 and AD 315.

Thus the site of Peter's burial had been known and had been preserved from the very beginnings. Whatever may have happened to the bones themselves[351] and to architectural developments on the site (which is again partly accessible even to non-archaeologists today), it can be said that there is uninterrupted evidence, from the date of the burial to the day when Constantine decided to build a basilica on the spot, for the existence of Peter's tomb on this southern slope of the Vatican.

III

Peter's career had led him, and leads those who follow its traces, away from the cradle of Christianity on the shores of the Sea of Galilee, away from the roots of Judaism in Galilee, Judaea and Jerusalem, to the centre of the pagan world, to the capital of the

Roman Empire. It not merely symbolizes, it also typifies the development of the Christian faith from its regional beginnings to the worldwide mission commanded by Jesus. More than anything else, however, the pages of this book have tried to demonstrate that Peter's life, traceable in reliable historical documents, in literature and in archaeology, presents a multifaceted example and encouragement to Christians today. Most obviously, there is the fact that a fisherman was able to become the solid rock of the Church through the power of the Holy Spirit. But there is a further lesson in the relationships within Peter's story: the relationship between Peter and Jesus, the relationship between Peter and John, Peter and Paul, Peter and Mark, Peter and the motley crowds of Jerusalem, the Christians of Antioch and those at Rome, between Peter and those he heals, those he binds and those he looses, between Peter and the tanner, Peter and the Roman army officer, Peter and the religious-political Sanhedrin, between Peter and the readers of his letters, between Peter and the Jews, and between Peter and the Gentiles. Peter was the man of relationships, the brother, the diplomat, the unifier.

All of these, of course, supply good topics for research and study. But research and study can never suffice in a Christian's life. Prayer has to take over. The example of Peter's life from Galilee to Rome should cause us to pray that the unity of all Christians in the Lord and the preaching of the gospel to everyone, regardless of race, nationality or social status do not remain separate goals, the one theoretical, the other practical, but become mutually dependant realities. When our individual weaknesses are fermented into purposeful strengths, our vacillations will give way to an inward solidity that can help to change lives. This is what happened to Peter. And he believed it could happen to every follower of Jesus. For, as Peter put it himself (2 Pet. 1:3):

> 'His divine power has given us everything we need for life and godliness through our knowledge of him who called us by his own glory and goodness.'

Bibliography

Select Bibliography

(Further references to secondary literature may be found in the notes)

Where a short title has been used in the notes, it is here shown in capital letters.

Aland, K., 'Petrus in Rom', *Historische Zeitschrift* 183 (1957), 497–516.
Aland, K. & Aland, B., *Der Text des Neuen Testaments* (Stuttgart, 1982).
Allen, W. C., *The Gospel According to St. Mark* (London, 1915).
Anderson, F. I., *Job* (Leicester, 1976).
Atzberger, L., *Geschichte der christlichen Eschatologie innerhalb der vornicäischen Zeit* (Freiburg, 1896).
Auerbach, E., 'Fortunata', in *Mimesis. Dargestellte Wirklichkeit in der abendländischen Literatur* (Bern/Munich 1946), 28–52.
Bailey, K. E., *Poet and Peasant. A literary-cultural approach to the parables in Luke* (Grand Rapids, 1976).
Bammel, E. & Moule, C. F. D., (eds.), *Jesus and the Politics of His Day* (Cambridge 1984).
Barnard, L. W., 'The Judgement in II Peter iii'. *Expository Times* 68 (1958), 302.
Barnett, P. W., *Opposition in Corinth* (JSNT, 22, 1984).
Barrett, C. K., *Things Sacrificed to Idols* (NTS, 11, 1964/65).
Barrett, C. K., 'Cephas and Corinth', in Betz, O., Hengel, M. & Schmidt, P. (eds.), *Abraham unser Vater. Festschrift für Otto Michel* (Leiden/Cologne, 1963), 1–12.
Bassin, F., *L'Évangile de Marc* (Vaux-sur-Seine, 1984).
Bauckham, R. J., *Jude/2 Peter* (Waco, 1983).
Bauer, W., *Griechisch-Deutsches Wörterbuch zu den Schriften des Neuen Testaments und der übrigen urchristlichen Literatur* (Berlin/New York, 1971).
Beare, F. W., 'The Sequence of Events in Acts 9–15 and the Career of Peter', *Journal of Biblical Literature* 62 (1943), 295–306.

197

Beasley-Murray, G. R., 'Second Thoughts on the Composition of Mark 13', *New Testament Studies* 29 (1983) 414–20.

Bell, F. K. A. & Deissmann, A., *Mysterium Christi* (Berlin, 1931).

Bénétreau, S., *La Première épître de Pierre* (Vaux-sur-Seine, 1984).

Bénétreau, S. F., *La deuxième épître de Pierre et le problème du proto-catholicisme dans le Nouveau Testament*, Paris. Unpublished doctoral thesis, Institut Protestant de Théologie, 1978.

Best, E., '1 Peter and the Gospel Tradition', *New Testament Studies* 16 (1970), 95–113.

Betz, O., 'Felsenmann und Felsengemeinde', *Zeitschrift für die neu-testamentliche Wissenschaft* 48 (1957), 49–77.

Beyschlag, K., *Simon Magus und die christliche Gnosis* (Tübingen, 1974).

Bickermann, E., 'Utilitas Crucis', *Revue de l'histoire des religions* 112 (1935), 169–241.

Bieder, W., *Grundkraft der Mission nach dem. 1. Petrusbrief* (Zürich, 1950).

Bieler, L., *Theios aner* (Vienna, 1935–36, repr. Darmstadt, 1967).

Bigg, C., *The Epistles of St. Peter and St. Jude* (Edinburgh, 2nd ed., 1902).

Black, M., *An Aramaic Approach to the Gospels and Acts* (Oxford, 3rd. ed., 1967) (*Aramaic*).

Black, M., *Die Muttersprache Jesu. Das Aramäische der Evangelien und der Apostelgeschichte* (Stuttgart, 1982).

Blaiklock, E. M., *The Acts of the Apostles* (London & Grand Rapids, 1959).

Blintzler, J., *Der Prozess Jesu* (Regensburg, 4th ed., 1969).

Bonnard, P., *L'Évangile Selon Saint Matthieu* (Paris, 1963).

Boomershine, T. E. & Bartholomew, G. L., 'The Narrative Technique of Mark 16.8', *Journal of Biblical Literature* 100 (1981), 213–23.

Brandon, S. G. F., *The Fall of Jerusalem and the Christian Church* (London, 2nd. ed., 1957).

Braun, H., *Spätjüdisch häretischer und frühchristlicher Radikalismus II* (Tübingen, 1957).

Brown, R. E., Donfried, K. P. & Reumann J. (eds.), *Peter in the New Testament* (London, 1974).

Brown, R. E. & Meier, J. P., *Antioch and Rome: New Testament Cradles of Catholic Christianity* (New York, 1983).

Brownrigg, R., *The Twelve Apostles* (London, 1974).

Brox, N., *Falsche Verfasserangaben: Zur Erklärung der frühchristlichen Pseudepigraphie* (Stuttgart, 1975).

Brox, N. (ed.), *Pseudepigraphie in der heidnischen und jüdisch - christlichen Antike* (Darmstadt, 1977).

Bruce, F. F., *The Speeches in the Acts of the Apostles* (London, 1944), (SPEECHES).

Bruce, F. F., *New Testament History* (London 2nd ed. rev.), 1977 (HISTORY).

Bruce, F. F., *Men and Movements in the Primitive Church, Studies in Early Non-Pauline Christianity* (Exeter, 1979) (MEN).

Bruce, F. F., *The New Testament Documents* (Leicester, 5th ed., 1960).

Bruce, F. F., *The Epistle of Paul to the Romans* (London, 1963).

Bruce, F. F., *The Epistle to the Galatians* (Exeter & Grand Rapids, 1982).
Bruce, F. F., *The Acts of the Apostles* (Leicester, 2nd ed., 1952) (ACTS).
Buchheim, K., *Der historische Christus*. *Geschichtswissenschaftliche Überlegungen zum Neuen Testament* (Münich, 1974).
Cadbury, H. J., *The Making of Luke-Acts* (New York, 1927).
Capocci, V., 'Sulla concessione e sul divieto di sepoltura nel mondo romano ai condamnati a pena capitale', *Studia et Documenta Historiae et Juris* 22 (1956), 266–310.
Carmignac, J., *La naissance des Evangiles Synoptiques* (Paris, 1984).
Catchpole, D. R., 'Paul, James and the Apostolic Decree', *New Testament Studies* 23 (1977), 428–44.
Chadwick, H., 'St. Peter and St. Paul in Rome: The Problem of the Memoria Apostolorum ad Catacumbas', *Journal of Theological Studies* NS 8 (1957), 31–52. (ST. PETER).
Chadwick, H., 'Pope Damasus and the peculiar claim of Rome to St. Peter and St. Paul', *Neotestamentica et Patristica*. *Festschrift für Oscar Cullmann* (Leiden, 1962), 313–18 (POPE DAMASUS).
Chadwick, H., *The Early Church* (Harmondsworth, 1967) (EARLY).
Chadwick, H., *Early Christian Thought and the Classical Tradition* (Oxford, 1966), repr. 1984.
Chaine, J., 'Cosmogonie aquatique et conflagration finale d'après la Secunda Petri, *Revue biblique* 46 (1937), 207–16.
Charlesworth, J. H., 'The Discovery of a Dead Sea Scroll' (*4Q Therapeia*). 'Its Importance in the History of Medicine and Jesus Research' (Lubbock, 1985).
Chilton, B. D. (ed.), *The Kingdom of God* (London, 1984).
Cladder, H. J., *Unsere Evangelien: Zur Literaturgeschichte der Evangelien* (Freiberg, 1919).
Clark, A. C., *The Acts of the Apostles* (Oxford, 1933).
Codrington, H. W., *The Liturgy of St. Peter* (Münster, 1936).
Cole, R. A., *The Gospel According to St. Mark* (London, 1961).
Cole, R. A., *The Epistle of Paul to the Galatians* (Leicester, 1965).
Conzelmann, H., *Die Apostelgeschichte* (Tübingen, 1963).
Corbo, V., *The House of St. Peter at Capharnaum* (Jerusalem, 1969).
Cousins, P., 'Stephen & Paul', *Evangelical Quarterly* 33 (1961), 157.
Craig, W. L., 'The Guard at the Tomb', *New Testament Studies* 30 (1984), 273–81.
Craig, W. L., 'The Historicity of the Empty Tomb of Jesus', *New Testament Studies* 31 (1985), 39–67.
Crehan, J., 'New Light on 2 Peter from the Bodmer Papyrus', in E. A. Livingstone (ed.), *Studia Evangelica VII* (Berlin, 1982), 145–49.
Cullmann, O., *Le problème littéraire et historique du roman pseudo-Clémentine* (Paris, 1930).
Cullmann, O., *Peter, Disciple, Apostle, Martyr* (London, 2nd ed. rev., 1962) (PETER).
Daube, D., 'Three notes having to do with Johanan ben Zaccai', *Journal of Theological Studies* 11 (1960), 53–62.

D'Arcais, F., Brezzi, P. & Ruysschaert J. (eds.), *Pietro a Roma* (Rome, 1967).

Deissmann, A., *Bible Studies* (Edinburgh, 1901).

Delclaux, A., 'Deux témoignages de Papias sur la composition de Marc?', *New Testament Studies* 27 (1981), 401–11.

Delehaye, H., 'Le Sanctuaire des Apôtres sur la Voie Appienne', *Analecta Bollandiana* 45 (1927), 294–304.

Delehaye, H., *Cinq leçons sur la méthode hagiographique* (Brussels, 1934).

Demus-Quatember, M., *Est et alia Pyramis* (Rome/Vienna, 1974).

Derrett, J. D. M., *The Making of Mark. The Scriptural Bases of the Earliest Gospel* (2 vols., Shipston-on-Stour, 1984/85).

Dibelius, M., *Studies in the Acts of Apostles* (London, 1956).

Dietrich, W., *Das Petrusbild der lukanischen Schriften* (Stuttgart, 1972).

Dinkler, E., 'Die Petrus-Rom-Frage', *Theologische Rundschau* NF 25 (1959), 189–230, 289–335; NF 27 (1961), 33–64.

Dinkler, E., 'Petrus und Paulus in Rom. Die literarische und archäologische Frage nach den *tropaia ton apostolon*', *Gymnasium* 87 (1980), 1–37.

Dockx, S., *Chronologies néotestamentaires et Vie de l'Eglise primitive* (Paris-Gembloux, 1976).

Dodd, C. H., *The Apostolic Preaching and its Development* (London, 1936).

Dodd, C. H., *According to Scripture* (London, 1965) (SCRIPTURE).

Dodd, C. H., *The Epistle to the Romans* (London, 1932).

Dunn, J. D. G., *Unity and Diversity in the New Testament* (London, 1977).

Dupont, J., 'Pierre et Paul à Antioche et à Jerusalem', *Id.*, *Etudes sur les Actes des Apôtres* (Paris, 1967), 185–215.

Edersheim, A., *The Life and Times of Jesus the Messiah* (London, 1890, repr. 1927).

Edmundson, G., *The Church in Rome in the First Century* (London, 1913).

Elliott, J. H., *A home for the homeless: A sociological exegesis of 1 Peter, its situation and strategy* (Philadelphia, 1981).

Ellis, E. E., *Prophecy and Hermeneutic in Early Christianity* (Tübingen, 1978) (PROPHECY).

Ellis, E. E., 'Dating the New Testament', *New Testament Studies* 26 (1980), 487–502 (DATING).

Ellis, E. E., *Paul and his Co-Workers* (NTS 17, 1970/71).

Ellis, E. E., 'New Directions in Form Criticism' in G. Strecker, *Jesus Christus in Historie und Theologie* (Tübingen, 1975).

Elton, G. E., *Simon Peter. A Study of Discipleship* (London, 2nd ed., 1967).

Farmer, W. R., *The Last Twelve Verses of Mark* (Cambridge, 1974).

Fasola, U. M., *Petrus und Paulus in Rom* (Rome, 1980).

Feldmeier, R., 'Die Darstellung des Petrus in den synoptischen Evangelien' in Stuhlmacher, P. (ed.), *Das Evangelium und die Evangelien* (Tübingen, 1983), 267–71.

Féret, H.-M., *Pierre et Paul à Antioche et à Jerusalem. Le 'conflit' des deux Apôtres* (Paris, 1955).

Ferrua, A., 'Pietro in Vaticano', *La Civilta Cattólica* 135 (1984), 573–81.

Feuillet, A., 'La découverte du tombeau vide en Jean 20. 3–10, *Hokhma* 7 (1978), 1–45.

Fiebig, P., *Die Gleichnisreden Jesu* (Tübingen, 1912).

Fink, J., 'Das Petrusgrab - Glaube und Grabung', *Vigiliae Christianae* 32 (1978), 255–75.

Fitzmyer, J. A., *Essays on the Semitic Background of the New Testament* (London, 1971).

Fitzmyer, J. A., 'Crucifixion in Ancient Palestine, Qumran Literature and the New Testament' *Catholic Biblical Quarterly* 40 (1978), 498–513 (CRUCIFIXION).

Fitzmyer, J. A., *A Wandering Aramean. Collected Aramaic Essays* (Missoula, 1979).

Fitzmyer, J. A., 'The Aramaic Language and the Study of the New Testament', *Journal of Biblical Literature* 99 (1980), 5–21.

Fitzmyer, J. A., *Jerome Biblical Commentary* (Englewood Cliffs/London, 1968).

Foakes-Jackson, F. J., *Peter, Prince of the Apostles* (London, 1927).

Fornberg, T., *An Early Church in a Pluralistic Society. A Study of 2 Peter* (Lund, 1977).

France, R. T., *Jesus and the Old Testament* (London, 1971).

France, R. T., *The Gospel According to Matthew* (Leicester, 1985).

France, R. T. & Wenham D. (eds.), *Gospel Perspectives* 5 vols. (Sheffield 1980–1985).

Fuchs, E. & Raymond, P., *La Deuxième épître de Saint Pierre/L'épître de Saint Jude* (Neuchatel, 1980).

Gaechter, P., *Petrus und seine Zeit* (Innsbruck/Vienna/Munich, 1958).

Garofalo, S., Maccarone, M. & Ruysschaert J. (eds.), *Studi Petriani* (Rome 1968).

Gasque, W., 'The Speeches of Acts. Dibelius Reconsidered' in Longenecker, R. N. & Tenney, M. C. (eds.), *New Dimensions in New Testament Studies* (Grand Rapids, 1974), 232–50.

Géoltrain, P., 'Esséniens et Hellénistes', *Theologische Zeitschrift* 15 (1959), 241–54.

Gerhardsson, B., *Memory and Manuscript. Oral Tradition and Written Transmission in Rabbinic Judaism and Early Christianity* (Lund/Kopenhagen, 2nd ed., 1964) (MEMORY).

Gerhardsson, B., *Die Anfänge der Evangelientradition* (Wuppertal, 1977) (ANFANGE).

Gewalt, D., *Petrus. Studien zur Geschichte und Tradition des frühen Christentums.* (Heidelberg, Doctoral thesis), 1966.

Ghetti, B. M. A. (ed.), *Saecularia Petri et Pauli. Conferenze per il centenario del martirio degli Apostoli Pietro e Paolo.* (Vatican City, 1969).

Goetz, K. G., *Petrus als Gründer und Oberhaupt der Kirche* (Leipzig, 1927).

Goodspeed, E. J., *Matthew, Apostle and Evangelist* (Philadelphia, 1959).

Goppelt, L., *Typos. Die typologische Deutung des Alten Testaments im Neuen* (Gütersloh, 1939).

Goppelt, L., *Christentum und Judentum im ersten und zweiten Jahrhundert. Ein Aufriss der Urgeschichte der Kirche* (Gütersloh, 1954).

Goppelt, L., 'Prinzipien neutestamentlicher Sozialethik nach dem 1. Petrusbrief', in Baltensweiler, H. & Reicke B. (eds.), *Neues Testament und Geschichte. Oscar Cullman zum 70. Geburtstag* (Zürich/Tübingen, 1972), 285–96.

Goppelt, L., *Theologie des Neuen Testaments* (Göttingen, 1975/76).

Goulder, M., *Midrash and Lection in Matthew* (London, 1974).

Grayston, K., *The Translation of Matthew 28:17* (*JSNT* 21, 1984).

Grazzi, L., *Ricerche sui 'Fideles', ossia nomi e famiglie d'inchiesta archeologica nonche da fonti comparata sopra i primi Cristiani di Roma per gli anni 41– 155* (Rome, 1981).

Green, E. M. B., *2 Peter Reconsidered* (London, 1961).

Green, E. M. B., *Second Epistle General of Peter* (Leicester) 1968, now 2nd ed. rev., 1987. (2 PETER/JUDE).

Grundmann, W., 'Die Apostel zwischen Jerusalem und Antiochia', *Zeitschrift für neutestamentliche Wissenschaft* 39 (1940), 110–37.

Grundmann, W., *Des Evangelium nach Lukas* (Berlin, 3rd. ed., 1966) (LUKAS).

Guarducci, M., *The Tomb of St. Peter* (New York, 1960).

Guarducci, M., *Le Reliquie di Pietro sotto la Confessione della Basilica Vaticana* (Rome, 1965).

Guarducci, M., *Pietro ritrovato. Il martirio, la tomba, le reliquie* (Milan, 2nd. ed., 1970).

Guarducci, M., 'Die Ausgrabungen unter Sankt Peter', in Klein, R. (ed.), *Das frühe Christentum in römischen Staat* (Darmstadt, 2nd. ed., 1982). 364–414.

Guarducci, M., *Pietro e Paolo sulla Via Appia e la tomba di Pietro in Vaticano* (Vatican City, 1983).

Guelich, R., 'The Gospel Genre', in Stuhlmacher, P. (ed.), *Das Evangelium und die Evangelien* (Tübingen, 1983), 183–219.

Gundry, R. H., 'The Language Milieu of First Century Palestine. Its Bearing on the Authenticity of the Gospel Tradition', *Journal of Biblical Literature* 83 (1964), 404–08.

Gundry, R. H., ' "Verba Christi" in 1 Peter. Their Implications concerning the authorship of 1 Peter and the authenticity of the Gospel Tradition', *New Testament Studies* 13 (1967), 336–50.

Gundry, R. H., 'Further "Verba" on "Verba Christi" in First Peter' *Biblica* 55 (1974), 211–32.

Gunther, J. J., *St. Paul's Opponents and Their Background. A Study of Apocalyptic and Jewish Sectarian Teachings* (Leiden, 1973) (ST. PAUL'S).

Gunther, J. J., 'The Association of Mark and Barnabas with Egyptian Christians', *Evangelical Quarterly* 54 (1982), 219–33, 55 (1983), 21–29.

Guthrie, D., 'Epistolary Pseudepigraphy' Id., *New Testament Introduction* (Leicester, 1970), 671–84.

Guthrie, D., 'Questions of Introduction', in Marshall, I. H. (ed.), *New Testament Interpretation* (Exeter, 1977), 105–116.

Guthrie, D., *New Testament Introduction* (Leicester, 1970).

Haacker, K., 'Dibelius und Cornelius. Ein Beispiel formgeschicht-licher Überlieferungskritik', *Biblische Zeitschrift* 24 (1980), 234–51.

Haenchen, E., *The Acts of the Apostles* (Oxford, 1982).

Hahn, S., *Die Darstellung der Verleugnung Petri. Ikonographische Studie* (Munich, Doctoral thesis, 1977).

Hahn, F., *Christologische Hoheitstitel* (Gottingen, 4th ed., 1974).

Harnack, A. v., *Neue Untersuchungen zur Apostelgeschichte und zur Abfassungszeit der synoptischen Evangelien* (Leipzig, 1911).

Harnack, A. v., *Date of Acts and the Synoptic Gospels* (London, 1911).

Harnack, A. v., *Beiträge zur Einleitung in das neue Testament* IV (Leipzig, 1911).

Harnack, A. v., *Zur Revision der Prinzipien der neutestamentlichen Textkritik: Die Bedeutung der Vulgata für den Text der katholischen Briefe* (Leipzig, 1916).

Harnack, A. v., *Die Mission und Ausbreitung des Christentums in den ersten drei Jahrhunderten* (Leipzig, 4th ed., 1924) (MISSION).

Hedinger, H. W., *Subjektivität und Geschichtswissenschaft. Grundzüge einer Historik* (Berlin, 1969).

Hemer, C. J., 'The Address of 1 Peter', *Expository Times* 89 (1977/78), 239–43.

Hengel, M., 'Anonymität, Pseudepigraphie und "literarische Fälschung" in der jüdisch-hellenistischen Literatur', in Reverdin, O. (ed.), *Entretiens sur l'antiquité classique* vol. 18, *Pseudepigrapha* 1 (Vandoeuvres-Geneva, 1972, 231–329.

Hengel, M., *Judentum und Hellenismus* (Tübingen, 2nd ed., 1983) (JUDENTUM).

Hengel, M., 'Probleme des Markusevangeliums', in Stuhlmacher, P. (ed.), *Das Evangelium und die Evangelien* (Tübingen 1983), 221–65 (PROBLEME). See also p. 211 below.

Hengel, M., 'Entstehungszeit und Situation des Markusevangeliums' in Cancik, H. (ed.), *Markus-Philologie* (Tübingen, 1984), 1–45 (ENTSTE-HUNGSZEIT). See also p. 211 below.

Hengel, M., *Die Evangelienüberschriften* (Heidelberg, 1984) (EVANGELIEN-ÜBERSCHRIFTEN). See also p. 211 below.

Hengel, M., *Zur urchristlichen Geschichtsschreibung*, Stuttgart, 2nd ed., 1984.

Hennecke, E., *New Testament Apocrypha* I (London, 2nd ed., 1973).

Hill, D., *The Gospel of Matthew* (London, 1972).

Holzmeister, U., 'Vocabularium Secundae epistolae S. Petri erroresque quidam de eo divulgati', *Biblica* 30 (1949), 339–55.

Horst, P. W. van der, 'Can A Book End with *gar*?', *Journal of Theological Studies* 23 (1972), 121–24 (CAN A BOOK).

Horst, P. W. van der, 'Peter's Shadow. The Religio-Historical Background of Acts 5.15', *New Testament Studies* 23 (1977), 204–12 (PETER'S SHADOW).

Howard, W. F. (revd. C. K. Barrett), *The Fourth Gospel in recent criticism and Interpretation* (London, 1955).

Hunger, H., *Zur Datierung des Bodmer II* (Anzeiger der phil hist. Klasse der Österr. Akad. d. Wiss, 4, 1960), 12–23.

Hunzinger, C. L., 'Babylon als Deckname für Rom und die Datierung des 1 Petrusbriefes' in H. Graf Reventlow (ed.) *Gottes Wort und Gottes Land* (Göttingen, 1965).

Jeremias, J., *Golgotha* (Leipzig, 1926).

Jeremias, J., *New Testament Theology*, I (London, 1971) (THEOLOGY).

Jeremias, J., *Jerusalem in the Time of Jesus* (London, 1969).

Jewett, R., 'The Agitators and the Galatian Congregation' *New Testament Studies* 17 (1971), 198–212.

Judge, E. A., *The Social Pattern of Christian Groups in the First Century* (London, 1960).

Judge, E. A. & Thomas, G. S. R., 'The Origin of the Church at Rome— A New Solution?' (*Reformed Theological Review* 25, 1966).

Juster, J., *Les Juifs dans l'empire romain* (Paris, 1914), 2 vols.

Kamlah, E., *Die Form der katalogischen Paränese im Neuen Testament* (Tübingen, 1964).

Katzenmayer, H., 'Die Beziehungen des Petrus zur Urkirche von Jerusalem und Antiochia', *Internationale Kirchliche Zeitschrift* 35 (1945), 116–30.

Kelly, J. N. D., *The Epistles of Peter & Jude* (London, 1969).

Kilpatrick, G. D. *Origins of the Gospel According to St. Matthew* (Oxford, 2nd ed., 1950).

Kim, S., *The 'Son of Man' as Son of God* (Tübingen, 1983).

Kirschbaum, E., *Die Gräber der Apostelfürsten St. Peter und St. Paul in Rom* (Frankfurt 3rd ed. rev., 1974).

Kittel, G., *Theological Dictionary of the New Testament* (Grand Rapids, 1964–77).

Klauser, Th., *Die römische Petrustradition im Lichte der neuen Ausgrabungen unter der Peterskirche* (Cologne, 1956).

Klein, G. I., 'Die Verleugnung des Petrus. Eine traditionsgeschichtliche Untersuchung' *Id.*, Rekonstruktion und Interpretation (Munich, 1969), 49–98.

Klein, G., 'Der zweite Petrusbrief und der neutestamentliche Kanon' *Id.*, *Ärgernisse. Konfrontationen mit dem Neuen Testament* (Munich, 1970), 109–114.

Knoch, O., *Die Testamente des Petrus und Paulus. Die Sicherung der apostolischen Überlieferung in der spätneutestamentlichen Zeit* (Stuttgart, 1973).

Körtner, U. H. J., *Papias von Hierapolis. Ein Beitrag zur Geschichte des frühen Christentums* (Göttingen, 1983).

Kopp, C., *Die heiligen Stätten der Evangelien* (Regensburg, 2nd ed., 1964).

Kosnetter, J., *Zur Geschichtlichkeit der Verleugnung Petri. Dienst an der Lehre. Festschrift für Kardinal König* (Vienna, 1965), 127–43.

Kürzinger, J., *Papias von Hierapolis und die Evangelien des Neuen Testaments* (Regensburg, 1983).

Lampe, P., *Die stadtrömischen Christen in den ersten beiden Jahrhunderten* (Bern, Doctoral thesis, 1984), now Tübingen (WUNT 2/18), 1987.

Lane, W. L., *The Gospel According to Mark* (London, 1974).

Leipoldt, J. & Grundmann, W. (eds.), *Umwelt des Urchristentums* (3 vols., Berlin, 1966–67).

Lenski, R. C. H., *Interpretn. of Epp. of SS. Peter/John/Jude* (Columbus, Ohio 1945, 1960²).

Leon, H. J., *The Jews of Ancient Rome* (Philadelphia, 1960).

Lindars, B., *Jesus Son of Man—A fresh examination of the Son of Man sayings in the gospels in the light of recent research* (London, 1983).

Loffreda, S., *Capharnaum: The Town of Jesus* (Jerusalem, 1985).

Longenecker, R., *Biblical Exegesis in the Apostolic Period* (Grand Rapids, 1975).

Lowe, J., *Saint Peter* (London/New York, 1956).

Ludwig, J., *Die Primatworte Mt. 16, 18–19 in der altkirchlichen Exegese* (Münster, 1952).

Lyonnet, S., 'De ministerio romano S. Petri ante adventum S. Pauli', *Verbum Domini* 33 (1955), 143–54.

McCant, J. W., 'The Gospel of Peter. Docetism Reconsidered', *New Testament Studies* 30 (1984), 258–73.

Maier, G., 'The Church in the Gospel of Matthew. Hermeneutical Analysis of the Current Debate', in Carson, D. A. (ed.), *Biblical Interpretation and the Church. Text and Context* (Exeter, 1984).

Manson, T. W., *Studies in the Gospels and Epistles* (Manchester, 1962).

Marco, A. A. de, *The Tomb of St. Peter. A representative and annotated bibliography of the excavations* (Leiden, 1964).

Marrou, H.-I., *De la connaissance historique* (Paris, 1975).

Marrou, H.-I., *Histoire de l'éducation dans l'antiquité* (Paris, 1981), 2 vols. (HISTOIRE).

Marshall, I. H., 'Palestinian and Hellenistic Christianity. Some Critical Comments, *New Testament Studies* 19 (1973), 271–87.

Marshall, I. H., *The Origins of New Testament Christology* (Leicester, 1976) (ORIGINS).

Marshall, I. H., *Luke. Historian and Theologian* (Exeter, 2nd rev. ed., 1979) (LUKE).

Marshall, I. H., *Last Supper and Lord's Supper* (Exeter, 1981).

Marshall, I. H., *The Gospel of Luke* (Exeter, 1978) (GOSPEL).

Marshall, I. H., *The Acts of the Apostles* (Leicester, 1980).

Martin, R. P., *Mark. Evangelist and Theologian* (Exeter, 1972).

Marucchi, O., *Eléments d'Archéologie chrétienne* 3 vols. (Paris, 1899–1903).

Marucchi, O., *The Evidence of the Catacombs for the Doctrines and Organisation of the Primitive Church* (London, 1929) (EVIDENCE).

Marucchi, O., *Pietro e Paolo a Roma* (Torino/Roma, 4th ed., 1934) (PIETRO).

Marxsen, W., *Mark the Evangelist* (Nashville, 1969).

Mayer, R., *Die biblische Vorstellung vom Weltenbrand* (Bonn, 1956).

Maynard, A. H., 'Peter in the Fourth Gospel' *New Testament Studies* 30 (1984), 534–43.

Mayor, J. B., *The Epistle of St. Jude and the Second Epistle of St. Peter* (London, 1907).

Metzger, B. M., *The Text of the New Testament. Its Transmission, Corruption and Restoration* (Oxford, 2nd edn., 1968).

Metzger, B. M., *A Textual Commentary on the Greek New Testament* (London/New York, 1971).

Metzger, B. M., *Manuscripts of the Greek Bible* (Oxford, 1981).

Meyer, E., *Ursprünge und Anfänge des Christentums* II (Berlin, 1923).

Michaelis, J. R., 'Eschatology in 1 Peter iii 17', *New Testament Studies* 13 (1967), 394–401.

Milik, J. T., *The Books of Enoch, Aramaic Fragments of Qumran Cave 4* (Oxford, 1976).

Millauer, H., *Leiden als Gnade. Eine traditionsgeschichtliche Untersuchung zur Leidenstheologie des 1. Petrusbriefes* (Bern/Frankfurt, 1976).

Moffatt, J., *Introduction to the Literature of the New Testament* (Edinburgh, 3rd ed., 1918).

Mohrmann, Ch., 'À propos de deux mots controversés de la latinité chrétienne: tropaeum - nomen', *Vigiliae Christianae* 7 (1954), 154–173.

Morris, L., *The Gospel According to John* (London, 1972).

Morris, L., *Studies in the Fourth Gospel* (Grand Rapids, 1969).

Morton, A. Q., *The Authorship and Integrity of the New Testament* (London, 1965).

Moule, C. F. D., 'The Nature and Purpose of 1 Peter', *New Testament Studies* 3 (1956), 1–11.

Mühlenberg, E., 'Spätantike Geistlichkeit und altchristliche Kunst', in Blume, H.-D./Mann, F. (eds.), *Platonismus und Christentum. Festschrift für Heinrich Dörrie* (Münster, 1983), 162–83.

Munro, W., *Authority in Paul and Peter. The identification of a pastoral stratum in the Pauline Corpus and 1 Peter* (Cambridge, 1983).

Murphy-O'Connor, J., 'The Essenes and their History' *Revue Biblique* 81 (1974), 215–44 (ESSENES).

Murphy-O'Connor, J., *The Holy Land. An archaeological guide from the earliest times to 1700* (Oxford, 1980).

Murray, J. O. F., *Jesus according to St. John* (London, 1936).

Mussies, G., 'Greek as the Vehicle of Early Christianity', *New Testament Studies* 29 (1983), 356–69.

Mussner, F., Petrus und Paulus—Pole der Einheit (Freiburg, 1976).

Neugebauer, F., *Die Entstehung des Johannes-Evangeliums* (Stuttgart, 1968).

Neugebauer, F., 'Zur Deutung und Bedeutung des 1. Petrusbriefes', *New Testament Studies* 26 (1980), 61–86. (DEUTUNG).

Nineham, D. E., *Studies in the Gospels* (Oxford, 1955).

Obrist, F., *Echtheitsfragen und Deutung der Primatstelle Mt. 16, 18 f. in der deutschen protestantischen Theologie der letzten 30 Jahre* (Münster, 1961).

O'Callaghan, J., 'Papiros neotestamentarios en la cueva 7 de Qumrân?', *Biblica* 53 (1972), 91–100 (PAPIROS).

O'Callaghan, J., 'Tres probables papiros neotestamentarios en la cueva 7 de Qumrân', *Studia papyrologica* 11 (1972), 83–89 (TRES PROBABLES).

O'Callaghan, J., *Los papiros griegos de la cueva 7 de Qumrân* (Madrid, 1974) (GRIEGOS).

O'Connor, D. W., *Peter in Rome. The literary, liturgical and archeological evidence* (New York, 1969).

Overbeck, F., *Über die Auffassung des Streits des Paulus mit Petrus in Antiochien (Gal. 2, 11 ff.) bei den Kirchenvätern* (1877, repr. Darmstadt 1968).

Perrot, Ch. (ed.), *Etudes sur la première lettre de Pierre* (Paris, 1980).

Pesch, R., 'Das Messiasbekenntnis des Petrus (Mk 8, 27–30). Neuverhandlung einer alten Frage', *Biblische Zeitschrift* 17 (1973), 178–95; 18 (1974), 20–31.

Pesch, R., *Simon Petrus. Geschichte und geschichtliche Bedeutung des ersten Jüngers Jesu Christi* (Stuttgart, 1980).

Pesch, R., *Die Echtheit eures Glaubens. Biblische Orientierung: 1. Petrusbrief* (Freiburg, 1980).

Philipps, K., *Kirche in der Gesellschaft nach dem 1. Petrusbrief* (Gütersloh, 1971).

Phillips, J. B., *Peter's Portrait of Jesus* (London, 1976).

Pickering, W. N., *The Identity of the New Testament Text* (Nashville, 2nd ed. rev., 1980).

Piper, J., 'Hope as the Motivation of Love: 1 Peter 3: 9–12', *New Testament Studies* 26 (1980), 212–31.

Pixner, B., 'An Essene Quarter on Mount Zion?' *Studia Hierosolymitana. Festschrift B. Bagatti* (Jerusalem, 1976), 245–84.

Plümacher, E., 'Acta-Forschung 1974–82', *Theologische Rundschau* 46.1 (1983), 1–56; 49.2 (1984), 105–69.

Ramsay, W. M., *St. Paul, The Traveller and Roman Citizen* (London, 1895, repr. 1942).

Reicke, B., *The Disobedient Spirits and Christian Baptism: A Study of 1 Pet. III 19 and its Context* (Copenhagen, 1946).

Reicke, B., 'Der geschichtliche Hintergrund des Apostelkonzils und der Antiochia-Episode Gal. 2, 1–14', in Sevenster, J. N. & van Unnik, W. C. (eds.), *Studia Paulina in honorem Johannis de Zwaan Spetuagenarii* (Haarlem, 1953), 172–87.

Reicke, B., *The New Testament Era* (London, 1968) (ERA).

Richter, W., *Exegese als Literaturwissenschaft* (Göttingen, 1971).

Ridderbos, H. N., *The Speeches of Peter in the Acts of the Apostles* (Cambridge/London, 1962).

Riesenfeld, H., *The Gospel Tradition and its Beginnings* (Berlin, 1959) (GOSPEL).

Riesenfeld, H., 'The Text of Acts 10:36' in Best, E. & Wilson, R. McL. (eds.), *Text and Interpretation* (Cambridge 1979), 191–94 (TEXT).

Riesenfeld, H., 'Hur fick vi våra evangelier?', in *Festskrift till Bertil E. Gärtner* (Goteborg, 1984), 54–67.

Riesner, R., 'Wie sicher ist die Zwei-Quellen-Theorie?', *Theologische Beiträge* 8 (1977), 49–73.

Riesner, R., 'Der Aufbau der Reden im Matthäus-Evangelium', *Theologische Beiträge* 9 (1978), 172–82 (AUFBAU).

Riesner, R., 'Wie steht es um die synoptische Frage?' *Theologische Beiträge* 11 (1980), 80–83.

Riesner, R., *Jesus als Lehrer. Eine Untersuchung zum Ursprung der Evangelien-Überlieferung* (Tübingen, 2nd ed., 1984) (JESUS).

Riesner, R., *Formen gemeinsamen Lebens im Neuen Testament und heute* (Giessen/Basel, 2nd ed. rev., 1984).

Riesner, R., 'Der zweite Petrus-Brief und die Eschatologie' in Maier, G. (ed.), *Zukunftserwartung in biblischer Sicht. Beiträge zur Eschatologie* (Wuppertal/Giessen/Basel, 1984, 124–43) (PETRUSBRIEF).

Riesner, R., 'Golgota und die Archäologie', *Bibel und Kirche* 1 40 (1985), 21–26 (GOLGOTA).

Riesner, R., Essener und Urkirche in Jerusalem, *Bibel und Kirche* 40 (2)/1985, 64–76.

Robertson, A. Th., *Epochs in the Life of Simon Peter* (New York/London, 1933).

Robinson, B. P., 'Peter and his Successors. Tradition and Redaction in Matthew 16. 17–19'. *Journal for the Study of the New Testament* 21 (1984), 85–104 (PETER).

Robinson, J. A. T., *Redating the New Testament* (London, 1976) (REDATING).

Robinson, J. A. T.: *The Priority of John* (London, 1985) [published after the completion of this present book].

Roller, O., *Das Formular der paulinischen Briefe* (Stuttgart, 1933).

Ruysschaert, J., 'À propos de quelques textes romains du IVe siècle relatifs à Pierre et à Paul', *Archivum Historiae Pontificae* 7 (1969), 7–41.

Ruysschaert, J., 'Les premiers siècles de la tombe de Pierre', *Revue des Archéologues et Historiens d'Art de Louvain*, 8 (1975), 7–41.

Ruysschaert, J., 'La tomba di Pietro. Nuove considerazioni archaeologiche e historiche' *Studi Romani* 25 (1976), 322–30.

Schadewaldt, W., 'Die Zuverlässigkeit der synoptischen Tradition', in *ibw journal*, Sonderbeilage zu Heft 3, März 1983, und *Theologische Beiträge* 13 (1982), 201–23.

Schlatter, A., *Geschichte der ersten Christenheit* (Stuttgart, 1926) (GESCHICHTE).

Schlatter, A., *Petrus und Paulus nach dem ersten Petrusbrief* (Stuttgart, 1937).

Schlatter, A., *Der Evangelist Matthäus. Seine Sprache, sein Ziel, seine Selbständigkeit* (Stuttgart, 1957) (MATTHÄUS).

Schmid, J., 'Petrus "der Fels" und die Petrusgestalt der Urgemeinde', in Roesle, M. & Cullmann, O. (eds.), *Begegnung der Christen* (Frankfurt, 1960).

Schmithals, W., *Neues Testament und Gnosis* (Darmstadt, 1984).

Schnackenburg, R., 'Das Petrusamt. Die Stellung des Petrus zu den anderen Aposteln', *Wort und Wahrheit* 26 (1971), 206–16.

Schnackenburg, R. S., *The Gospel According to St. John* II (London, 1980) (JOHN).

Schneider, R., *Petrus* (Freiburg, 1955).

Schneider, R., 'Der Glaube des Petrus', *Id.*, *Das Unzerstörbare. Gesammelte Werke 9* (Frankfurt, 1978), 89–96.

Schoeps, H.-J., *Theologie und Geschichte des Judenchristentums* (Tübingen, 1949).

Schröger, F., *Gemeinde im erstem Petrusbrief* (Passau, 1981).

Schulze-Kadelbach, G., 'Die Stellung des Petrus in der Urchristenheit', *Theologische Literaturzeitung* 81 (1956), 1–14.

Selwyn, E. G., *The First Epistle of Peter* (London, 2nd ed., 1947).

Sevenster, J. N., *Do you know Greek? How much Greek could the first Jewish Christians have known?* (Leiden, 1968).

Smith, M., *Clement of Alexandria and a secret gospel of Mark* (Harvard, 1973).

Smith, T. V., *Petrine Controversies in Early Christianity. Attitudes towards Peter in Christian writings of the first two centuries* (Tübingen (WUNT), 1985).

Sotomayor, M., *San Pedro en la iconografia paleocristiana* (Granada, 1962).

Speyer, W., 'Fälschung, pseudepigraphische freie Erfindung und "echte religiöse Pseudepigraphie" ', in Reverdin, O. (ed.), *Entretiens sur l'antiquité classique, 8, Pseudepigrapha 1* (Vandoeuvres-Geneva, 1972), 331–72.

Stählin, G., *Die Apostelgeschichte* (Göttingen, 11th ed., 1970).

Stanton, G., *Jesus of Nazareth in New Testament Preaching* (Cambridge, 1974).

Staudinger, H., *The Trustworthiness of the Gospels* (Edinburgh, 1981).

Stauffer, E., 'Petrus und die Urgemeinde' *Id.*, *Die Theologie des Neuen Testaments* (Stuttgart/Berlin, 1941), 14–19 (PETRUS).

Stauffer, E., *Jesus. Gestalt und Geschichte* (Bern, 1957) (JESUS).

Stauffer, E., 'Petrus und Jakobus in Jerusalem', in Roesle, M. & Cullmann, O. (eds.), *Begegnung der Christen* (Frankfurt, 1960), 361–72.

Stempvoort, P. V. van, *Petrus en zijn graf te Rome* (Baarn, 2nd ed., 1960).

Stibbs, A. N., *The First Epistle General of Peter* (Leicester, 1959).

Stier, H.-E., 'Prämissen, Methoden und Tragweite der historischen Wissenschaft', in Hollenbach, J. M. & Staudinger, H. (eds.), *Moderne Exegese und historische Wissenschaft* (Trier, 1972), 49–57, 135–42, 151.

Strack, H. L. & Billerbeck, P., *Kommentar zum N.T. aus Talmud und Midrasch* (Munich, 5th ed., 1969).

Strange, J. F. & Shanks, H., 'Has the House Where Jesus Stayed in Capernaum been found?' *Biblical Archeology Review* 7 (1982), 26–37.

Stuhlmacher, P., 'Zum Thema. Das Evangelium und die Evangelien', *Id.* (Ed.), *Das Evangelium und die Evangelien* (Tübingen, 1983), 1–26.

Talbert, C. H., *Again: Paul's Visits to Jerusalem* (Novum Testamentum 9, 1967).

Tasker, R. V. G., *The Gospel According to St. Matthew* (Leicester, 1961).

Taylor, R. O. P., *The Groundwork of the Gospels* (Oxford, 1946).

Taylor, V., *The Gospel According to St. Mark* (London, 2nd ed., 1969).

Theissen, G., *Soziologie der Jesusbewegung* (Munich, 1977).

Thiede, C. P., '7Q—Eine Rückkehr zu den neutestamentlichen Papyrus-fragmenten in der siebten Höhle von Qumran', *Biblica* 65 (1984), 538–59 and 66 (1985), 261 (7Q).

Thiede, C. P., 'A Pagan Reader of 2 Peter: Cosmic Conflagration in 2 Peter 3 and the "Octavius" of Minucius Felix'; *Journal for the Study of the New Testament*, 26, 1986, 79–96 (PAGAN).

Thiede, C. P., *Die älteste Evangelien-Handschrift? Der Fund des Markus-Fragments von Qumran und die Anfänge der schriftlichen Überlieferung des Neuen Testaments* (Wuppertal, 1986) (ÄLTESTE).

Thiede, C. P.: 'Babylon, der andere Ort: Anmerkungen zu 1. Petr. 5, 13 und Apg. 12, 17', *Biblica* 67 (1986), fasc. 4 pp 532–538

Thiede, C. P. (ed.), *Das Petrusbild in der neueren Forschung* (Wuppertal, 1987).

Thiede, C. P., *The Oldest Manuscript of the Gospels? The Qumran Fragment of Mark and the Beginnings of the Textual Tradition of the New Testament* (Exeter, forthcoming).

Thompson, D. B. & Griswold, R. E., *Garden Lore of Ancient Athens* (Princeton, 1963).

Torrey, C. C., *The Composition and Date of Acts* (Cambridge, Mass., 1916).

Torrey, C. C., *The Four Gospels: A New Translation* (London, 2nd ed., 1947).

Toynbee, J. & Perkins, J. W., *The Shrine of St. Peter and the Vatican Excavations* (London, 1956).

Trocmé, E., *The Formation of the Gospel According to Mark* (London, 1975).

Turner, C. H., 'St. Peter in the New Testament', *Theology* 13 (1926), 66–78.

Unnik, W. C. van, 'The Teaching of Good Works in 1 Peter' *New Testament Studies*, 1 (1954), 92–110.

Unnik, W. C. van, 'Christianity According to 1 Peter', *Expository Times* 68 (1956), 79–83.

Unnik, W. C. van, 'Sparsa, collecta. The collected essays. I: Evangelica. Paulina. Acta', *Novum Testamentum* Suppl. Vol. 29 (1973), 'II: 1 Peter. Canon. Corpus Hellenisticum, Generalia', *Novum Testamentum* Suppl. Vol. 30 (1980).

Veit, K., *Die synoptischen Parallelen und ein alter Versuch ihrer Enträtselung mit neuer Begründung* (Gütersloh, 1897).

Vermes, G., *The Dead Sea Scrolls. Qumran in Perspective* (London, 1977).

Vermes, G., *Jesus the Jew* (London, 2nd ed., 1977).

Vögtle, A., 'Die Schriftwerdung der apostolischen Paradosis nach 2 Petr. 1, 12–15', Baltensweiler, H. & Reicke B. (eds.), *Neues Testament und Geschichte. Oscar Cullman zum 70. Geburtstag* (Zürich/Tübingen, 1972), 297–305.

Vögtle, A., 'Messiasbekenntnis und Petrusverheissung' Id., *Das Evan-*

gelium und die Evangelien. Beiträge zur Evangelienforschung (Düsseldorf, 1974), 137–70.

Walsh, J. E., *The Bones of St Peter* (London, 1983).

Warfield, B. B., 'The Canonicity of Second Peter', *Southern Presbyterian Review* 34 (1883), 390–445.

Wehnert, J., 'Literarkritik und Sprachanalyse. Kritische Anmerkungen zum gegenwärtigen Stand der Pseudo-Klementinen- Forschung', *Zeitschrift für die neutestamentliche Wissenschaft* 74 (1983), 268–301.

Weiss, J., *Das älteste Evangelium* (Göttingen, 1903).

Wenger, L., *Die Quellen des römischen Rechts* (Vienna, 1953).

Wenham, D., *The Rediscovery of Jesus' Eschatological Discourse (Gospel Perspectives* Vol. 4, Sheffield, 1984).

Wenham, J., 'Did Peter go to Rome in AD 42?' *Tyndale Bulletin* 23 (1972), 94–102 (DID PETER).

Wenham, J., 'Gospel Origins', *Trinity Journal* 7 (1978), 112–34.

Wenham, J., 'Synoptic Independence and the Origin of Luke's Travel Narrative', *New Testament Studies* 27 (1981), 507–15.

Wenham, J., 'Gospel Origins. A Rejoinder'. *Trinity Journal* NS 2 (1981), 37–39 (REJOINDER).

Wenham, J., 'Why do you ask me about the Good? A Study of the Relation between Text and Source Criticism', *New Testament Studies* 28 (1982), 116–25.

Wenham, J., *Easter Enigma* (Exeter, 1984) (EASTER).

Werdermann, H., *Die Irrlehrer des Judas- und 2. Petrusbriefes* (Gütersloh, 1913).

Wernle, P., *Die synoptische Frage* (Freiburg, 1899).

Wibbing, S., *Die Tugend- und Lasterkataloge im Neuen Testament und ihre Traditionsgeschichte unter besonderer Berücksichtigung der Qumrantexte* (Berlin, 1959).

Wilckens, U., *Die Missionsreden der Apostelgeschichte* (Neukirchen, 2nd ed., 1963).

Wohlenberg, G. *Der erste und zweite Petrusbrief und der Judasbrief* (Leipzig, 1923³)

Wuellner, W. H., *The Meaning of 'Fishers of Men''* (Philadelphia, 1967).

Zahn, Th., *Einleitung in das Neue Testament* II (Leipzig, 2nd ed., 1900).

Zahn, Th., *Der Brief des Paulus an die Galater*, (Leipzig, 1905).

Zahn, Th., *Das Evangelium des Matthäus* (Leipzig, 4th ed., 1922).

Zuntz, G., 'Wann wurde das Evangelium Marci geschrieben?' in Cancik, H. (ed.), *Markus-Philologie* (Tübingen, 1984), 47–71.

NOTE After the completion of this book three papers by M. Hengel referred to on p. 203 were published in slightly expanded English versions as

Hengel, M., *Studies in the Gospel of Mark* (London, 1985).

Indexes

Notes

Works referred to by author only, or by author and short title (e.g. Riesner, Aufbau), will be found listed in the Bibliography. Where reference is made to a work not listed in the Bibliography, details of author and title are given in full in the first instance only. Subsequent mention of such works will refer back to their first appearance in the Notes.

1 See Papias, in Eusebius, HE 3, 39:15; Justin, Dial. 106:3; Irenaeus, Haer. 3, 1:1–2; the Anti-Marcionite Prologue; Tertullian, Adv. Marc. 4:5; Origen, in Eusebius, HE 6, 25:5; Clement of Alexandria, in Eusebius, HE 2, 15:1–2 and 6, 14:5–7 and Sketches on 1 Peter 5:13; Eusebius himself, Theophany (Syr.) 5:40; Jerome, On Famous Men 8; Letter 120:11; Commentary on Matthew, Preface, 6.

2 Irenaeus, Haer. 3, 1:1–2, referred to by Eusebius, HE 5, 8:1–4. This appears to be an interpretation of 2 Pet. 1:15 as alluding to and announcing the Gospel of Mark. M. Green, The Second Epistle General of Peter and the General Epistle of Jude (Leicester, 1968) 80–81, interprets the similarities and concludes: 'It is hard to escape the conclusion that Irenaeus knew this passage in 2 Peter, and took the implicit promise to refer to Mark's gospel.' See also Crehan, New Light, 145–49.
   Among recent critics, Hengel, Probleme, 252–57, underlines the dependence of Mark on Peter; see also Riesner, Jesus, 20–24.

3 Cf. Thiede, 7Q and Älteste, recently S. Daris, in Biblica 68 (1987), fasc. 3, 431–33; G. Ghiberti, in Aegyptus 66 (1986), 297–98; B. Schwank, in Erbe und Auftrag 63/1 (1986), 54-56; M. Fernández-Galiano, in Una Voce 23 (1987), 3–5; H. Riesenfeld, in Signum 12/4–5 (1986), 105–109, and in Signum 13/6 (1987), 204–205; B. Zay, in Theologiai Szemle XXX/5 (1987), 283–86; H. Staudinger/J. Schlüter, An Wunder glauben? (Freiburg/Basel/Wien 1986, 85–86). M. Green, The Second Epistle General of Peter and the General Epistle of Jude (London/Grand Rapids, 2nd ed., rev., 1987), 16-17. H. Hunger, in Tyche 2 (1988), 278–80.

4 For example there are no traces of Pauline theology in Mark. Cf. Robinson, Redating, 94–117, and, for a later, but nonetheless pre-AD 70 date, Hengel, Entstehungszeit.

5 For the number of appearances of Peter in the gospels, see Hengel, Probleme, 253–54, and Feldmeier, Darstellung, 267.

6 E.g., Conrad Witz, 'La Pêche Miraculeuse' (Geneva, Musée d'Art et d'Histoire); Gentile da Fabbriano, 'Christ and Peter' (National Gallery of Scotland); Poussin, 'Sacrament of Ordination' (National Gallery of Scotland). Historically slightly more plausible are Raphael's portrayals in his cartoons

215

'Christ's Charge to Peter' and 'The Miraculous Draught of Fishes' (London, Victoria and Albert Museum; tapestries: Vatican, Pinacoteca).

7 *Ant.* 18, 2:1. Cf. Reicke, *Era*, 126–27.

8 Cf. Kopp, 230–43; Riesner, *Jesus*, 412. Most recently B. Pixner, 'Searching for the New Testament Site of Bethsaida', in *Biblical Archeologist*, 48 (1985), 207–16.

9 I. H. Marshall, *The Gospel of Luke* (Exeter, 1978), 134.

10 Josephus, *Ant.* 18, 5:4. Mk. 6:17 calls Herod Boethius, first husband of Herodias and half-brother of Herod Antipas, by the name of Philip: cf. Reicke, *Era*, 111, 125.

11 *Clouds*, 351; see A. Fick/F. Bechtel, *Die griechischen Personennamen* (Göttingen, 1894).

12 See S. Lieberman, *Greek in Jewish Palestine* (2nd ed., New York, 1965); Sevenster; Mussies.

13 The geographer Strabo (c. 63 BC – AD 21) credits Gadara with the birth of Menippos, the philosophers Meleager and Philodemos, and the rhetor Theodoros, in his *Geography* 16, 759. Cf. Reicke, *Era*, 97; Riesner, *Jesus*, 207.

14 Riesner, *Jesus*, 123–99.

15 Cf. the Italian Cohort mentioned in Acts 10:1 and the very recent discovery of the remains of the garrison implied by Mt. 8:5–13 par.

16 The solid foundation of the Jewish population in the history and tradition of their culture is testified to by Seneca, in his treatise *On Superstition*, Fragment 41f., quoted by Augustine in his *City of God* 6:11: 'They, admittedly, know the reasons and origins of their customs, but the majority of our people are doing things the reasons of which they do not understand' (*Illi tamen causas ritus sui noverunt; maior pars populi facit quod cur faciat ignorat.*)

17 See Mk. 10:28; Mt. 19:27; Lk. 5:11, 18:28.

18 By inference, the other one is John, Son of Zebedee, who tells the story with his customary relish for detail: 'it was about the tenth hour' (1:39).

19 Jn. 1:43–45; see Stauffer, *Jesus*, 56.

20 See below, p. 43.

21 'Lake of Gennesaret' is an alternative designation of the Sea of Galilee. In the form 'Gennesar' it occurs as the local name for the lake: cf. Josephus, *War* 2, 20:6; 3, 10:7–8. In the Greek version of the Old Testament, the LXX, it is called 'Sea Chenereth' (cf. Nu. 34:11). 'Lake of Gennesaret' is the version given only by Luke in the NT; Matthew (14:34) and Mark (6:53) know 'Gennesaret' as the name of the region on the north-western shore of the lake they call 'Sea of Galilee' (Mk. 1:16, 7:31, Mt. 4:18, 15:29). John informs us of a third name, 'Sea of Tiberias', after the city on its western shore (6:1, 21:1).

22 The title 'Master' (*epistátes*) suggests a previous acceptance of Jesus' position. Luke had in fact placed the healing of Peter's mother-in-law before the actual calling of the disciples (4:38–39). See below, p. 24.

23 Cf. Marshall, op. cit. n. 9, 203.

24 One of the more amusing results of unrealistic NT scholarship can be seen in the attempt to place the incident on the shore, as Jesus could not have 'gone away' from a boat at sea. (Cf. R. Pesch, *Der reiche Fischfang* (Düsseldorf, 1969), 71, 116. Such a strange misinterpretation of the context remains astonishing even if we did not allow for the fact that Jesus *was* able to walk on water according to Mk. 6:48, Mt. 14:25, and Jn. 6:19.

For the address 'Lord', see below p. 48, and Marshall, *Origins*, 97–100.

25 See Lk. 14:1.
26 Cf. Marshall, op. cit. n. 9, *Luke,* 195.
27 *Peregrinatio ad loca sancta,* in *Corpus Scriptorum Ecclesiastorum Latinorum (CSEL),* Wien 1898, XXXIV, 112f.; O. Prinz (Ed.), *Itinerarium Egeriae (Peregrinatio Aetheriae)* (5th ed., Heidelberg 1960).
28 Cf. Corbo; Riesner, *Jesus,* 438–39; Strange/Shanks.
29 Strange/Shanks, 37.
30 Luke's rephrasing of his list in Acts is also interesting for another reason: whereas in his gospel, as in Matthew's, Andrew follows his brother Simon, he is now followed by John, with James coming third in both lists, so that the arrangement in Acts begins with the inner circle of the three as it had developed during the period covered by the gospel. For Luke's 'Judas (Son) of James' in the place of the other evangelists' 'Thaddaeus', see Jeremias, *Theology,* 232f., and F. F. Bruce, *The Acts of the Apostles* (Leicester, 2nd ed., 1952), 73.
31 Cf. G. D. Kilpatrick, *The Origins of the Gospel According to St. Matthew* (Oxford, 2nd ed., 1950), 40f.
32 For a detailed discussion of the different attitudes towards authorship, see D. Guthrie, *New Testament Introduction* (Leicester, 1970), 33–44.
33 Cf. Robinson, *Redating,* 300f., and D. A. Carson, 'Historical Tradition in the Fourth Gospel', in France/Wenham, 83–145.
34 For a similar use of *ei,* cf. Mt. 12:28 and Rom. 5:17. For 'Lord', see Marshall, *Origins,* 97–110.
35 Attempts to show that he did not actually walk, as the Greek word, *peripátesen,* should be constructed as an inceptive aorist, 'began to walk' (R. V. G. Tasker, *The Gospel According to St. Matthew* (Leicester, 1961), 145–46), and that Peter therefore never really exercised Jesus' power, are not convincing, as v. 30 demands a certain interval of time to have passed in which Peter did make at least a few steps towards Jesus.
36 Others had done so before them: God himself (Mk. 1:11, Mt. 3:17, Lk. 9:35), temptingly the devil (Mt. 4:3–6), as well as the demon-possessed man (Mk. 5:7, Mt. 8:29, Lk. 8:28); in John's gospel, Nathanael uses the title the very moment he is called by Jesus to become a disciple (1:49): 'Rabbi, you are the Son of God, you are the King of Israel'. See also below, p. 44 and note 62, end.

When Mark does not record the appellation 'Son of God'—which he could have done even without the episode of Peter simply on the strength of Jesus walking on the water as an added impetus after all the other miracles the disciples had already witnessed—but says of the men in the boat that 'they were completely amazed, for they had not understood about the loaves, their hearts were hardened', this is not necessarily contrary to what Matthew says about the insight they had into the true identity of Jesus. The kind of worshipping Matthew mentions is in itself not free of conflict (see p. 30)—Jesus does not react to it; and even in Jn. 1:49, where he reacts to Nathanael's appellation, he is at pains to explain that Nathanael called him 'Son of God' for wrong, or at least insufficient, reasons. In this sense, Mark is giving a fair description of the disciples at this stage of their intellectual and spiritual development: they were as yet 'stubborn' (*peporoménos*); 'their hearts were hardened' by preconceived ideas about the 'Son of God' as well as about Jesus himself.
37 For those who favour the priority of the so-called Majority Text, the longer version is the original one. *Kai hoi met autou* has therefore been reinstated in

the passage by the editors of *The Greek New Testament According to the Majority Text* (Nashville/Camden/New York, 1982), 216.

38 Peter, of course, gets his first practical opportunity when Cornelius, the Roman centurion, asks him to come to Caesarea (Acts 10:1, 22f.).

39 Some textual witnesses have the longer version, 'You are the Christ, the Son of God' (Codex Sinaiticus, Codex Regius (L019), and others), or even 'You are the Christ, the Son of the living God' (Codex Washingtonensis (W032), Codex Beratinus (Φ043), and others, including old Latin, Syriac and Sahidic versions). It is natural to assume that the shorter text is the original, and that the longer variants have been added in order to comply with the testimony of Mt. 16:16b. If so, it underlines the importance given to Peter's statement by later scribes.

40 Outside the OT, a text from Qumran, 4Q Patriarchal Blessings 2–5, speaks of the righteous Messiah who is the sprout of David in a comment on Gn. 49:10. (See also 4Q Flor 1:11–13).

41 For the use of the expression 'Son of Man' as applied by Jesus to himself in v. 31, see in Mark also 2:10 and 2:28, and in the context of his foretold sufferings, 9:31 and 10:33–34. It is obvious from these passages that the prophecy of Dn. 7:13–14 is supplemented in Jesus' thinking by other messianic prophecies, such as Is. 53:7–12, to form a coherent picture of the suffering Christ based on OT writings and therefore recognisable to the 'careful hearer and (later) reader. It is significant that Peter and the others do not fully understand Jesus, either here or on the next occasion (Mk. 9:31).
   The 'Son of Man' question as such is discussed at length in two recent publications, by Kim and Lindars.

42 Cf. the Qumran 'War Scroll', 1QM 7:5–6, where prerequisites for the battle on the day of vengeance are listed, and where it says that holy angels will accompany the armies of the believers.

43 Mk. 3:16, cf. above p. 27–28. The text implies that Jesus gave Simon his by-name Peter on this occasion. That the naming as such is not linked with Peter's confession is corroborated by Jn. 1:42, where Jesus uses the name as early as their first meeting. Even if the usage in Jn. 1:42 could possibly point to the future ('and you will be called Petros'), Jesus utters the name prior to Peter's confession which he records in 6:69.

44 Recent commentaries have hinted in this direction: cf. W. L. Lane, *The Gospel According to Mark* (London, 1974), 295; and F. Bassin, *L'Évangile de Marc* (Vaux-sur-Seine, 1984), 191.

45 This passage is remarkable for two reasons: Peter uses the term 'Satan' himself (and this is the only instance in the NT where he does so); and it is reported by Luke, who did not include the 'Satan' rebuke in his account of the scene in Lk. 9:18–22. See below, p. 42.

46 Cf. Robinson, *Redating*, 313–19. Others still date the letter to around AD 130: cf. K. Wengst, *Schriften des Urchristentums II* (Darmstadt, 1984), 114–118.

47 As Origen puts it in *Contra Cels.* 1:63, commenting on this passage: Jesus chose them to show to mankind how great his power to heal souls was when he took such people 'to the point where they became examples of the purest ethos for those who were led by them to the Gospel of Christ'.

48 See P. Bonnard, *L'Évangile selon Saint Matthieu* (Paris, 1963), 243, and Tasker, op. cit., n. 35, 157: 'Of all the historical characters of the Old Testament, Jeremiah approximates most closely to Jesus as an outstanding example of patient endurance of undeserved suffering.'

49 See D. Hill, *The Gospel of Matthew* (London, 1972), 259. In a recent paper, Bernhard P. Robinson (*Peter*) tries to analyze it as inauthentic patchwork but fails to do so not least because of an incomplete grasp of how literary history works (e.g. op. cit. p. 87 below). His paper is noteworthy, however, for a suggestion taken from Michael Goulder's *Midrash and Lection in Matthew*, 387, and developed further by him, that the appellation in 16:17, 'Simon, Son of Jonah' (Bar Yona), is not an abbreviation of 'Son of John' (Jn. 1:42; 21:15, 16, 17), but an allegorical reference to Jonah, who has 'survived the assault of the sea, the "bars of Sheol" not being able to hold him fast' (Jonah 2:6, Robinson p. 90); 'Simon Peter will in some sense enjoy protection against the destructive forces of Sheol, for, as the son of Jonah, he will, like Jesus his master, prevail over death.' (p. 91). In view of Matthew's particular interest in the prophet Jonah (Mt. 12:39–41; 16:4; cf. however, also Lk. 11:29–32), it is not wholly impossible that Matthew may have had an Aramaic pun in mind—similar to the one on 'kepa'/petra-petros in 16:18. It is, on the other hand, obvious that all the other references to Jonah are meant to prefigure aspects of Christ's role, not Peter's, and since Jesus did not predict an identical resurrection, i.e. victory over the gates of Sheol on the third day, for Peter, one should not push the analogy too far. The same, of course, holds true for earlier attempts to turn Peter into a terrorist or zealot (*baryôna*=Akkadian/Aramaic for 'terrorist'). Cf. Cullmann, *Peter*, 23–24, on this suggestion by R. Eisler.

50 See Cullmann, *Peter*, 188–190.

51 See A. Vögtle, *Messiasbekenntnis*, 103.

52 Schlatter, *Matthäus*, 514.

53 Cf. Th. Zahn, *Das Evangelium des Matthäus* (Leipzig, 4th ed., 1922), 540.

54 And he may have known the rabbinical explanation of this passage, where God sees in Abraham the rock on which he can build and found the world. Cf. P. Fiebig, *Die Gleichnisreden Jesu im Lichte der rabbinischen Gleichnisse des neutestamentlichen Zeitalters* (Tübingen, 1912), 53; H. L. Strack/P. Billerbeck, *Kommentar zum N.T. aus Talmud und Midrasch* (Munich, 5th ed., 1969), 731.

55 Recent evidence from Qumran shows that *Petros* could be used as a proper name even in Aramaic-writing Essene circles: the name occurs in the medical document 4Q *Therapeia*, written between AD 26 and 60. See J. D. Charlesworth, 'The Discovery of a Dead Sea Scroll' (4Q *Therapeia*). 'Its Importance in the History of Medicine and Jesus Research' (Lubbock, 1985), here p. 6 and 30–32.

56 In the Greek, he would in any case have had to change the wording of the Septuagint he was quoting: it uses *lithos*, not *petros* or *petra* for 'stone'.

57 The connection between Mt. 16:17–19 and Lk. 22:29–31 was seen by Stauffer, *Petrus*, 16.

58 This *pars pro toto* for Hell is used once in the OT: Is. 38:10, cf. Ps. 9:13; 107:18; Job 38:17 and several apocryphal texts such as Wis. 16:13.

59 Cullman, *Peter*, 209–10. Cf. also, on the whole passage, Jeremias, *Golgotha*, 68–77.

59a Cf. Cullmann, *Peter*, 210–11.

60 Marshall, op. cit. n. 9, 367.

61 Cf. J. O. F. Murray, *Jesus According to St. John* (London, 1936), 159; L. Morris, *The Gospel According to John* (London, 1972), 388–89.

R. Schnackenburg, *The Gospel According to St. John* (London, 1980), II, 77 suggests that Peter, with his 'You are' words, takes up Jesus' 'I am' of 6:20, 35, 48, 51.

62 Paul later does the same in his speech in Pisidian Antioch (Acts 13:34–37). Luke therefore independently confirms Peter's (and Paul's) interpretation of the 'Holy One of God' as a synonym for Christ: The 'Risen One' gives the final meaning to a term the implications of which were only embryonic when applied to Aaron (Ps. 106:16) and by David (Ps. 16:10). In Jerusalem, after the Resurrection, Peter understands fully what he himself had hinted at in Capharnaum, and what Jesus had told him near Caesarea Philippi when he said that the gates of hades would not prevail (cf. Acts 2:27, 31 with Mt. 16:18b).

Philologically, there is a difference in the Greek passages: for 'The Holy One of God', Jn. 6:69 and Jdg. 13:7; 16:17 use *ho hagios [tou] Theou*; Ps. 106:16 has *ho hagios kuriou*; on the other hand, Ps. 16:10 and Acts 2:27; 13:35 have *ho hosios sou*. *Hagios* and *hosios*, however, can be used synonymously in the NT: e.g. 1 Pet. 1:15,16 speaks of Christ and God as *hagios* (Peter uses the *hosios* of Ps. 16:10 in his speech, Acts 2:27, but calls Jesus *hagios* in his speech in Acts 3:14).

Revelation uses both *hagios* (4:8) and *hosios* (15:4; 16:5) of God. In Hebrews, 7:26 *hosios* is used of Christ, in Rev. 3:7, a passage quoted above (p. 30), he is *hagios*, etc.

It has been suggested that John's use of *ho hagios tou Theou* for Peter's confession in Jn. 6:69 is an indirect attempt to belittle Peter, since the precise wording is used in this form only by demons in Mk. 1:24; Lk. 4:34 and as John has no demons in his gospel, 'their supernatural testimony about Jesus' divine origin is here made by Peter' (Maynard, 534, 543; cf. G. F. Snyder, 'John 13:16 and the Anti-Petrinism of the Johannine Tradition', *BR* 16, 1971, 11). Surprisingly, this overlooks Lk. 1:35, where the angel, not a demon, foretells the birth of Christ as *ho hagios huios Theou*; in Johannine literature itself, 1 Jn. 2:20 confirms the 'untainted' usage of Jn. 6:69 by calling Christ *ho hagios*. Quite apart from that, when the demons recognize Jesus as the Holy One of God, they do not thereby 'demonize' the confession, but rather are impelled to reveal that they know what is to come: the victory of Christ over their dominion. (For this last point, cf. Lane, op. cit., 73–74.)

63 Mk. 9:1; Mt. 16:28; Lk. 9:27. Luke and Matthew differ slightly from Mark: both omit 'with power' at the end, and Matthew adds 'the Son of Man', who will come in his kingdom. Strictly speaking, they all say the same, with Matthew simply underlining that it is Jesus himself who will be the ruler of the kingdom. For a recent discussion of the concept of the kingdom of God, see B. Chilton (ed.), *The Kingdom of God*.

64 None of the evangelists mentions the name of the mountain. But it seems obvious for geographical reasons that Mount Hermon is meant: the group was near Caesarea Philippi and Mount Hermon was within easy walking distance north-west of the villages where they had spent the previous time. It is definitely 'a high mountain' (Mk. 9:2; Mt. 17:1)—the highest anywhere in the vicinity (2,814 metres). And it had to be a 'high' mountain if Jesus wanted his disciples to understand the precedents set first of all by Moses on the high mountain Horeb in the Sinai and later by Elijah (Ex. 3:1–4:17; 24:15–18; 1 Kg. 19:11–18). Since it had been an ancient site of Baal worship (Jdg. 3:3), Jesus could also use it as a background against which his triumph over the kingdom of demons would be apparent once more.

See also Kopp, 300ff. A voice in favour of Mount Meron was raised by W. Liefield, 'Theological Motifs in the Transfiguration Narrative', in R. N.

Longenecker/M. C. Tenney (eds.), *New Dimensions in New Testament Studies* (Grand Rapids, 1974), 167, note 27.

65 Cf. W. Grundmann, *Das Evangelium nach Lukas* (Berlin, 3rd ed., 1966), 192.

66 Whereas Mark and Matthew expect their readers to understand the allusion, Luke expects his to understand that he is using a kind of compromise formula: '*About* eight days . . .'. That allows for a dual interpretation. For the inclusive method of counting (eight days=a week), cf. also Jn. 20:26.

67 There are of course 'metamorphoses' of gods into men or other beings (cf. Ovid, *Metamorphoseon;* Apuleius, *Metamorphoseon sive Asinus Aureus*) but, needless to say, they bear no resemblance whatsoever with what the New Testament is talking about. When Mark and the others wrote, most of this type of mythical story telling had not even seen the light of day.

However, Luke's acquaintance with the texts that did exist may well have prompted him to omit the word which could have caused misunderstandings among his educated readers (such as the dedicatee, Theophilus, himself). Instead, he simply says that 'the appearance of his face changed . . .'.

68 The supposed reference to 4 Ezra 9:97, where the motif of the face shining like the sun is used, seems difficult to maintain (*pace* Marshall, *Luke*, 383), unless it is regarded as an early example of Christian influence on Jewish apocalyptic, as 4 Ezra was written some time after Mark, Matthew and Luke.

69 Here is yet another instance where one may ask why Mark's sequence was changed by one or, as in this case, both of the other synoptics. In view of Mk. 8:28, Mark probably regarded it as natural to put Elijah first, as Moses was not even mentioned in that scene, and he was of course intimately linked with the coming of the Messiah. Matthew and Luke may have preferred the historical sequence, placing the representative of the law before the representative of the prophets.

70 After Jesus' ascension, another good reason for God's choice of Moses and Elijah as his messengers may have become apparent: both were credited with having been taken up into heaven, Elijah in 2 Kg. 2:11; Moses in the apocryphal 'Assumption of Moses'. Written in the late first century BC, this is alluded to by Stephen in his speech, Acts 7:36, in a passage which explains similarities between Moses and Jesus; by Paul, Rom. 1:25 and 9:16; and by Jude 9. Although the 'Assumption of Moses' was thus known to at least three New Testament writers, it is significant that they do not mention the actual assumption as such: in Christ's case, they dealt with an historical fact; with Moses, it was an apocryphal legend, and it would have been counter-productive to draw any parallels.

71 See W. Bauer, *Griechisch-Deutsches Wörterbuch zu den Schriften des Neuen Testaments und der übrigen urchristlichen Literatur*, (Berlin/New York, 6th ed., 1971), 362. As the word occurs here only in the NT, and nowhere in the LXX, parallels to explain its use have to be taken from secular literature.

72 Even if we take the Greek to mean that the three disciples had dozed off, the construction of Luke's sentence would not make it impossible for them to have been fully awake at least at the end of the conversation: Luke begins by saying (a) that Jesus was at prayer when the appearance of his face and his clothes changed; (b) Moses and Elijah appeared in glorious splendour; (c) they conversed with Jesus. Only then does Luke turn his attention to the disciples: (a) they had been very sleepy; (b) they became fully awake; (c)

they saw Jesus' glory and the two men standing with him. Methodologically, Luke would thus have reported two simultaneous events consecutively—the experience first of Jesus, then of the disciples. This allows the conclusion that Peter and the other two had felt sleep coming over them while Jesus was praying (a), but became fully awake when Moses and Elijah made their remarkable appearance (b) and began to pay full attention at some stage during the conversation (c).

73 'Exodus' in the sense of death is used in the apocryphal 'Wisdom of Solomon' (3:2; 7:6), a popular writing of the mid-second century BC which was known to Peter (cf. 1 Pet. 2:25 with *Wis.* 1:6; 1 Pet. 5:7 with *Wis.* 12:13; 2 Pet. 2:2 with *Wis.* 5:6 and 2 Pet. 2:7 with *Wis.* 10:6) and also to Luke who has twenty-two allusions, mostly indirect, to it (four in the gospel, eighteen in Acts; one such allusion occurs in a speech by Peter, at Acts 10:26/*Wis.* 7:1). As *Wis.* 3:2 shows, 'exodus' could mean death not merely in a terminal sense but as a transition to a new state, a meaning implicit in Lk. 9:31 and 2 Pet. 1:15.

Outside the Bible, but prior to the NT writings, Philo gives an example of 'exodus' meaning death in his *Virtutibus*, 77.

74 Luke does not use it anywhere. This is perfectly understandable, since his mainly Greek-speaking readers would not have understood it without explanation. He prefers one of the Greek synonyms, *epistatēs*, 'Master', which in fact only he uses. (When the other evangelists offer a 'translation' for Rabbi, it is *didaskalos*, 'teacher', but this is never used by the Twelve. For a discussion of forms of address, cf. Riesner, *Jesus*, 246–245).

75 For a detailed discussion of why the title of Jewish teachers acquired a special, higher connotation when used by the disciples, see F. Hahn, *Christologische Hoheitstitel* (Göttingen, 4th ed., 1974), discussed by Riesner, *Jesus*, 253–54.

76 Cf. C. H. Dodd, 'Jesus als Lehrer und Prophet', in F. K. A. Bell/ A. Deissmann, *Mysterium Christi* (Berlin, 1931), 67–86. Dodd argues (p. 69) that the preservation of the terms *rabbi* and *didaskalos*, inadequate for later theology, is proof of their historicity.

77 'Shelters'=NIV; AV has 'tabernacles'; RSV 'booths'. The Greek word *skēnē* had a wide range of meanings, from 'the tent of soldiers' or the 'dwelling-place of nomads' to the 'eternal dwellings' of Lk. 16:9. In the present context, several interpreters have seen a reference to the Feast of Tabernacles (for conclusions drawn from this interpretation, see Bonnard, op. cit., n. 48, 254). It is, however, much more plausible to assume that Peter, at a loss what to make of it all, wants Moses and Elijah to stay on for a while, with Jesus and with them; it is night; what could be more natural than to erect temporary shelters, the traditional type of leafy hut, for them and Jesus? While there certainly is an implicit eschatological element, Peter will not have grasped the full implications of *skēnē* when he used the word. If he was aware of the glory of the Lord that had filled the 'Tent of Meeting' in Ex. 40:34–35, he drew the wrong conclusions. (Cf. R. A. Cole, *The Gospel According to St. Mark* (London, 1961), 143.)

78 Luke rephrases the analysis: 'He did not know what he was saying' (9:33) and postpones the fear to the moment when Jesus, Moses and Elijah enter the cloud (9:34); Matthew places the moment of fear even later, when God addresses them (17:6).

79 The word employed by Matthew and Luke (*phobeomai*) conveys the same

meaning; Peter uses it in this sense in his first letter, 1 Pet. 2:17 ('Fear God!'), and Mark ends his whole gospel with it, *ephobounto gar* (16:8).

80 Luke's different apposition ('This is my son whom I have chosen. Listen to him.') is confirmed by some of the most valuable textual witnesses, p45, p75, Codex Sinaiticus (Aleph 01), Codex Vaticanus (B 03). A number of others, among them the Codex Alexandrinus (A 02), the Codex Ephraemi Rescriptus (C 04), the Codex Washingtonensis (W 032), Syriac, Coptic and Latin versions, as well as quotations by Tertullian, Clement and Epiphanius, have 'whom I love' (=/'beloved'), as in Mk. 9:7 and Mt. 17:5—and as Luke himself in 3:22, when the voice coming from heaven made a pronouncement foreshadowing the one in 9:35. The editors of *The Greek New Testament According to the Majority Text* saw good reason to reinstate *agapētos* in the main text (p. 221).

This does not answer the question why, when and by whom the participle *ho eklelegmenos* (which occurs only here in the NT) was chosen to rephrase God's words. Indeed, many later scribes did not understand it and changed it into the more familiar form *ho eklektos*. This does make sense, for the text would thus refer to OT prophecies of the Messiah as Servant (Is. 42:1; 44:1, where the word is used), and to those of the Son of Man (the apocryphal 1 Enoch 39:6 and fourteen other verses in 1 Enoch). The account of the transfiguration in 2 Pet. 1:17, is explicit that 'beloved', not 'chosen', was the word used by the voice. See below, p. 53.

Matthew adds, '. . . with him I am well pleased' (*en hō eudokēsa*) after 'whom I love'. Mark (and Luke) do not have this statement; it is, however, present in the Baptism voice at Mk. 1:11; Mt. 3:17; Lk. 3:22; and in 2 Pet. 1:17 it may be a conscious allusion to Is. 42:1.

81 Cf. (among the more recent ones), M. Green, op. cit. n. 2, 82, pointing to Mt. 24:30 as a parallel; E. Fuchs/P. Reymond, *La deuxième épître de Saint Pierre/L'épître de Saint Jude* (Neuchâtel, 1980), 68; R. J. Bauckham, *Jude/2 Peter* (Waco, 1983), 215.

82 Cf. Green, op. cit. n. 2, 83, n. 1.

83 See W. Dittenberger, *Sylloge Inscriptionum Graecarum* (4 vols., Leipzig, 3rd ed., 1915–24), III, 1052f. The use of *epoptēs* with this meaning is independently confirmed by Plutarch, 50 years after 2 Peter (*Lives*, 'Alcibiades' 22:4, published c. AD 115).

84 A title also given to Artemis, as we can see from Acts 19:27, 28b.

85 In the NT it also occurs in Lk. 9:43, for the greatness of God, and in Acts 19:27b, in the mouth of the pagan silversmith Demetrius, for the goddess Artemis (see above, n. 84).

86 It should not remain unnoticed that Paul uses *megalos Theos* of Christ in Tit. 2:13, in a context not unlike that of 2 Pet. 1:16: '. . . while we wait for the blessed hope—the glorious appearing of our great God and Saviour Jesus Christ'. He does so in a letter that pursues its own controversy with the myth-makers, even though of a different kind (1:14). Finally, Tit. 2:13, like 2 Pet. 1:17, also refers to Christ's *glory*, (*hē doxa*). Cf. Lk. 9:32 and Lk. 21:27 for the use of *doxa* to describe first the Transfiguration and then the Second Coming.

87 It is used in Dt. 33:26 and in 2 Macc. 8:15; 15:13; and in 3 Macc. 2:9, interestingly enough in a prayer of the high priest Simon, where it is followed immediately by the verse which has *epoptēs*, 'onlooker', for God (2:21)!

88 S. J. N. D. Kelly, *The Epistles of Peter and Jude* (London, 1969), 319.

89 Bauckham, op. cit. n. 81, 218.
90 Mark: *Houtos estin ho huios mou ho agapētos*. Peter (in the p72 and the Codex Vaticanus): *Ho huios mou ho agapētos mou houtos estin*.
91 Consequently, *The Greek New Testament According to the Majority Text* has reinstated the original wording, as given in Mk. 9:7.
92 Cf. Bauckham, op. cit. n. 81, 207–9.
93 This is not to say, of course, that 'my beloved one' could not itself be a Messianic title (cf. Mt. 12:18). But to construct this into 2 Pet. 1:17 is simply not warranted by the textual evidence.
94 There is in fact another difference of little significance: Peter constructs *eis hon ego eudokēsa*, instead of Matthew's *en hō eudokēsa*. *Ego* merely intensifies the verb; and the unfamiliar *eis hon* is quite possible in NT Greek as a synonym of *en hō*: cf. Mt. 12:18.
95 Cf. the point made by Bauckham, *op cit.* 207.
96 For *bebaioteron* as an elative ('very sure' or 'very firm', instead of the usual comparative 'more sure', 'more certain'), see Fuchs/Reymond, *Saint Pierre/Saint Jude*, 71–72; more elaborately J. H. Neyrey, 'The Apologetic Use of the Transfiguration in 2 Peter 1:16–21', in *Catholic Biblical Quarterly*, 42 (1980), 515.
97 See Ex. 30:11–16, 2 Chr. 24:6 and other, non-biblical texts. Cf. Bruce, *History*, 134. The half-shekel had the value of a two-drachma coin in the Attic 'Eurodollar' currency of the time (Mt. 17:24).
98 So Hill, op cit. n. 49, 271.
99 Bruce, *History*, 134.
100 It is on the political repartee in Mt. 22:21, not on the question about the temple tax, that Peter bases his call for obedience to the 'kings of the earth' in 1 Pet. 2:13, 17.
101 The Danish traveller A. Falk-Rønne witnessed the catch of such a stone-carrying fish in the Sea of Galilee a few years ago: *Auf Petrus' Spuren* (Frankfurt/Berlin/Wien, 1980), 51.
102 The story helps us to date Matthew's gospel: as the temple tax was abolished after the destruction of the temple in AD 70, or rather was turned by the Emperor Vespasian into a Roman tax dedicated to the temple of Jupiter Capitolinus (cf. Josephus, *War*, 7, 6:6), the gospel must be dated earlier than AD 70—to insert it after the destruction of the temple would have rendered it practically meaningless, as the 'moral' would have lost its whole point. For an analysis, see Robinson, *Redating*, 104–5. Robinson also quotes the Mishnah (Shekel 8:8): '(The laws concerning) the Shekel dues . . . apply only such time as the Temple stands.'
103 Cf. Strack/Billerbeck, op. cit. n. 54, I, 795–97; and H. Braun, *Spätjüdisch-häretischer und frühchristlicher Radikalismus* (Tübingen, 1957), II, 87.
104 Seven times=*heptakis*. Cf. Bauer, op. cit. n. 71, 605–6.
    In Luke's rendering of the same (or perhaps a similar) occasion, where Peter does not appear, Jesus himself uses the 'seven times' twice in this sense (Lk. 17:4).
105 A. H. McNeile, *The Gospel According to St. Matthew* (London, 1915), 268, remarks that the unlimited spirit of vengeance represented by Gn. 4:24 has given way to 'the unlimited forgiveness of Christians'.
106 Characteristically, Matthew has an additional sentence: 'What then will there be for us?' (19:27).
107 One should not be too surprised to find the word translated as 'gospel', *euangelion*, on Jesus' lips before the first gospel was written: Jesus had used

it before in 8:35, and in the sense of 'good news', it had been in use since Homer and can be found in the LXX (cf. 2 Sa. 4:10; 18:22, 25).

108 Cf. Lane, op. cit. n. 44, 372.

109 It may also have reminded the disciples of the persecutions suffered by the prophets: cf. La. 3:19. *et al.*

110 Cf. Bailey, *Poet and Peasant*; Riesner, *Aufbau*, 172–182.

The particular saying, Mk. 10:31, was a favourite one of Jesus: it occurs not only in the Matthean parallel, 19:30, but also in Mk. 9:35, Mt. 20:16 and Lk. 13:30.

111 *Tis ho sōzomenos plousios?* 21:4–7. The English translation is quoted from 'The Rich Man's Salvation', in Clement of Alexandria, ed. and trans. F. W. Butterworth (London, 1919), 315.

Clement's commentary is of textual interest for a variant reading of Mk. 10:30 (What Rich Man? 4:10; 25:1), only found elsewhere in the Codex Bezae Cantabrigensis (D05), and old Latin versions (Vercellensis, Veronensis, Corbeiensis II, as well as the early Vulgate), so-called Western witnesses, which make the passage mean that there is no point in having possessions in time of persecution.

112 For a comparison of the Christians to the 'twelve tribes' in the diaspora, the 'dispersion', see 1 Pet. 1:1. In Peter's view, the characteristics of the people of Israel are now those of the Christians. Cf. also Jas. 1:1.

113 Peter would inevitably have been reminded of his dialogue with Jesus about forgiveness (Mt. 18:21–22, see above p. 57). The final verse of the fig tree passage, v. 26, is omitted from most modern translations, as several old textual witnesses do not have it. (E.g. the Codex Sinaiticus, the Codex Vaticanus, some other codices, minuscules, and several Latin, Syriac, and Coptic translations.) It has been regarded as a gloss under the influence of Mt. 6:15 (cf. H. F. D. Sparks, 'The Doctrine of the Divine Fatherhood in the Gospels', in D. E. Nineham (ed.), *Studies in the Gospels* (Oxford, 1955), 243–5. This may be so—notwithstanding the fact that an overwhelming number of manuscripts, beginning with the Codex Alexandrinus, include it—but in spite of its Matthean character, it is certainly a fitting conclusion to the passage, and a thought which would not have been alien to Mark's informant Peter (see beginning of note). Hodges and Farstad reinstate it in *The Greek New Testament According to the Majority Text*, 152.

Peter's exclamation is dropped by Matthew in his account, which is condensed and has changed its location (Mt. 21:18–22); Luke has no parallel but gives a different story with a similar message, also without mentioning Peter (Lk. 13:6–9). As Luke's parable is about a fig tree in a a vineyard, an additional allusion to Is. 5:1–7 in the context of God's judgement becomes possible.

114 *Hist.* 5,8:2. He did not like the Christians, either, calling their faith an *exitiabilis superstitio*, 'a pernicious superstition', in his account of the persecutions after the Fire of Rome, *Ann.* 15, 44:2.

115 Many attempts have been made to dissect the discourse into elements belonging to different parts of Jesus' ministry or to Mark's own redaction. (E.g. W. Marxsen, *Mark the Evangelist* (Nashville, 1969), 151–206; V. Taylor, *The Gospel According to St. Mark* (London, 2nd ed., 1969), 522–5; G. R. Beasley-Murray. The unity of the speech must however be regarded as safely established from the literary critical point of view; cf. France, 227–39; Lane, op. cit. n. 44, 444–450; Bassin, op. cit. n. 44, 254–56.

116 There is a striking parallel between 2 Peter and Matthew's account of the discourse on the Mount of Olives, which is all the more remarkable as Matthew does not name Peter—or any of the other disciples—in that scene. Apart from the usual differences in the wording, two of the additions have a Petrine quality: there is the reference to Noah and the flood (Mt. 24:37–39), the only one in the gospels (outside the isolated parallel Lk. 17:26–27), which is also used by Peter in 1 Pet. 3:20 and 2 Pet. 2:5 (cf. Heb. 11:7). There is also the oblique reference to the day of the Lord coming like a thief in the night: Mt. 24:42–44/2 Pet. 3:10, cf. 1 Thes. 5:2 and the displaced Lukan parallel to Matthew, Lk. 12:30–40. The latter parallel in Luke is particularly interesting, as it offers an idiomatic near-parallel to 1 Peter (cf. Lk. 12:35/ 1 Pet. 1:13), and as it is followed by a question from Peter (Lk. 12:41), 'Lord, are you telling this parable to us, or to everyone?' This is a characteristic 'spokesman's question', which is answered here by the parable of the absent householder (cf. Mk. 13:33–37; Mt. 24:43–51) which Luke places before the entry into Jerusalem (19:28), as he had already done with the Noah episode (see above). Luke has of course preserved the discourse on the end times (21:5–36), like Matthew without naming any disciples. As may be seen by looking at the evidence, he has also drawn on different incidents, probably a *public* speech made by Jesus on the same subject (cf. Marshall, op. cit. n. 9, 759–62).

117 On the cosmic catastrophe in 2 Pet. 3, its literary precedents and successors, see Thiede, *Pagan.*

118 For recent interpretations of 2 Pet. 3, see also Bénétreau, 288–348; Riesner, *Petrusbrief*, 124–43.

119 Or so the modern tourist might think at first glance. It is however possible that the gesture refers to the second part of the scene, and signifies his erroneous understanding: 'I see, Lord—not just the feet, but my hands and my head as well!'

120 For the most desperate attempts to turn John's account into an anti-Petrine polemic, see G. F. Snyder, op. cit. n. 62, and A. H. Maynard.

121 AV 'supper being ended' is wrong; for even if the alternative manuscript reading *genomenou* instead of *ginomenou* is correct, it is an inceptive aorist ('supper having been served'). There is no doubt that the meal continued after the washing of the feet: see v. 26!

122 *lention* was found in rabbinical usage also. As a Latin loan-word, it may have
come to Palestine with the Romans. Bauer, op. cit. n. 71, 932, offers the intriguing information that the *Vita Aesopi* (I 61) tells of a woman going to wash another woman's feet and uses the same term for the towel she wraps around her waist. This lexicographical detail is all the more remarkable if one adds to it that the *Life of Aesop*, originally not much later than John's gospel, received a revision by the rhetor Libanios in the fourth century, who, although himself anything but a Christian, had John Chrysostom, Basil the Great and Gregory of Nyssa among his students. The possibility exists that the near-identical idiom crept into the novel because of a Christian influence; could it be safely established, it would be yet another example of the influence Christian teaching had on hellenistic secular literature (another one is the 'empty tomb' story in Chariton's novel *Chaireas and Kallirrhoe*, a work of the early second century; cf. C. P. Thiede, 'Die Glaubwürdigkeit der neutestamentlichen Schriften', *Factum* 11/12 (1979), 19–20).

123 For further discussion, see L. Morris, *Studies in the Fourth Gospel* (Grand Rapids, 1969), 246f; Guthrie, op. cit. n. 32, 245–49; cf. also Robinson, *Redating*, 310.
124 Cf. Morris, op. cit. n. 61, 169–170.
125 Mark ends his depiction of the Lord's Supper with the traditional singing of the Passover-Hallel section of the Psalter (Psalms 113–118), perhaps only the last one (*a* hymn writes Mark, 14:26, followed in this by Matthew, 26:30), which would have been particularly appropriate, as it contains a note of final triumph; see Ps. 118:17, 22–24. He then writes that they went out to the Mount of Olives. Lane, op. cit. n. 44, 510, has pointed out that the following section, 14:27–31 (the prediction of the denial), interrupts the flow of the narrative; v. 32 would follow more naturally immediately after v. 26. To Lane, it remains difficult to determine whether this paragraph depicts an event taking place in the upper room or on the way to Gethsemane. One might tentatively suggest that Mark wishes it to be seen in the context of the meal and that he has set it in a separate paragraph precisely in order to underline its individual importance, which would otherwise have interrupted the careful structure of the preceding sequence on the institution of the Lord's Supper. Matthew, who follows Mark's order, has a word which is significantly missing from Mark, *tote* (Mt. 26:36), which is usually translated as 'then', but should perhaps rather be rendered by 'at that time', as in 2:17; 3:5; 3:13, where it is clearly used to describe concurrent events, in the sense of Matthew's alternative *en ekeinō tō kairō*. In other words, Mark does not state explicitly when the event took place, and Matthew, understanding Mark's concern, tries to help by inserting *tote* to signify that it was not a consecutive, but a concurrent one.
   Both John (13:36–38) and Luke (22:31–34) make it quite clear, at any rate, that the prediction of the denial took place indoors, and there are no stringent reasons to assume that Mark disagrees. To see him as disagreeing, however, could have been a case in point for the famous, early second century remark of Papias, that Mark did not report certain events in their correct chronological order (*ou mentoi taxei*, in Eusebius, *HE* 3, 19, 15).
126 The Roman satirist Juvenal, writing some 50 years after Mark, confirms this usage as idiomatic: 'Yet what that one does at the second crow of the rooster, the nearest grocer knows it before daybreak' (*quod tamen ad cantum galli fecit ille secundi/proximus ante diem caupo sciet . . .*). *Sat.* 9, 107–08.
127 On Satan's role see F. I. Andersen, *Job. An Introduction and Commentary* (Leicester, 1976), 82–83; W. Foerster, art. *Satanas, Theological Dictionary of the New Testament* (Grand Rapids, 1971) VII , 151–63; and H. Bietenhard, art. 'Satan', *Theologisches Begriffslexikon zum Neuen Testament* (Wuppertal, 2nd ed., 1979), II, 1057–64.
128 Stauffer, *Petrus*, 16.
129 Cf. Cicero, *Ad Att.* 5, 11.19; *Ad Fam.* 13.3, on Epicurus and the Epicureans. Cf. also the grove-like Lyceum of Socrates and Aristotle, and Plato's olive in the valley of the Kephissos (see D. B. Thompson/R. E. Griswold, *Garden Lore of Ancient Athens* (Princeton, 1963), 6–7).
130 Cf. Riesner, *Jesus*, 356.
131 The attempt of G. Vermes, *Jesus the Jew* (London, 2nd ed., 1977), 210–11, to demonstrate that God was *Abba* for a charismatic like Chanin Hanechba, falls flat, as the text from the Babylonian Talmud, Ta'anith 23b, says nothing of the sort: the school-children(!) come to Chanin, call him *Abba* and ask him to give them rain, whereupon he says to God: 'Lord of the Universe

(!), do it for the sake of those who cannot yet distinguish between an *abba* who can give rain and an *abba* who cannot give rain.' In other words, Chanin simply copies the 'abba' the children had used to address *him* without employing it in any way to speak to God: for him, God is, as he would be for any praying Jew, the 'Lord of the Universe'. Chanin's means of addressing God proves the very opposite of what Vermes wants it to.

132 Lane, op. cit. n. 44, 520, suggests, following earlier exegesis, that the spirit is not man's own spirit fighting against the weakness of the flesh, but God's Holy Spirit who is the source of power in a time of crisis—as indicated in Ps. 51:12b.

133 For an interesting foray into this area, see also Black, *Aramaic*, 225.

134 Even so, the editors of *The Greek New Testament According to the Majority Text* have found enough textual evidence to keep them in their place. Among the witnesses one could list the Codex Aleph (the Sinaiticus) and its first corrector (the second corrector has omitted them), the Bezae Canta-brigiensis (D05), the Parisianus (K017), the Regius (L019), the Monaclusis (X033), the Sangallensis (Δ037), the Koridethianus (Θ038), the Petropolitanus (Π041), the Athous Laurensis (Ψ044), as well as several minuscules and Church Fathers.

135 John, who had chosen other prayers of Jesus in the last chapter of his long section following the prediction of Peter's denial (14–17), goes straight into the arrest at the beginning of ch. 18.

136 This reconstruction of the composition of the armed crowd presupposes a particular understanding of the Greek words used by John for what has been translated by 'temple guard' (*speira*) and 'commanding officer of the temple guard' (*chiliarchos*). It is based on the assumption that the normal NT meanings of these words, 'Roman cohort' or 'maniple', and its commanding officer, could not apply here, as the participation of Roman officials at the arrest of Jesus was highly unlikely. Would a Roman officer have taken orders from Jewish priests (Jn. 18:12, 24)? Would they not have taken a prisoner straight to a Roman prison instead of to the house of Annas (Jn. 18:13)? Furthermore, Pilate did not appear to know anything about the arrest when Jesus was finally taken to him (Jn. 18:29–31). This case, strongly argued by Blinzler, 87–101 etc., and accepted by (among others) Lane, op. cit. n. 44, 524, has its problems which should not be overlooked: without exception, the term *speira* is used for Roman contingents in the New Testament, remarkably so in the aftermath of the arrest: cf. Mk. 15:16/Mt. 27:27, and also Acts 10:1; 21:31; 27:1. And with one exception (Mk. 6:21, where it is used for officers of Herod), *chiliarchos* always describes the leader of such a unit, originally of the rank of a military tribune. It is, however, true that John uses both words only here, so that one cannot compare his usage to other occurrences in his own gospel, and it is also true that when he speaks of Roman soldiers elsewhere, he uses the term *stratiōtai*, 'soldiers' (Jn. 19:2, 23, 24, 32, 34). Even so, it is noteworthy that he would seem to ignore the accepted usage of his contemporaries. Flavius Josephus, born some 40 years after John but writing not much later than he (the *Jewish War* was published between AD 75 and AD 79, the *Antiquities* followed c. AD 93) is a contemporary Jewish witness for the use of both terms for Jewish forces, in his description of actions undertaken by Archelaus, the son of Herod and Malthake: *War* 2, 1:3 (cf. 2, 20:7), and *Ant.* 17, 9:3. Strictly speaking, however, this confirms Mk. 6:21 rather than a non-Roman interpretation of Jn. 18:3, 12. If one adds to this that Roman co-operation with local

authorities in matters of policing, even acting on request of the locals, was in accordance with Roman law (see Bickermann, 172) and was carried out regularly (cf. Wenger, 288), the case against Roman involvement is weakened considerably. A Roman contingent at the arrest of Jesus would not contradict Mark, Matthew and Luke, who say only that the armed group was sent on behalf of the Sanhedrin, the Jewish court of law, which would be historically correct. That the leader of the detachment acted on orders from the Jews during and after the arrest is equally plausible historically. And Pilate was not as ill-informed as he is made out to be: Jn. 18:29–31 simply and accurately tells us that, having obligingly helped out with some soldiers, probably because the Sanhedrin had told him of the threat Jesus offered, Pilate now wants to find out if their interrogation has confirmed their suspicions: was there a legal charge to be answered?

If it was a Jewish detachment after all, it can, according to Blinzler, only have been the temple guard, but there is no corroborative evidence for the terminology. If it was a Roman contingent, it was probably part of (not the whole: *totum pro parte!*) cohort stationed at the fortress Antonia next to the temple (cf. E. A. Abbott, *Johannine Grammar* (London, 1905), 1994b: John uses the definitive article, *the* cohort).

137 In Luke's account, *two* of the disciples ask Jesus if they should draw the swords which they had had for some time, but only one acts, without waiting for the answer (Lk. 22:49, cf. Lk. 22:38). The disciples had not understood his figurative language predicting the dangers ahead (Lk. 22:36–37); his reply in 22:38b, 'That is enough', was not a comment on the number of swords they already had, but a way of telling them to stop talking like that.

138 *Heis de tis* (Mk. 14:47) and *heis tis* (Lk. 22:50) means 'a certain one', in the sense of 'one we know but do not want to identify': cf. the usage in Sophocles, *Oedipus Rex*, 118, where Kreon, in his conversation with Oedipus, calls the known witness who had survived Oedipus' killing of his father *heis tis*. Cf. Mk. 14:51 (!).

139 It is of course the very same reason that prevents Luke from identifying 'the other place' in Acts 12:17, when Peter had just become an escaped prisoner on the run.

140 E.g. Morris, op. cit. n. 61, 745, n. 16.

141 See Daube, 59–62.

142 The case of the young man who tried to follow Jesus but was apprehended and fled naked (Mk. 14:51) has remained unsolved. The church fathers are divided—some think it was the evangelist himself, who appends his signature in this way, while others state that Mark never met Jesus personally (cf. Weiss, 405–7). It depends entirely on how far one wants to go in piecing together the available information. The 'certain young man' (see above, n. 138) was known to the evangelist; he was no disciple, but a follower who had been alarmed and had not the time to dress properly: underneath his outer garment he was naked. The piece of clothing is described as a *sindōn*, a valuable linen, which points to a well-to-do owner. Mark's family owned a house in Jerusalem which became the meeting place of the first Christians (Acts 1:13/12:12) and which may well have been the place where the Last Supper had taken place (cf. Weiss, as above, and Bruce, op. cit. n. 30, 73 and 246–7). One does not have to go as far as suggesting that Mark's father was the owner of the olive grove Gethsemane at the Mount of Olives (cf. Wenham, *Easter*, 47) to see that a case can be

made for the identification of the young man as the evangelist. Bassin, op. cit. n. 44, 276, is the most recent author to assert that the text demands neither this interpretation nor that of an eschatological prophecy from Am. 2:16 (or Gn. 39:12), let alone that of seeing in the young man the symbolical young Christian initiate (cf. R. Scroggs/K. I. Groff, 'Baptism in Mark. Dying and Rising with Christ', *Journal of Biblical Literature* 92 (1973), 531–48). For Bassin, the passage has no special significance and is merely yet another 'memory of Peter's'.

143 That this pedigree shows John to have been a relative of Jesus—which helps to understand why he was the so-called beloved disciple—does not concern us here. Cf. for some recent material on the family relationships of Jesus, Wenham, *Easter*, 34–36 and 132–139.

144 Brownrigg, 85–88, explains the fact that John was *personally* known to the acting high priest and to his servants by the interesting theory that 'the firm of "Zebedee and Sons, of Galilee" ' was contracted to supply fish to the high priest's palace in Jerusalem. However, Peter himself would have been a leading partner in this business: cf. Lk. 5:10!

145 See, for example, Stier, 49–57, 135–42, 151.

146 *Emblepō* can be translated by 'to look straight, closely at . . .'; but it may also quite simply mean 'to look at', as in Mk. 10:21, 27. It does not necessarily imply an inquisitive look.

147 RSV and NIV do not include the crowing of the cock in v. 68b, as it is omitted by several textual witnesses, among them the Codex Sinaiticus and Codex Vaticanus. It is, however, retained by the Codex Alexandrinus (A02), Ephraemi Rescriptus (C04), the Bezae Cantabrigiensis (D05), and other independent codices, together with more than twenty minuscules and most translations, and it appears to be demanded by 14:72, where the cock crows for the second time (and only the Sinaiticus, together with the Regius (L019) omits this second crowing, too).

148 Lane, op. cit. n. 44, 542, suggests that Peter's first denial is made according to the form common in rabbinical law for a formal, legal denial—cf. Mishnah Shebuoth 8:3 and 6, and 'Testament of Joseph' 13:1.

149 At first sight, the general outline of John's account seems to imply that Jesus was taken to Caiaphas after Peter's first denial. Like the others, however, John is reporting two simultaneous events (hearing and denials) consecutively, only with a different technique and differentiating between two hearings. Thus there is no conflict. Within John's own account, it is remarkable that nothing is said about what happened before Caiaphas. This led different scribes to adopt different solutions, e.g. placing v. 24 after v. 13, so that the hearing would have taken place in front of Caiaphas, after a courteous detour via the house of Annas. It seems, however, that all four gospels refer to a hearing before Annas (nowhere in Mark, Matthew and Luke is the high priest and questioner identified as Caiaphas, and Jn. 18:19 points to the use of the title for Annas, too: cf. v. 19 with v. 13—a usage confirmed by Jn. 18:35; Lk. 3:2 and Acts 4:6, as well as, by analogy, Josephus, *War* 4, 3:8 with 4, 3:10!). He will have been sent to Caiaphas with the results of that hearing, whereupon Caiaphas, who, as the legally acting high priest, had the responsibility of decision, and sent him to Pilate (Jn. 19:28) at the earliest opportunity. One should not be too surprised at the importance thus given to Annas: for tradition-conscious Jews, he was still the real high priest, though he had been removed from office by the Roman governor Valerius Gratus, Pilate's immediate predecessor. (See Josephus,

Ant. 18, 2:2). Caiaphas seems to have been keen on playing second fiddle for tactical reasons (he must have been a more than average diplomat, otherwise he would not have survived in his job for nineteen years (AD 18–37) under two governors). First, he planted the idea of an indictment of Jesus into the minds of the Sanhedrin (Jn. 11:49–51), then he withdrew into the background until the situation was clear enough for him to act officially, i.e., after the initial hearing before Annas. Although he would normally have presided over sessions of the Sanhedrin, exceptions were possible (cf. Edersheim, I, 264), and we must not forget that this session at night was very unusual and untraditional anyway. It is equally unnecessary to assume that Mark means all seventy-one members of the Sanhedrin when he says (14:53 and 55) that the whole Sanhedrin was assembled: cf. Mk. 1:5 for his *totum pro parte* technique. According to the Mishnah, twenty-three members were sufficient to constitute a quorum (see M. Wolff, 'De samenstelling en het karakter van het groote synedrion te Jeruzalem voor het jaar 70 n Chr', *Theologisch Tijdschrift* 51 (1917), 299–320, referred to by Lane, op. cit. n. 44, 531).

150 Mark does not specify where Peter broke down; Matthew and Luke state that it was 'outside', and that he wept *bitterly*.

151 For a recent, debatable attempt to disentangle the identities of these women mentioned in a non-uniform way by the four evangelists, see Wenham, *Easter,* 23–67. Stauffer, *Jesus,* 104, has pointed out that Jesus put Mary under John's protection in the formal language of traditional Jewish family law.

152 For a recent summary of archaeological results, see Riesner, *Golgotha,* 21–25: 'From up there', Riesner writes, referring to the Second Wall, 'one could indeed watch the gruesome spectacle as from the circles of an amphitheatre.'

153 The use of 'tree', literally 'wood' or 'piece of wood' (*xulon*) for the cross as gibbet is peculiar to these five NT passages. It is based on an OT precedent (Dt. 21:22–23) and has a parallel in the Qumran writings: cf. 11Q Temple Scroll 64:6–13. (See Fitzmyer, *Crucifixion,* 493–513).

154 Gospel of Peter 7:26, in E. Hennecke (ed.), *New Testament Apocrypha,* (London 2nd ed., 1973), I. 185.

155 Josephus, *Ant.* 4, 8:15 relates as Mosaic law that 'one witness shall not suffice, but there must be three or at least two, whose love of the truth is vouched for by the irreproachable life they lead; and the witness of women shall not be admissible because of the frivolity and imprudence typical of their sex.' See also Mishna Rosh Ha-Shanah 1:8, etc. The mere fact that all four gospels tell of the initial revelation of the Resurrection as given to women in spite of this is of course proof of the historicity of the event in itself. In addition, it is a further reminder of the special esteem in which Jesus held women.

156 Cf.Hengel, *Probleme,* 264, n. 97. For a recent discussion, see Bassin, op. cit., n. 44, 59–65.

157 The oft-repeated theory that a sentence, let alone a whole work, cannot end with *gar* has been due to insufficient knowledge of Greek literature. Recent evaluation of texts has shown examples in Plotinus (Enneads V:5, last sentence *Teleioteron gar*); Menander (*Dyscolos* 437–8, *nai ma ton Dia/To goun probaton mikrou tethnēke gar*); Musonius Rufus (Discourse XII, end: *gnōrimon gar*). See K. Aland, 'Der Schluss des Markusevangeliums', in M. Sabbe (ed.), *L'Évangile selon Marc. Tradition et rédaction* (Gembloux, 1974), 435–470; Lane, op. cit. n. 44, 583; F. W. Danker, 'Menander and the New Testament', in *New Testament Studies* 10 (1964), 365–8.

This seemingly abrupt ending of Mark is consistent with certain aspects of his style, in particular his brevity in ending a report; cf. 5:20; 12:12; and the emphasis on the 'holy uncanny' (cf. p. 49 and n. 79 above on Mk. 9:6, and p. 74 on Mk. 14:40); and generally the element of fear: cf. Mk. 4:41, 5:15; 5:33; 5:36; 6:50; 9:32; 10:32; 11:18. For 'abrupt' endings in other writings, see the Pentateuch, ending *before* its culmination, the acquisition of Canaan, and even the Gospel of John, ending without the oft-predicted Ascension (cf. Jn. 14:3, 28; 16:5–7, 17; 20:17).

Without going into the textual-critical details of the later date of the shorter and longer additional endings, one point seems noteworthy to the observer looking at the gospel from a Petrine point of view: neither the shorter additional ending, transmitted on its own only in one Old Latin version, the Codex Bobiensis, nor the longer ending, which has a vast number of textual witnesses to its credit but is equally non-Marcan in style and form, add anything to our knowledge of Peter's role after the Resurrection: Peter is not even mentioned in the longer ending, and all the shorter addition has to say is that the women reported the news of the empty tomb 'to Peter and those with him'—but this is merely a logical consequence of 16:7! If any of the additional endings had come into being in Mark's time and under Peter's own authority, such an omission would be difficult to explain.

For other contributions to the debate, see Horst, *Can a Book;* Boomershine/Bartholomew; and, in favour of the longer ending, Farmer; Wenham, *Easter,* 45–46 and 147–48.

Even if the longer ending is a non-Marcan addition, it is, as its contents betray, very early and uninfluenced by later theological reflection. One has to allow with Brown/Donfried/Reumann, 71, that it is canonical. Metzger emphasized its importance as we have it: 'Since Mark was not responsible for the composition of the last twelve verses (. . .), and since they undoubtedly had been attached to the Gospel before the Church recognized the fourfold Gospels as canonical, it follows that the New Testament contains not four but five evangelic accounts of events subsequent to the Resurrection of Christ (Metzger, *The Text* 229).

158 It goes without saying that 16:8b does not mean that they did not tell anyone anything at all, otherwise we would not have this gospel account. They quite literally did not tell anyone they were not meant to; but once they had got over their initial trembling and bewilderment of v. 8a, they would have looked for the disciples at once, as Jn. 20:3 implies. For a recent analysis of the Empty Tomb accounts and the role of the women in them, see Craig, *Historicity.*

159 RSV omits Lk. 24:12. It is however extremely well attested. (The only ancient witnesses without it are the Bezae Cantabrigiensis D05, six variant Latin translations, Palestinian Syriac manuscripts, the heretic Marcion, and Tatian in his *Diatessaron.*) In view of the overwhelming evidence of all textual witnesses in favour of v. 12, reasons suggested for its omission are inevitably rather far-fetched. The untenable claim that Lk. 24:12 is too close to Jn. 20:6–7 to be originally Lucan, is one of them. AV and NIV are right in retaining v. 12.

160 For a detailed analysis of the correct technical meaning of *othonia, soudarion* and *sindōn,* see Feuillet.

161 This, at any rate, is what the Greek text suggests, see Feuillet, 18–21.

162 Cf. Marshall, op. cit. n. 9, 893.

163 This is, of course, a conclusive argument against the oft-repeated contention that Christ appeared only to those who believed in him anyway. We need not mention Paul and James, who came to faith after a long time of doubt, and, in Paul's case, open enmity: even the closest circle of followers had to be convinced first. For a recent analysis of the kind of doubt expressed by some on the mountain of Mt. 28:17, see K. Grayston, 'The Translation of Matthew 28:17', *JSNT* 21 (1984), 105–9.

164 Some writers suggest that this incident is derived from Lk. 5:1–11 (or vice versa), or that both go back to a common source of one single event (cf., for example, Brown/Donfried/Reumann, 114–119, 140–141). Such fragmentation is entirely unwarranted by the textual evidence. As should be obvious to any literary historian worth his spectacles, the differences are much more numerous and also much more important content-wise than the similarities, all of which are to be expected because of the comparable work situation and locality. The setting as such is historically plausible to begin with: the disciples had merely followed a command of Jesus when they went back to their roots.

165 Attempts have been made to explain the symbolism, if any, behind the number 153. If there is one, John gives us no clue. The most 'ingenious' explanation is one connected with the ichthyological expertise of a Galilean fisherman: according to Jerome, the late second-century (i.e. post-Johannine) writer Oppianos of Cilicia, author of the only extant Greek treaty on fishing, wrote that there were 153 different kinds of fish. All of these, Jerome says in his commentary on Ez. 47:9–12, were caught by the apostles. The 153 fish would thus symbolize the mission 'to all nations'. The problem is that this reference does not occur in our extant text of Oppianos, nor in any other ancient writer, and that it conflicts with the great natural historian Pliny the Elder, an exact contemporary of the NT writers (he was killed by the eruption of Vesuvius in AD 79), who claims that there were only 74 known kinds of fish (*Natural History* 9, 43). For this and a list of other more or less far-fetched allegorisations of '153', see W. F. Howard, *The Fourth Gospel in Recent Criticism and Interpretation* (rev. C. K. Barrett, London, 1955), 184, and Morris, op. cit. n. 61, 867, n. 28.

166 As in the earlier instance, Jn. 1:42, the three appellations of Peter as 'Son of John' (*ho huios Iōannou*) are not shared by all textual witnesses; some important ones, such as the Codex Alexandrinus (A02) have 'Jonah' (*Iōna*) instead. Among the important codices, only the Alexandrinus (A02) and Athous Laurensis (Ψ044) are consistent in their use (cf., however, the verdict in favour of *Iōna* in both passages by the editors of *The Greek New Testament According to the Majority Text*).

An original *Iōna* would confirm the usage of Mt. 16:17, and since our earliest witnesses, the p66, p75 and the Codex Siniaticus, have *Iōannēs*, critical opinion tends to assume that the 'majority text' is a later adaptation to Matthew.

John, as a life-long colleague, must have known who Peter's father was; there remains the question whether *Iōna* or *Iōannēs* is the original form (*Iōna* can at any rate be explained satisfactorily only as an abbreviation for *Iōannēs*). The emphatic, formal address of Jn. 21:15–17 makes it quite impossible that the other two instances, Mt. 16:17 and Jn. 1:42, could either refer to the OT prophet Jonah, or be an epithet for 'terrorist' (cf. n. 49 above).

167 There has been much debate whether the pairs of different words used for 'love', 'sheep' and 'tend' have any deep exegetical significance, and

opinions continue to differ. Peter uses *phileō* throughout for his love; Jesus uses *agapaō* in the first two questions and then switches to Peter's *phileō* in the last one. Both words are used interchangeably by John in his gospel—cf. Jn. 11:5 and Jn. 13:23, 19:26 with Jn. 20:2, etc; and Jn. 3:35 with Jn. 5:20, etc. If one wishes to press the point, *phileō* is generally the wider, all-encompassing term, whereas *agapaō* tends to imply a more reverential love. (This is how the Vulgate sees it, using *diligo* for *agapaō* and *amo* for *phileō*). Peter insists on his all-encompassing love for Jesus, and Jesus takes this up in his final, decisive, conclusive question. It is, however, much more probable that this is just the attempt of two speakers (and indeed their chronicler) to employ synonyms for the sake of variation, as we would all probably do in a conversation where the same thing has to be said several times.

　　The different words for the members of the flock, *arnia* (v. 15, 'lambs', but also 'sheep' and even 'rams'), and *probata* (v. 16 and 17, 'sheep' or even *probatia*, 'little sheep', as in the Codex Vaticanus B03 and the Ephraemi Rescriptus C04 for v. 16, and in the Codex Alexandrinus (A02), the Vaticanus and the Ephraemi Rescriptus for v. 17) appear to support the view that the words are synonyms, as much as the words for 'feeding', *boskō* (vv. 15, 17), which means quite explicitly the tending of sheep (or lambs) in Greek literature, and 'tending', *poimainō*, (v. 16), which is the more technical term for the tending of a flock and is used as such, e.g., by Peter in 1 Pet. 5:2.

168　E. M. Blaiklock, *The Acts of the Apostles* (London and Grand Rapids, 1959), 89. For a more recent assessment, see Marshall, *Luke*, 1979.
169　For a detailed survey, see Plümacher.
170　Cf. Eusebius, *HE* 2, 25:5; 3, 1:3, *et al*; see also pp. 185–91 below on the context of Peter's death.
　　　There is, of course, no parallel between the 'abrupt' ending of Mark and that of Acts. Mark stops short of reporting the culmination of Jesus' ministry, his resurrection (or rather the resurrection appearances). Paul's death would not have been the triumphant conclusion to Acts, it would have been an obligatory historical datum, like the deaths of Stephen (Acts 7:60) and of James (Acts 12:2), had it happened by the time Luke wrote. For the death of James, the 'brother of the Lord', see Josephus 20, 9:1.
171　Attempts to argue this away have signally failed time and again. Even the famous 'Theudas' episode (Acts 5:36), allegedly based on Josephus *Ant.* 20, 5:1, published in c.AD 93), is inconclusive. Luke and Josephus are so different in their relative accounts, that any dependence, even a reference to the same person, is less than likely. The mere fact that Gamaliel, portrayed here in a situation that cannot have taken place later than AD 36, refers to Theudas (the Theudas of Josephus rose against the Romans c. AD 45), settles the matter. Cf. also A. von Harnack, *Date of Acts and the Synoptic Gospels* (London, 1911), 114–5, and below, n. 206.
172　Surprises can never be ruled out. The identification of a papyrus fragment of Mk. 6:52–53 from c. AD 50 (see n. 3 above) is a case in point. The *tentative* identification of a fragment from Acts 27:38 from the same seventh cave at Qumran, archaeologically to be dated before AD 68 (when the caves were sealed) and suggested by O'Callaghan (*Tres probables*), should serve as a gentle reminder.
173　The evangelists do not report in detail any of the missionary expeditions of the disciples (cf. Mk. 6:7–13, 30; Lk. 9:2–6, 10), but the overall evidence

points to such a verbal imparting of Jesus' teaching, see Lk. 19:31, 34, where the disciples answer a question by repeating literally what Jesus had said to them. The same verbal identity of message and repetition is implied by Lk. 22:10–11; Mk. 14:13–14. For a discussion of this custom in the New Testament (cf. also Lk. 7:18–20!) see G. Theissen, *Soziologie der Jesusbewegung. Ein Beitrag zur Entstehungsgeschichte des Urchristentums* (Munich, 1977), 87; Riesner, *Jesus*, 467–471.

174 Bruce, *Men*, 19, suggests that the doubly anarthrous Greek title should be translated as '(Some) Acts of (some) Apostles'. This would make sense grammatically and it would solve the problem why not all the apostles and only some of their actions are portrayed in the book—whoever first affixed that title to the first scroll of this book must, after all, have known that it did not contain *the* acts of *the* apostles. However, a caveat is demanded by the evidence of our earliest extant NT papyrus preserving the title of the work, the p66, written c.150 (for the date see H. Hunger, 'Zur Datierung des Bodmer II', *Anzeiger der phil hist. Klasse der Österr. Akad. d. Wiss*, 4 (1960), 12–23; R. Seider, *Paläographie der griechischen Papyri* (Stuttgart, 1970), II, 121), heads John's gospel with EUANGELION KATA IOANNEN, i.e. without the definite article. Cf. also Hengel, *Evangelienüberschriften*.

175 The number '120', even though it is explicitly only approximate, could be meant to comply with Jewish law requiring a minimum of 120 Jewish men to establish a community with its own council (Marshall, *The Acts of the Apostles* (Leicester, 1980), 64); but it is difficult to see why the constitution of a community was required for the election of a twelfth apostle—none of the other Petrine or apostolic decisions, such as sending Peter and James to Samaria (Acts 8:14) or Barnabas and Paul to Judaea (Acts 11:30) are decisions taken by a minimum quorum of 120. According to 1 Cor. 15:6, there were more than five hundred Christians even before the Ascension.

'Brothers' is here used for the first time in Acts, but had always meant those belonging to the family of faith (unless, of course, it was literally applied to physical brothers): see, e.g., Mk. 3:31–35 for Jesus' own explanation.

Peter takes up his usage of Acts 1:15 in his second letter, 2 Pet. 1:10, where, interestingly enough, he is also talking about 'calling and election' (*hē klēsis kai eklogē*), though of course in a spiritual sense; cf. 1 Pet. 5:12 and 2 Pet. 3:15. He uses the term for 'brotherhood', *adelphotēs*, in the sense of Acts 1:15, in 1 Pet. 2:17; 5:9—the only NT author to use this term derived from his preaching experiences in Jerusalem.

For some interesting recent remarks on *adelphos* in the NT, see E. E. Ellis, 'Prophecy and Hermeneutic in Jude', in: *id, Prophecy*, 223–36.

176 Cf. on this aspect Dodd, *Scripture*, 58.

177 Whereas the legend linking Paul with a school where he is supposed to have taught (now part of the Church San Paolo alla Regola) is discounted by the fact that not a single stone there is pre-medieval, the rooms discovered underneath Santa Maria in Via Lata are in an old Roman residential area of the period concerned, and had been in use as a granary for several centuries before they were turned into a deaconry for the down-and-out in the early sixth century. We may have here what is commonly called a 'local tradition', but it is too vague and too late to even demand more serious investigation. What is historical about its context, however, is the fact that Christians could well have lived in this particular quarter of Rome (another early Judaeo-Christian quarter was on the other side of the Tiber, in Trastevere,

but no place there claims Petrine connections, even though the church Santa Maria in Trastevere claims to be the first Christian church built with official permission in Rome), and, as stated above, Peter, Paul and Luke were in Rome at the same time. A similar local tradition exists in the case of the house of Senator Pudens, allegedly to be identified in 2 Tim. 4:21. Pudens, whose social status is not even so much as hinted at in Paul's letter, makes a late and sudden appearance in church history; he and his daughters are presented as having been close friends of Peter, the Senator as Peter's host for seven years, the daughters as Peter's protegées, led by him to the Christian faith. The garbled account in the *Liber Pontificalis*, relating the building of the church Santa Pudenziana, the so-called *Acts of Praxedes and Pudentiana*, and the entry in the sixth-century guide, the *Notitia Ecclesiarum Urbis Romae*, on the tombs of these daughters, Pudentiana and Praxedes, in the Catacombs of Priscilla, have all contributed to the story that the Senator's house stood at the Vicus Patricius (today's Via Urbana) and was later a part of the mid-second century Baths of Novatus which in turn became the building ground of today's Santa Pudenziana in the fourth century—thereby preserving the local tradition of Pudens' house. Recent archaeological research has established that the Baths of Novatus were indeed underneath the church, and that a first-century private house was also on the spot alleged by tradition. Whatever the later legendary embellishments may have been, the historical kernel has become visible again: there was a private house (which could have belonged to a Senator), there were public baths (which must have been those of Novatus), and there still is the church, on the very spot, 'recognizable' in spite of countless alterations over the centuries. (For a recent archaeological survey, see A. Henze, 'Santa Pudenziana', *Osservatore Romano*, German weekly edition, 4 March 1983, 9).

178 The most influential critics to doubt the authenticity of the speeches in Acts have been M. Dibelius, *Studies in the Acts of the Apostles* (London, 1956); H. Conzelmann, *Die Apostelgeschichte* (Tübingen, 1963); E. Haenchen, *The Acts of the Apostles* (Oxford, 1982). Long before the more recent return to a serious analysis of the historical background of these speeches (for a survey, see Plümacher, 131–38), the classical philologist E. Norden accepted Harnack's verdict in his *Die Apostelgeschichte* (Leipzig, 1908), 110, that 'the genius for selecting the thoughts is here as great as the historical faithfulness when what mattered was to summarise in a few words what Paul had, in all probability, demonstrated to the pagans in his fundamental, missionary speeches' (E. Norden, *Agnostos Theos* (Berlin, 1912, repr. Darmstadt, 1974), 9–10).

179 Cf. Riesenfeld, *Gospel, id.*, The Gospel Tradition (Philadelphia, 1970); Gerhardsson, *Memory*; *id.*, *Tradition and Transmission in Early Christianity* (Lund, 1964); *id.*, *Anfänge*; Riesner, *Jesus*, 119–23, 371–79, 392–406, 440–71.

180 Cf. E. E. Ellis, 'New Directions in Form Criticism', in G. Strecker, *Jesus Christus in Historie und Theologie. Festschrift für H. Conzelmann* (Tübingen, 1975), 304–9; G. A. Kennedy, 'Classical and Christian Source Criticism', in W. O. Walker, *The Relationships among the Gospels* (San Antonio, 1978), 130–37; Riesner, *Jesus*, 491–98; see also E. J. Goodspeed, *Matthew, Apostle and Evangelist* (Philadelphia, 1959), 16–17, 101–9; F. F. Bruce, *The New Testament Documents* (Leicester, 5th ed., 1960), 45; Wenham, *Gospel*, 121–122. If Wenham's daring theory that Luke was one of the 'seventy' were to be

substantiated, he could of course also have been a note-taking witness of the Jerusalem events of Acts.

181 That he was employed not only as a younger fellow-evangelist, but also as a kind of secretary or scribe, seems to follow from Acts 13:5, and *huperetes* may even identify him as an evangelist (cf. the usage in Lk. 1:2; see R. O. P. Taylor, GROUNDWORK, 21–30, F. F. Bruce, ACTS, 255). The remarks by Papias (in Eusebius, *HE* 3, 39:15) and others (see above, n. 1), seem to point in this direction, at least as far as following Peter and recording his teaching is concerned (cf. 1 Pet. 5:13).

182 See E. G. Selwyn, *The First Epistle of Peter* (London, 2nd ed., 1947), 33–36.

183 Thucydides claims that it was difficult for him to record the exact words which he had heard himself or which had been passed on to him by others. But, he goes on to say, 'I have used language in accordance with what, as far as I can see, the speakers most probably had said in each case, remaining as close as possible to the general sense of what was really said.' This is certainly not a justification for having invented speeches; on the contrary he is claiming that he did not merely invent any speeches.

184 *Hist.* 2, 56:10 and 12, 25:1.

185 See Bruce, *Speeches*, 7; cf. also T. F. Glasson, 'The Speeches in Acts and Thucydides', *Expository Times* 76 (1964–5), 165; H. J. Cadbury, *The Making of Luke-Acts* (New York, 1927), 76–98, 157; C. F. D. Moule, 'The Christology of Acts', in L. E. Keck/J. L. Martyn, *Studies in Luke-Acts* (London, 1976), 159–85; Gasque; 'Dibelius Reconsidered', in R. N. Longenecker/M. C. Tenney (eds.), *New Dimensions in New Testament Studies* (Grand Rapids, 1974), 232–50.

186 There is nothing peculiar in Peter's rephrasing of this part of Joel's text. Since most of his readers would have remembered the original as well as he did, they would have seen his point. He had used the same technique in his 'election address', where he had turned a plural into a singular (Acts 1:20). Jesus himself had felt free to differ slightly from the quoted text at least three times: see Mk. 10:19 with Ex. 20:12–16 and Dt. 5:16–20, or Mk. 14:27 with Zc. 13:7; or Lk. 4:18–19 with Is. 61:1–2.

Other instances depend on whether one wants to rely on the Hebrew text or the Greek LXX; and in all these cases, including those in Acts, one has to keep in mind that Jesus and his apostles were concerned with concrete, interpretative applications of the Old Testament: see Longenecker, 57–66 ('The Phenomena of the Quotations'), 70–75 ('Pesher Interpretations'), and 96–103 ('Exegetical Practices and Patterns').

187 The development is even more obvious in the Greek, as Peter uses the same introductory appellation (*andres*, 'men') all three times: *andres Ioudaioi, andres Israēlitai, andres adelphoi* (For *adelphoi* see also n. 175 above).

188 Peter makes it clear enough that his fellow-Israelites are responsible; even so, the inclusion of the 'wicked men' who had helped them (2:23b) may be an allusion to the Romans. (Cf. Bruce, op. cit. n. 30, 91–2.)

189 It must be pointed out that the identity of the titles works only in the Greek (and English or other translations): where *kurios* is used in all instances, the Hebrew text differentiates between 'Yahweh' (Joel 2:30, 31; Ps. 16:8; Ps. 110:1, first 'Lord') and 'Adon' (Ps. 110:1, second 'Lord'). It is safe to assume that Peter would have refrained from calling Jesus 'Yahweh' directly; but even if he differentiated—supposing that he spoke Aramaic on this occasion and quoted Joel and the Psalms in Hebrew or Aramaic—between 'Jahweh' and 'Adon', the attentive listener would not have missed the point he was trying to make, simply because his interpretations of the quotations were

speaking for themselves. Peter, at any rate, could well have spoken Greek on that day: in view of an international multi-racial audience, the lingua franca of the time would have been the obvious choice. (There is no indication that Peter spoke in (a) tongue(s) during his speech.)

In his first letter, Peter twice makes similar use of Old Testament passages referring to 'Yahweh' by applying them to the Lord Jesus Christ: see Ps. 34:8 as used in 1 Pet. 2:3, and Is. 8:13 as used in 1 Pet. 3:15.

190 The Greek text for 'be baptized in the name of Jesus Christ', *baptisthētō . . . epi tō onomati Iēsou Christou,* implies the form of a solemn contract (cf. on this aspect L. Hartmann, 'Into the Name of Jesus', *NTS* 20 (1973), 432–40, and J. A. Ziesler, 'The Name of Jesus in the Acts of the Apostles', *JSNT* 4 (1979), 28–41). The formula recurs in Acts 10:48—where it is again Peter who calls for baptism—with a minute alteration: the *epi* has become an *en* (which has probably led the scribes of the Codex Vaticanus B03 and the Codex Bezae Cantabrigiensis D05—and those of some minuscules—to substitute *en* for *epi* in 2:38). It is, however, rather a good example of Luke's faithfulness in sticking to his sources: if Peter had used *epi* in his Jerusalem speech (assuming, of course, that he did speak Greek that day), so be it. When Luke was free to formulate for himself, he used the more elegant *en*!

191 The name 'Beautiful Gate' (. . . *pros tēn thuran tou hierou tēn legomenēn Hōraian . . .*) is not documented outside the NT; the epithet is, however, unambiguous enough to identify it as the beautiful Nicanor or Corinthian Gate, opposite the main entrance to the temple itself. Josephus mentions it several times in his *Jewish War*; in 5, 5:3 he describes it in detail—it was fifty cubits high; the doors were forty cubits high and embellished with silver and gold plates. Peter's words to the cripple gain in poignancy at such a gate: 'Silver and gold I do not have, but what I have I give you' (3:6). One may see this as yet another indication of Jesus' superiority over the temple: if Peter can make that cripple walk again *in the name of Jesus,* what are the outward splendours of the Beautiful Gate compared to such inward healing strength?

192 In v. 16 Luke preserves a somewhat misshapen and repetitive Greek structure. The structural problem may be due to the shifting of an originally Aramaic speech into vernacular Greek (see Torrey, 14–16, for a solution that still carries weight), but even the possible Aramaic would be open to debate, so we are on safer grounds if we assume that this is simply one of many instances where Luke remains faithful to his source: Peter, as his second letter shows quite abundantly, has a way of concocting unusual sentences (2. Pet. 1:3, quoted above, is a case in point in the original Greek); and what is not untypical of him in writing may even be more typical of his speaking style—not always, of course, but now and then, as Luke's example would thus appear to demonstrate faithfully. As for the repetition in 16a and 16b, it is characteristic of public speaking and may even be a virtue: as any broadcaster or orator knows, 'redundance' *can* be an art if one wants to drive home a vital point.

193 Hippocrates, in his essay *On Fractures,* 25, uses the term to denote the drying-out and healing of an open wound which has been left exposed to the open air by the surgeon; cf. A. Dihle, *'anapsuxis'* (Grand Rapids, 1974), IX, *TDNT,* 664.

194 Reicke, who dates the crucifixion in AD 33, assumes AD 34–35 for the events described in Acts 3:1–5:42 (Reicke, *Era,* 189).

195 Cf. J. Jeremias, *Jerusalem in the time of Jesus* (London, 1969), 83: between 55,000 and 95,000 inhabitants.
196 Cf. Bruce, op. cit. n. 30, 122; Gerhardsson, *Memory*, 25 and n. 50; Ellis, art. cit. n. 180, 305; Marshall, op. cit. n. 175, 101.
   The verdict of E. E. Ellis sums up the critical discussion: 'The picture of Jesus' followers as simple illiterate peasants is a romantic notion without historical basis.'
197 Marshall, op. cit. n. 175, 102, notes 'an illustrious precedent' for the apostles' defiance of the Sanhedrin: Socrates' speech before the Athenian constitutional court in 399 BC. Socrates indeed said (*Apology* 29d): 'I shall obey the God rather than you, and as long as I breathe and am capable of it, I shall not cease to look for wisdom and to admonish you.'
   The precedent set by Socrates is bettered by the apostles, in that they do not have to look for 'wisdom' any more; but his attitude towards the state authority highlights, as Marshall rightly points out, for all times, not just for Socrates or Peter and John, that the higher obedience due to God stands above the commands of any religious or political system.
198 Marshall, op. cit. n. 176, 103.
199 The self-appellation as 'slave of Christ', *doulos tou kuriou Christou*, is of course not peculiar to Peter. Paul copies the apostolic usage, which is also documented in Jas. 1:1 (with 2 Pet. 1:1 therefore in two letters of the pillars of the second stage of the Jerusalem community!) in e.g. Rom. 1:1; Phil. 1:1; 1 Cor. 7:22; Gal. 1:10; Eph. 6:6.
200 Jude uses some of this Petrine thinking in his letter, v. 4.
201 The classical philologist E. M. Blaiklock, who thinks that this is Peter's own prayer, anyway, uses Acts 4:28 as an opportunity to state that 'a study of Peter's thought and vocabulary in utterances reported in Acts and in his own writing demonstrates most convincingly their unity.' (op. cit. n. 168, 67).
202 On this continuous 'famine relief', see D. R. Hall, 'St. Paul and Famine Relief: A Study in Galatians 2:10', *Expository Times* 82 (1970–71) 309–11, Bruce, op. cit. n. 30, 38–40; and *id.*, *The Epistle to the Galatians. A Commentary on the Greek Text* (Exeter, 1982), 126–28.
203 Some textual witnesses insert *en tē ekklēsia* at the end of 2:47 (the Codex Bezae Cantabrigiensis D05 and minuscules). But although the editors of *The Greek New Testament According to the Majority Text* have accepted it, the combined evidence of the earliest extant papyrus, p74, and all other major codices point to the assumption that the addition to 2:47 is only a scribal gloss.
204 For an analysis of magic and superstition behind belief in the power of a man's shadow, see Horst, *Peter's Shadow*. This passage must not be bracketed with Acts 19:12, where not the shadow, but aprons and handkerchiefs touched by Paul are credited with miraculous powers, and where Paul obviously condones the practice.
205 It is not certain if the Greek word used here and in Acts 13:45 (the only two occurrences in Acts), *zēlos*, is correctly translated by 'jealousy', (AV, 'indignation'). Jealousy may of course have played a part, but that alone does not appear to be sufficient motivation for the action of the high priest and the others. They are offended in their authoritative dogmatism and their own religious fervour. Ps. 69:9 may give the clue: here *zēlos* is used for 'zeal'—'For zeal for your house consumes me, and the insults of those who insult you fall on me.' One can easily see the Sadducees encouraged by such

a verse as they saw it—cf. Paul about himself in Phil. 3:6! (The disciples had applied Ps. 69:9 to Jesus, after the cleansing of the temple, Jn. 2:17).

206 For the characteristically Petrine expression of 'the tree' for the cross of Jesus (5:30), see p. 187 and n. 153 above.

207 Gamaliel's speech has contributed to confusion over the date of Acts 5:36, as he mentions a certain Theudas whom Josephus (*Ant.* 20, 5:1) clearly dates to the period when Fadus was procurator of Judaea (i.e. AD 44–46). The non-identity of the Theudas in Josephus and the Theudas in Acts (see above, n. 171) is beyond reasonable doubt, as Gamaliel goes on to speak of the revolt of Judas the Galilean which, as he states quite explicitly, happened afterwards (5:37); there is only one Judas the Galilean who opposed the census, and he led his revolt in AD 6. (Theudas is an equally common name, but neither Gamaliel nor Josephus identify him by topographical or other epithets). While Josephus got it right with Judas the Galilean (cf. *Ant.* 18, 1:1; 20, 5:2; *War* 2, 8:1; 7, 8:1), it is noteworthy that Gamaliel is more accurate in detail: only he stresses that Judas the Galilean was killed (5:37), and only he specifies the number of insurgents (400) in the band of 'his' Theudas. It is therefore obvious that Gamaliel and indeed Luke know what—and who—they are talking about, something that we know was not always the case with Josephus. In the context of these revolts Josephus also speaks vaguely of 'various other unrests' (*Ant.* 17, 10:4). The only alternative to the non-identity of the two Theudas is a chronological error by Josephus.

208 Bruce, op. cit. n. 30, 146, suggests that Paul could have been present (cf. his own allusion to membership of the Sanhedrin in 28:10), or that Gamaliel informed his pupil Paul. (It was, after all, a remarkable event which would have provided useful teaching and discussion material!) Either way, Paul could have been Luke's source.

209 Joseph's potential as a figure of legend carried him as far as Glastonbury and linked him with relics such as the Holy Grail and the Holy Thorn.

210 On the differences between the Grecian Judaeo-Christians and the Aramaic-speaking ones, Stephen's role and his martyrdom, see in particular M. Hengel, 'Zwischen Jesus und Paulus', *ZThK* 7/2 (1975), 151–206, and Bruce, 'Stephen and other Hellenists', *Men*, 49–85.

211 As Blaiklock, op. cit. n. 168, 79, puts it, 'The account sets this time of tribulation in encouraging perspective. The forcible dispersion of the Jerusalem church was a rich source of evangelization. The chapter will show its influence reaching distant Ethiopia.'

212 That Samaria was to be one of the target areas of apostolic mission had of course been emphasized by Jesus in the Ascension address of Acts 1:18; it is also implicitly included in Mt. 28:19 and Lk. 24:47.

213 Once the authority of Philip to act *fully* on behalf of the apostles had thus been vindicated, he could work entirely on his own. His conversion and baptism of the Ethiopian (8:37–38) does not need any apostolic confirmation.

214 See L. Bieler, *Theios anēr* (Vienna, 1935–36, repr. Darmstadt, 1967). Bieler calls Simon Magus 'a real *theios anēr*, 48.

215 E.g. Leipoldt/Grundmann, I, 401; W. Schmithals, *Neues Testament und Gnosis* (Darmstadt, 1984), 131–33.

216 For a circumspect analysis of the available evidence, see Beyschlag.

217 *Apōleia* is used in this sense of perdition or damnation by Jesus himself: Mt. 7:13.

218 The sentence is difficult to translate, but the NEB version comes closest to the Greek original, behind which there is a Hebrew turn of phrase or way of

thinking in the expression *cholē pikrias*, 'the gall of bitterness'. 'The phrase appears to be metaphorical of a person whose idolatry and godlessness lead to bitter results for himself and the people whom he deceives' (Marshall, op. cit. n. 175, 159).

219　The first source outside the New Testament is Justin Martyr (who died c AD 165 in Rome) in his two-part *Apology*, an invaluable source for information about the struggle of the church to define and assert itself over external and internal enemies. (For his role in early Roman Christian literature, see H. Chadwick, *Early Christian Thought and the Classical Tradition* (Oxford, 1966), 9–23; Thiede, *Pagan*.

Justin (*Apology* 1, 26, 56) writes that Simon went to Rome under Claudius (AD 41–54) and protests against his public standing as a Christian. The Church Fathers are unanimous in their condemnation of Simon as an arch-heretic. Eusebius, in his *Ecclesiastical History*, 2, 13:1–15:1, compiles the story, drawing on Acts, Justin, Irenaeus and possibly other sources; Justin's information is particularly valuable as he had been born in Samaria himself. His identification of Gitta as Simon's birth-place may point to the unnamed city of Acts 8:5, 9; and his story of the altar dedicated to Simon on a Tiber island, 'To Simon the Holy God', is particularly revealing. *If* the altar discovered on the island of San Sebastiano in 1574 is the one Justin alluded to, it demonstrates the recklessness of the Simonians in Rome—for the (fragmentary) inscription reads *Semoni Sanco Deo (Fideo)*, 'To Semo Sancus God (of Oaths)'. Since one of the earliest literary sources for the cult of this Sabine deity, which seems to have flourished in the 5th century BC (Propertius, 4, 9:71–74, written c.20 BC) is transmitted with the scribal corruption of Sancus into Sanctus—one may assume that by then, and by the time of Simon's death, let alone Justin's writing, the original deity had been forgotten, so that the Simonians could happily claim the altar to be Simon's, or at least Semo Sancus to have been a prefiguration of Simon the Holy. And to confound -e- with -i- would not have caused any problems—such itacisms were common, as is demonstrated the other way round by Suetonius, who calls Christ *Chrestus* (*Life of the Caesars, Claudius*, 25). During the second century, then, Simon was still an influential cult-figure—see also Tertullian, *Apology*, 13:9 (written c. AD 197). Eusebius states (*HE* 1, 14:6–15:1) that Peter, when he came to Rome during the reign of Claudius, brought about the extinction of Simon's power 'and of the man himself').

Peter's attacks against Simon are related in detail in the late second century *Acts of Peter* (c.AD 180), chs. 12–32. This is entertaining fiction. Peter's miracle contest with Simon before the prefect Agrippa on the Forum, chs. 23–28, and Simon's attempt to fly to God—whom he calls his father, ch. 31—are not without their hilarious moments: when Simon manages to fly over Rome, watched by everyone like one of those commercial airships that attract Romans today, Peter prays to the Lord to let him fall down and break his leg in three places. This duly happens, Simon is stoned by the people, and dies later in exile (ch. 32).

The problem with the *Acts of Peter*, as with all comparatively early apocryphal material, is that it is almost impossible to disentangle fact and fiction. There is no good reason to doubt that Simon and Peter could have met in Rome; the sparse but unembellished evidence for their respective stays in Rome during the reign of Claudius is historically credible, and it may well have been the very lack of further information which gave rise to the legendary embroidery some 130 years later. We are not entitled to dismiss everything out of hand. Probability and improbability will have to be weighed up with care, as will two other famous incidents reported in the *Acts of Peter*, the 'Quo Vadis' story, ch. 35, and the crucifixion of Peter head downwards, ch. 37–38, the latter being confirmed by Eusebius, *HE* 3, 1:2. Eusebius seems to have had independent corroborative evidence, *perhaps* Origen's now lost *Commentary on Genesis*, III, mentioned in 3, 1:3. He knew the *Acts of Peter*, but rejected them as unreliable, since 'no accepted writer, neither ancient nor contemporary, has made use of their testimonies' (*HE*, 3,3:2).

Further material on confrontations between Peter and Simon is provided by the so-called *Pseudo-Clementines*, later than the *Acts of Peter*, and originally written at the beginning of the third century. In their present state, they are divided into two parts, the *Homilies* and the *Recognitions*. Peter appears in these stories, which also contain information on his travels, his sermons, his conversion of Clement of Rome and his role in the reuniting of Clement's family, as the protagonist of a hellenistic novel. Classical philology has always regarded the *Pseudo-Clementines* as novelistic literature; cf. K. Kerény, *Die griechisch-orientalische Romanliteratur in religionsgeschichtlicher Bedeutung* (Tübingen, 1927), 67–69, and R. Helm, *Der antike Roman* (Berlin, 1948), 61; see also J. Wehnert, 'Literarkritik und Sprachanalyse, Kritische Anmerkungen zum gegenwärtigen Stand der Pseudo-Klementinen – Forschung', *ZNW* 74 (1983), 268–301.

220 See Gal. 1:17–18. *Meta etē tria* could mean, literally, 'after three years'. It may, however, be a way of inclusive reckoning (so Marshall, op. cit. n. 175, 174). Bruce, op. cit. n. 202, 97, explains that 'in the third year' could be justified by gospel usage. Mk. 8:31 and 10:34, *meta treis hēmeras*, is specified as *tē tritē hēmera* or *tē hēmera tē tritē* by Luke, Lk. 9:22 and 18:33, i.e. not 'after three days' but 'on the third day'.

221 Paul's concept of the apostolate appears to be wider than that of Acts 1:21–22: he calls himself an apostle (Gal. 1:1) and applies the title to James (1:18), and also to Andronicus and Junias (Rom. 16:7). But Luke himself uses the title for Barnabas and Paul (Acts 14:14). Cf. H. Riesenfeld, *Apostel*, in *RGG* (Tübingen, 3rd ed., 1956), I. 497–99.

222 Even if Aeneas' parents did not have the Graeco-Roman hero in mind, the namesakes in Jewish history were equally lofty: e.g. the son of Antipater the Idumaean (Josephus, *Ant.* 14, 10:22, and Aeneas turned Aretas, king of Petra, *Ant.* 16, 9:4).

223 There is no noun for 'mat' or 'pallet' in the Greek text of Acts 9:34 (Lk. 5:18 *klinē*, Mk. 2:4, 9, 11, 12 *krabbatos*). Peter's command is merely verbal: *anastēthi kai strōson seautō*. This has led some interpreters to the suggestion that Peter means Aeneas to get up and have a meal. (Bruce, op. cit. n. 30, 210–11, refers to the use of *strōnnumi* in Mk. 14:15 and the interest shown by Luke and other NT writers in nourishment for convalescents, as with Paul in Acts 9:19a, also Lk. 8:55, a parallel noted by Marshall, op. cit. n. 175, 178–9.) The use of the reflexive pronoun *seautou* does appear to indicate that Aeneas is meant to prepare something for himself, to readjust the *krabbatos* of v. 33, and then 'stretch it out for himself' in the appropriate position for a meal (cf. *strōnnumi* in Mk. 11:8 and Mt. 21:8).

224 The Aramaic could of course be rendered both by *egeirō* and *anisthēmi*. It may well be that Luke, by using two different words for the same Aramaic

one in Lk. 8:54 and Acts 9:40, subtly points to a residual difference between the power of Christ the Lord and Peter, the trustee of his keys.

225 'Godfearer', here *phoboumenos ton Theon* (cf. 10:22; 13:16, 26), elsewhere also *sebomenoi ton Theon* (16:14; 18:7) or *sebomenoi* (13:50; 17:4, 17) is Luke's term for Gentiles who had accepted the Jewish faith, observed the laws and the Sabbath, and attended the synagogue but were not circumcised and were therefore still regarded as 'Gentiles' by mainstream Judaism. These technical terms for a non-circumcised believer in Jewish monotheism are all renderings of the rabbinical expression *jir'e schamaijim*. Josephus, *Ant.* 14, 7:2, gives the form *sebomenoi ton Theon* for God-fearers who contributed to the splendours of the temple.

226 The Cohors II Italica Civium Romanorum, mentioned on an inscription published in H. Dessau (ed.), *Inscriptiones Latinae Selectae* (Leipzig, 1982), no. 9168.

227 So Haenchen, op. cit. n. 178, 346.

228 For the first date, see Reicke, *Era,* 215; for the second date, Dockx, 135.

229 The possibility that he was a retired officer by the time of Acts 10 is taken into consideration by Marshall, op. cit. n. 175, 183. He is, however, still in command of soldiers: with two servants, he sends a 'pious soldier' (10:7) to fetch Peter.

230 The oldest textual witnesses have the number three that follows logically from 10:7—so the p74, the Sinaiticus, the Alexandrinus, the Ephraemi Rescriptus, the Laudianus E08. (This is one of the more fascinating codices of the New Testament: written in the sixth century, it is the oldest extant one to contain the Book of Acts alone; now in the Bodleian Library Oxford, where it was deposited by Archbishop Laud—hence its name—in 1636, it had belonged to the Venerable Bede and to Boniface; it is bilingual, with the Latin text in the left column, the Greek text in the right. It is also the oldest extant manuscript to contain the disputed verse 8:37. See A. C. Clark, *The Acts of the Apostles* (Oxford, 1933), 234–46, and B. M. Metzger, *Manuscripts of the Greek Bible* (Oxford, 1981), 96–7.) 'Two' instead of 'three' is the number given by the Codex Vaticanus, where the scribe apparently did not take the soldier seriously as a messenger, but merely as a guard; other codices and minuscules omit the number altogether, which has led the editors of *The Greek New Testament According to the Majority Text* and the translators of the NEB to omit it, too. AV and RSV opt for 'three'; so does NIV, which reflects the differing evidence in a footnote.

231 The first person form—'for I have sent them' (10:20)—used by 'the Spirit' may point to this voice as identical with that in the vision, or at least to Peter's realisation—once again—that the Spirit is the promised emanation of Jesus Christ.

232 Suggested by G. Stählin, *Die Apostelgeschichte* (Göttingen, 11th ed., 1970), 151.

233 See R. Meyer, *katharos,* in G. Kittel (ed.), *Theological Dictionary of the New Testament* (Grand Rapids, 1966, repr. 1982), III, 418–23; cf. F. Hauck, *ibid.,* pp. 423–31.
    Peter used the word *allophulos* for the Gentiles. It strictly means 'foreigner', which is of course the appropriate term for his dealings with members of a Roman household. It is the only occurrence of the word in the NT.

234 The Greek in v. 30 is very unusual, giving rise to many suggested improvements yet with no general agreement. For the explanation that it is

an acceptable form of colloquial (*koine*) Greek or a Semitism, see Torrey, 34–5. The *meaning* of the sentence is unambiguous, as in all modern translations.

235 For the question of Cornelius' prior degree of knowledge, see Stanton, 19–26.

236 For the end of this sentence, cf. 1 Pet. 4:5!

237 E.g. Marshall, op. cit. n. 175, 193.

238 On the use of the OT and Peter's exegetical thinking in this passage, see S. Bénétreau, *La première épître de Pierre* (Vaux-sur-Seine, 1984), 128–31.

239 Ridderbos, 27.

240 Torrey, 27 and 35–6, points out that parts of the speech can be translated back into literally-correct Aramaic. Cf. also Riesenfeld, *Text*, 191–94.

241 See Josephus, 1, 21:7, *Ant.* 16, 5:1.

242 Josephus, *War*, 3, 2:4, and on the correlations between Greeks and Jews in Antioch *ibid.*, 7, 3:3. Josephus writes that the Jews had the same civic rights as the Greeks, and that 'many Greeks' converted to Judaism and became members of the Jewish community of the city.

243 Such a comprehensive understanding of the term seems to be the most satisfactory interpretation of a difficult passage. Standard editions of the Greek New Testament (Nestle/Aland 26, UBS 3, Hodges/Farstad Majority Text) have opted for *Hellēnistai*, the word given by the Codex Vaticanus, the second corrector of the Bezae Cantabrigiensis, the Laudianus Oxoniensis and the group of 'majority text' manuscripts. The problem caused by this reading is obvious: Luke uses *Hellēnistai* on two other occasions in Acts (6:1; 9:29), and he is the only NT (or for that matter biblical) author to use the word at all; the meaning in the other two passages in unambiguous: the word refers to Greek-speaking Jews from the Diaspora who were resident in Jerusalem—people like Joseph Barnabas, 'a Levite from Cyprus' (4:36). Some of these had become Christians (6:1), while others were still violently opposed to the Christian message (9:29). While these groups were able at least to understand, if not to speak each other's language, the difference was apparent. If Luke uses the term a third time in 11:20, one would therefore expect him to mean the same thing—i.e. Greek-speaking Jews. This would, however, detract from the impact of the Antioch story, as there seems to be a marked contrast between the 'Jews' (*Ioudaioi*) of v. 19 and the 'Greek-speakers' (*Hellēnistai*) of v. 20 who are apparently seen as a *new* target group, not merely as the Greek-speaking Jews that had been reached before, anyway. But why did Luke use a word he had previously employed to denote not Gentiles, but Greek-speaking Jews or Judaeo-Christians? Some scribes have seen the answer in substituting *Hellēnas*, 'Greeks'—so the third corrector of the Codex Sinaiticus, the Codex Alexandrinus, the original hand of the Codex Bezae Cantabrigiensis, p74, several translations and some Fathers, suggesting that this was in fact the original word. Luke does use *Hellēn* nine times; eight times it is contrasted with Jews or Jewishness, and once (17:4) it stands for 'God-fearing' Greeks in Thessalonica—the Greek equivalents to Cornelius and his household. And this last group reminds us of the Greeks Josephus knew of in Antioch (see above, n. 241)—whereas 'many' of Josephus' God-fearing Greeks had become Jewish proselytes, some of Paul's Thessalonian Greeks would become Christian proselytes.

We should simply take the word used by Luke in 11:20 in its basic, literal sense, i.e. 'Greek-speaking ones', allowing its respective meanings to be illuminated by the immediate historical context in each passage. We thus see the *Hellēnistai* of 11:20 as the large group of Greek-speakers who comprised, among others, God-fearers, or even, according to Josephus, fully-fledged proselytized (and thus also circumcised) members of the Jewish community. If this last sense is the one implied by Luke, he would elegantly cover both the Greeks, the Greek-speaking Gentiles as such, and the Jews of Gentile origin, and *Hellēnistai* would therefore be indeed the appropriate term.

244 Dockx, 135, dates a first visit to Antioch to March 41-April 42, i.e. after his escape from Herod's prison.

There is a relatively early and varied tradition that Peter was or became the official founding father, or 'overseer' (*episkopos*) of the church of Antioch—which he could of course have been even if he was not the first to evangelize in Antioch. Cf. Origen, the first extant written source, but going back to an earlier local tradition (*On Luke*, Homily 6); Eusebius, *HE* 3, 36:2 (where Ignatius is mentioned as third bishop of Antioch after Peter, whereas in 3, 22, he is the second bishop after Evodius—pointing, it seems, to a special meaning of Peter's 'bishopric', not identical with the office as held later by Evodius and Ignatius); cf. also Eusebius, *Chronicle*, On the 212th Olympiad; John Chrysostom (himself educated in Antioch and ordained deacon and priest in the city), in his *Homily on Ignatius*; Jerome, *On famous men*, 1, *et al.* Cf. also the Pseudo-Clementines, *Recognition* 10, 69–72!

245 The news of the pro-Gentile activities of men like Philip, Peter and Barnabas will have reached the Jewish hierarchy in Jerusalem; it was certainly the last straw. Herod, eager to please the Sanhedrin, would have used their displeasure to start a persecution, thus winning their good will.

246 Pre-Lukan parallels to such miraculous escapes (Euripides *Bacch.* 443–8, Ovid, *Met.* 3, 696–700), where chains drop off and doors open by themselves, differ in two vital aspects: they do not deal with historical persons (Herod Agrippa, Peter) and circumstances, but with Greek mythology, and they happen 'on their own', as though the persons concerned (the Bacchae in Euripides and Acoetes in Ovid) had those miraculous powers in themselves, whereas Luke makes it quite clear that only God's direct intervention saved Peter from trial and certain execution.

247 There is some evidence for a *much later* belief in Judaism that guardian angels could assume the physical likeness of their protégés (cf. Strack/Billerbeck, op. cit. n. 54, II, 707); Rhoda does not think of a physical likeness—she has not 'seen' Peter, but *only* heard his voice.

248 For the view that the 'brothers' are the (apostolic) leaders of the church, see E. E. Ellis, 'Paul and his Co-Workers', *NTS* 17 (1970/71), 437–52.

249 The most instructive (if not complete) survey is Selwyn's, op. cit. n. 182, 243–44, 303–05. Cf. Cullmann, *Peter*, 84–87; G. K. Kuhn, *Babulōn*, in Kittel, op. cit. n. 233, I, 514–17.

C. H. Hunzinger's helpful and influential analysis of Jewish usage of 'Babylon' for 'Rome' ('Babylon als Deckname für Rom und die Datierung des 1. Petrusbriefes', in: H. Graf Reventlow (ed.), *Gottes Wort und Gottes Land, Festschrift H. W. Hertzberg* (Göttingen, 1965), 67–77) is marred by methodologically dubious presuppositions. When both Jews and Christians used the same cryptogram, we have no right to ignore the possibility of independence and to assume that one group (the Christians) must have copied the other. It is entirely unwarranted to claim that a usage which occurs in the New Testament has to be later than its earliest Jewish/ Rabbinical occurrence (in this case, according to Hunzinger, post AD 70). *Pace* Hunzinger, there are, not least in Isaiah, ample illustrations of Babylonian moral and political loathsomeness that could have inspired the parallelism long before AD 70 and the destruction of the temple (see also n. 250 below). And as so often, a New Testament writer could have quite different reasons for using a particular OT concept than a Jewish/Rabbinical author. Besides, it is noteworthy that Hunzinger does not even mention Ezekiel 12 (cf. op. cit., p. 73) as a possible link between 1 Pet. 5:13 and the passage in Acts 12:17, apparently written after 1 Peter.

Within the NT, Revelation 14–18 is obvious enough; in church history, the line can be drawn from Papias (in: Eusebius, *HE* 2, 15:2) to Tertullian (*Against the Jews* 9; *Adv. Marc*, 3:13); it becomes commonplace in literature in the third and fourth centuries. Jewish and Judaeo-Christian texts confirm the usage from the late first century onwards: e.g. *Apocalypse of Baruch* 11:1; 67:7; *Sibylline Oracles* 5:143, 159. Old Testament reasons for choosing Babylon are manifold; cf. Isa. 13:1–14:23, Jeremiah 50:51. Cf. also C. P. Thiede, 'Babylon der andere Ort: Anmerkungen zu 1. Petr. 5:13 und Apg. 12:17', in *Biblica* 67 (1986) fasc. 4, and Thiede (ed.), *Das Petrusbild in der neueren Forschung*, Wuppertal (forthcoming). This includes an analysis of secular Roman authors using 'Babylon' symbolically or metaphorically for Rome before Peter and at his time. The scribes of three minuscule manuscripts of the eleventh century ('2138', dated 1072, now in the Gorky University Library) and of the fifteenth century (marginal note in '4', now in Basel University Library; and '1518', the old Lambeth Palace minuscule 1181) substituted Rome (*Rōmē*) for Babylon.

250 Ample evidence (even though not quite untainted by polemical attitudes) is provided by Tacitus, *Ann.* 11–12 for Claudius and *Ann.* 13–16 for Nero; Suetonius, *Life of the Caesars* 5 for Claudius and *Life of the Caesars* 6 for Nero; Dio Cassius, *Histories* 60 for Claudius and *Histories* 61–63 for Nero. Nero's tutor and advisor Seneca (whom he forced to commit suicide in AD 65) ridicules Claudius' deficiencies in his satire, *Apocolocyntosis* ('Pumpkinification').

Claudius was a gifted and common-sensical administrator, but quite apart from the moral decadence of Roman public life and that of the Emperor, his expulsion of most of the Judaeo-Christian community of Rome in AD 49, which forced them into a new 'exile', cannot have made him popular with those who had stayed on or returned during the following years. Nero's most 'Babylonian' action prior to the murder of his mother and his actual persecution of the Christians (which happened after Acts and 1 Peter had been written) was the erection of a god-like statue in his honour in the Temple of Mars in AD 55 (Tacitus, *Ann.* 13, 8:1) and the introduction of coins depicting him as Apollo with a lyre—a representation recorded by Suetonius, *Life of the Caesars* 6:53. This novel deification and self-deification of the Emperor was satirized by one of Nero's successors, Vespasian, who would say in times of illness or fear of approaching death, 'Woe is me! I think I am becoming a God' (Suetonius, *Life of the Caesars*, 10:23). Only Domitian, who became emperor in post-NT times, revived Nero's attitude (cf. Suetonius, *Life of the Caesars*, 12:13). (For the dating of 1 Peter in this Neronian situation, cf. Neugebauer, *Deutung*, 86.)

251 The full source material was assembled by Edmundson, 47–86. See also Marucchi, *Evidence*, and *Pietro*.

More recently, J. A. T. Robinson has re-examined the sources, confirming in particular Edmundson's results (*Redating*, 112–14).

252 The fact that the *Liber Pontificalis* is a garbled text of mixed historical value cannot detract from its reliance on independent earlier sources. J. Wenham, who advocated its importance (*Did Peter*, 94–102; *Gospel*, 115) may have overestimated its overall value (see his retraction, *Rejoinder*, 37), but it does nonetheless stand in an uncontradicted tradition. Harnack, *Mission*, 832–36, opted for the basic reliability of the lists in the *Liber Pontificalis*.

253 Wenham (*Did Peter*, 98) quite rightly points to the fact that Jerome was, for some time (probably from 382–384) the secretary to Pope Damasus, so he would have had direct access to the episcopal archives 'which in spite of losses during persecution, doubtless contained much information now lost to us'.

254 There is also no need to infer an anti-Petrine sentiment from this 'omission'. Apart from the obvious fact that Paul did not have to tell the Romans who had founded their church, one cannot escape noticing a certain idiosyncrasy in Paul's naming of names in given contexts: cf. 1 Cor. 1:14–16, where he is not quite sure whom he had baptized in Corinth and even corrects himself; Rom. 16:3; 2 Tim. 4:19; where the Priscilla of Acts 18:2, 18, 26 and 1 Cor. 16:19 has lost her diminutive and is simply Prisca (in 1 Cor. 16:19, a minority of manuscripts does have 'Prisca', but the evidence of the partly independent majority corroborates 'Priscilla'); Gal. 2:7–9, where he cannot decide whether to call Peter 'Kephas' or 'Petros', and Gal. 1:19; 2:9, where James has moved from last to first place.

Needless to say, there are good and sometimes not so good reasons for these occurrences (one *could*, but does not *have to* argue, e.g., that in the case of Gal. 2:9 Paul wants to reflect James's rise to authority after Peter's first departure)—but in view of such varied peculiarities, a further one, namely the omission of Peter's name in Rom. 15:20, is also probably without significance. (For an explanation of the different name-forms, see W. M. Ramsay, *St. Paul the Traveller and Roman Citizen* (London, 1942), 268.)

255 See J. Juster, *Les Juifs dans l'empire romain* (Paris, 1914), 2 vols, 1, 209–10; cf. Leipoldt/Grundmann, 1, 292–98.

256 The traditional understanding that Mark was quite literally Peter's interpreter, i.e. translator, was recently upheld by Hengel, *Probleme*, 252–53. The assumption that he would have needed an interpreter for his evangelization once he had left Palestine is of course tenable (particularly in view of the fact that he used an amanuensis, Silas/Silvanus, for his first letter—1 Pet. 5:12; although even Paul did made use of Tertius for Romans—Rom. 16:22), but not entirely satisfactory. Or did Cornelius give Peter some advice in Caesarea? 'Look here, my friend, your Greek won't do in Rome. Should you ever get there, make sure you have an interpreter with you'? Kürzinger offers an alternative solution: Papias, following earlier studies by R. O. P. Taylor, 20–30 and 36–45; van Unnik, 'First Century AD Literary Culture and Early Christian Literature', in Ned Tht 25 (1971), 36: Papias follows hellenistic rhetorical terminology, and by *hermeneutēs Petrou* means not Peter's 'translator', but his 'explainer', the man who passes Peter's message on in his own interpretative words. (Cf. also Riesner, *Jesus*, 20, 60). Mark could of course have been both Peter's interpreter *and* his catechist (cf. Robinson, *Redating*, 114). Indeed we might even conjecture that Mark might have translated Peter not into Greek, but into *Latin*. Even if the Jewish and Judaeo-Christian community of Rome was predominantly

Greek-speaking and would remain so into the second century (cf. Harnack, *Mission*, 799–800), native Romans, both from the working classes and of higher rank, would have appreciated a Latin approach: the former because they had little Greek, the latter as a gesture of politeness. (It is easy to assume, e.g. that Nero's pro-Jewish former mistress and later wife Poppaea would have been more at home in Latin than in Greek, and the same must have been true for many others.) Mark's affinity with the Latin language is well established—cf. Lane, op. cit. n. 44, 24–25.

257 Cf. Edmundson, 59–86; Wenham, *Did Peter*, 101–02; Robinson, *Redating*, 113. Cf. M. Hengel, 'Entstehungszeit und Situation des Markusevangeliums' in H. Cancik (ed.), *Markus-Philologie* (Tübingen, 1982), 2, n. 9.

258 Cf. A. von Harnack, *Beiträge zur Einleitung in das Neue Testament IV. Neue Untersuchungen zur Apostelgeschichte und zur Abfassungszeit der Synoptischen Evangelien* (Leipzig, 1911), 88–93; W. C. Allen, *The Gospel According to St Mark* (London, 1915), 5–6; Robinson, *Redating*, 114. Allen's argument and that of C. C. Torrey (*The Four Gospels: A New Translation* (London 2nd ed., 1947), 261–62, followed by Zuntz, is however hampered by the assumption of an Aramaic Gospel of Mark. In Torrey's case, the reliance on Mk. 13:14 as a reference to Caligula's plan of erecting his statue in the Jerusalem temple—which he could not carry out after his execution on the 24th January 41, so that the gospel must have been written before his death, when the prophecy was still 'fulfillable'—is somewhat tenuous and far-fetched. Zuntz, who takes up Torrey's case, can do so only by supposing that the gospel was not written in Rome at all, but in Jerusalem. Cf. Guthrie, op. cit. n. 32, 73–74.

259 It is not even certain that the *Anti-Marcionite Prologue* to the Gospel of Mark misunderstands Irenaeus when it says 'post excessionem ipsius', as the Latin is not confined to 'death', either. Cf. Manson, 38–40; Guthrie, 73. In one point, the Anti-Marcionite Prologue even corrects Irenaeus: whereas the latter had made those misunderstandable statements about both Peter and Paul and their death, the Prologue returns to the unambiguous singular: only Peter and only his 'excessio' are mentioned in connection with the Gospel of Mark. The Prologue(s) also refrain from repeating Irenaeus' misunderstanding of Papias: whereas Papias had simply said that *Matthew* wrote his gospel in a literary form that was 'hebraic' (cf. R. Riesner, *Der Aufbau der Reden in Matthäus-Evangelium, Theologische Beiträge* 9 (1978), 172–82), Irenaeus interprets this as though Matthew had actually written in Hebrew (or Aramaic).

260 One should not overemphasize the fact that in the paraphrased version, *HE* 2, 15:2 the Spirit informs Peter of what had been done: the text merely implies that the Spirit told him what had been achieved, i.e. it gave him good reasons for moving from neutrality to open encouragement at the appropriate moment. Eusebius was no simpleton: if these two accounts were flagrantly inconsistent, he would have been the first to notice it.

Clement's letter to Theodore, discovered by M. Smith (*Clement of Alexandria and a Secret Gospel of Mark* (Harvard, 1973), 19–33), underlines the tradition that Mark wrote his gospel during Peter's stay in Rome. Interesting as the whole letter and Smith's theories are, it may well be a forgery and should not be used in the debate until a final verdict on its provenance is possible.

261 On this aspect of the inability to fully obey the law see the discussion in Bruce, op. cit. n. 30, 294.

262 For the 'people from the Gentiles', *ex ethnōn laon,* see N. A. Dahl, 'A people for his Name', *NTS* 4 (1957/58), 319–27; cf. Marshall, op. cit. n. 175, 251–53, against

the assertation that James' speech here betrays his usage of the LXX instead of the (for him supposedly more likely) Hebrew text. Cf. also Bruce, *Men*, 93–97.

263 James adds a cryptic note on Moses who has been preached in every city from the earliest times and is read in the synagogues on every Sabbath (15:21)—in other words, the Gentile Christians should show consideration for their Judaeo-Christian brothers who have been thoroughly and regularly permeated by the traditional legalistic teaching.

264 The differences between some textual witnesses in the above passage have not been discussed, as they do not affect the impact of the matter under debate—for an analysis, see B. M. Metzger, *A Textual Commentary on the Greek New Testament* (London/New York, 1971), 429–38.

265 Cf. J. B. Lightfoot, *Saint Paul's Epistle to the Galatians* (London, 1865), 122–27, quoted affirmatively by Robinson, *Redating*, 41: 'The object of the decree was to *relieve* the Gentile Christians from the burden of Jewish observances. It said, "Concede so much and we will protect you from any further exactions." The Galatians sought no such protection. They were willing recipients of Judaic rights; and St. Paul's object was to show them, not that they need not submit to these burdens against their will, but that they were wrong and sinful in submitting to them.'

266 See Marshall, op. cit. n. 175, 242–47, with list of supporters (244–45, n. 2); cf. the enumeration of different options by C. H. Talbert, 'Again: Paul's visits to Jerusalem', *Novum Testamentum* 9 (1967), 26.

267 E. Meyer, *Ursprünge und Anfänge des Christentums* (Berlin, 1923), II, 178. Meyer, normally no friend of harmonization, points to the most striking similarities—the cause (the question of circumcision) is identical, the setting of the relationship between the Jewish mother community and the Gentile Christians is identical, as is the participation of Barnabas, Paul, James and Peter. Meyer adds that both accounts are of necessity one-sided.

The list of correspondences is of course even more extensive than Meyer in his aside cared to note. Cf. Lightfoot, op. cit. n. 265 above.

268 Cf. Robinson, *Redating*, 38.

269 *Pace* F. F. Bruce, op. cit. n. 202, 106: cf. its use in Jas. 4:14, and, most strikingly of course, in Galatians itself, 1:18, *epeita meta etē tria*—'then, after three years', or: 'then, in the third year'—as though he had not done anything in between. *Epeita . . . palin* is much too vague to be used as an argument for a second visit only.

270 Cf. R. A. Cole, *The Epistle of Paul to the Galatians* (Leicester, 1965), 61; Robinson, *Redating*, 40.

271 Harnack, who incidentally also presupposes the identity of the assemblies in Galatians 2 and Acts 15, calls it 'more wallowed down than written down' ('mehr hingewühlt als hingeschrieben', *Mission*, 68).

272 One should see not just the material poverty behind the term *ptōchoi*: it has a metaphorical, spiritual sense, as well (cf., e.g. Lk. 6:20; or, at Qumran, 1QH 5:13–22, 1QpHab 12:3–10, 1QM 11:9–13, 4QpPs. Ps. 37 2:9, 3:10 (where it is a self-designation of members of the Qumran-Community).

The Aramaic form of the word helped to create the name 'Ebionites', which returns as the designation of a second century (Judaeo)-Christian sect: cf. Origen, 4, 3:8; Irenaeus, *De. Prin. Haer.* 1, 26:2; 3, 11:7; Eusebius, *HE* 3, 27:1–6. See also the *Gospel of the Ebionites*, in Hennecke, *New Testament Apocrypha*, I, 153–58; and H. J. Schoeps, *Theologie und Geschichte des Juden-christentums* (Tübingen, 1949), 381–456, on the Ebionites and their 'Acts of the Apostles'.

On the connections between the Qumran Community and the Jerusalem mother church, see also R. Riesner, 'Essener und Urkirche in Jerusalem', *Bibel und Kirche* 2/40 (1985), 64–76.

There is also an interesting reference to the name *pauperes* for second century Roman Christians in Minucius Felix, *Octavius* 36:3, written c. AD 160: *Ceterum quod plerique pauperes dicimur.* (For the date, see Thiede, *Pagan*.)

273 Cf. Hemer; cf. also Neugebauer, *Deutung*, 61–66.

274 That this was one of the reasons for Peter's visit to Antioch is argued by Catchpole.

275 For a stimulating recent analysis of this group, see E. E. Ellis, 'The Circumcision Party and the Early Christian Mission', *Prophecy*, 116–28.

276 F. F. Bruce, who sees no need to equate the 'circumcision party' with the 'certain men from James' (op. cit. n. 210, 131) has an interesting explanation for the possible source of this fear: the mid-forties, he says, saw a revival of militancy among Judaean freedom-fighters, and 'in the eyes of such militants, Jews who fraternized with the uncircumcised were no better than traitors, and the leaders of the Jerusalem church may have felt themselves endangered by the reports of Peter's free-and-easy conduct at Antioch' (*Men*, 35–36; cf. Jewett, and Bruce, *Galatians* n. 202, 130. As we have seen, it is not necessary to go to such lengths in explaining the 'fear', quite apart from the problems surrounding the question of the real influence of these militants on the Jerusalem Church.

277 This translation of the Greek is suggested by G. D. Kilpatrick, 'Gal. 2, 14 *orthopodein*', in W. Eltester (ed.), *Neutestamentliche Studien für Rudolf Bultmann* (Berlin, 1954), 269–74; cf. F. F. Bruce, *Galatians*, n. 202, 132.

278 That it was a downright defeat is an assessment shared by Dunn, 254.

279 Dockx, 129–46, suggests that Peter stayed on in Antioch for another seven years, until AD 56.

280 Tertullian, *Adv. Marc.* 1:20, thinks that, while Paul was still immature in diplomatic techniques at the time of the Antioch clash, he learned quickly, as shown in his letter to the Corinthians. This would seem to demand a dating of Galatians before 1 Corinthians, though not necessarily presupposing the identification of Gal. 2:1–10 with Acts 15:16–29. See Dunn, 252–54. Cf. Th. Zahn, *Einleitung*, II, 139–42; *id Der Brief des Paulus an die Galater* (Leipzig, 1905), 9–21; J. Drane, *Paul: Libertine or Legalist?* (London, 1975), etc.

281 The Cephas party of 1 Cor. 1:12; 3:22 could have been inspired by Peter's promulgation of the Apostolic Decree which Paul studiously avoids mentioning; cf. C. K. Barrett, 'Things Sacrificed to Idols', *NTS* 11 (1964/65), 138–53.

It is much less likely that Peter (or any of the Jerusalem 'pillars') could be Paul's ironical 'super-apostles' in 2 Cor. 11:5, 11. For a survey of proponents of such an identification and the arguments against it, see Brown/Donfried/Reumann, 36–38; P. W. Barnett, 'Opposition in Corinth', *JSNT* 22 (1984), 3–17.

Dionysius of Corinth, in one of those characteristically inclusive, generalizing statements we find so often in early church history (cf. Irenaeus, *Haer.* 3:1–3 on Peter and Paul *both* having founded the church of Rome) writes that Peter and Paul (in that order) taught 'in our Corinth' and later likewise in Italy, where they became martyrs 'about the same time' (*kata tou autou kairon*, cf. Acts 19:23, Rom. 9:9 for similar expressions). Vague as the statement is for both the Corinthian teaching and the Roman martyrdom, it is, for Corinth, a local tradition which cannot easily be dismissed. (The statement, from Dionysius' letter to the Romans, c. AD 170, is quoted by Eusebius, *HE* 2, 25:8.)

282 This is not the place to discuss the 'authenticity' of 16:3–16 in the context of the letter to the Romans (which should be accepted); for surveys see Guthrie, op. cit. n. 32, 400–04; cf. also C. H. Dodd, *The Epistle to the Romans* (London, 1932), xvii–xx; F. F. Bruce, *The Epistle of Paul to the Romans* (London, 1963), 266–76.

283 Cf. Judge, 36–38; E. A. Judge/G. S. R. Thomas, 'The Origin of the Church at Rome—A new solution?' *Reformed Theological Review* 25 (1966), 91.

Whether the third (?) century church Santa Prisca on the Aventine preserves a valuable local tradition in this respect, is a question still under debate. See already Harnack, *Mission*, 838–40, who thinks that the central administrative seat of the Roman Church in the third century *could* have been there.

284 Cf. Bruce, *Men*, 44–45.

285 2 Pet. 3:1 appears to be the first reference—unless, that is, 2 Peter is in fact the earlier of the two letters, in which case 2 Pet. 3:1 must either refer to a lost letter (so Th. Zahn, *Einleitung in das Neue Testament* (Leipzig, 2nd ed., 1900, II 43–53) or to the Epistle of Jude (so Robinson, *Redating*, 195–99). For a detailed list of allusions, direct quotations and references to Peter's authorship, see C. Bigg, *The Epistles of St. Peter and St. Jude* (Edinburgh, 2nd ed., 1902), 7–15.

286 Most recently Neugebauer, *Deutung*; Bénétreau, op. cit. n. 238, 36–41.

287 Its direct attestation (i.e. by name) is sketchy, but the case has been exaggerated. Even those who record doubts expressed by others (Origen, *Commentary on John* 5:3, Eusebius, *HE* 3, 3:1–4) do not appear to share them wholeheartedly, or even reject them (Origen, *Homily on Joshua* 7:1 is an unreserved acceptance of the authenticity of both letters). Clement of Alexandria accepted it (in Eusebius, *HE* 6, 14:1), and so did Jerome (*Letter to Paulinus; Letter to Hedibia*). Attestation by direct quotation or allusion begins with the oldest post-Petrine Roman writing, Clement's first letter (1 Clement 9:2=2 Pet. 1:17, etc.), traditionally dated 95/96 but perhaps considerably younger (in AD 70: cf. Edmundson, 191–2; Robinson, *Redating*, 327–35). From then on, the list is as long as for 1 Peter or indeed most other NT letters (cf. C. Bigg, op. cit. n. 285, 199–215; Green, 5–10).

288 The majority case against 2 Peter is neatly presented by R. J. Bauckham, op. cit. n. 81 (with bibliographies); among recent commentaries only E. M. B. Green, *2 Peter and Jude* (Leicester, 2nd revised and enlarged edition forthcoming) comes out strongly in favour of its authenticity.

289 As Green puts it, 'The case against the Epistle does not, in fact, appear by any means compelling. It cannot be shown conclusively that Peter was the author; but it has yet to be shown convincingly that he was not' (Green, 37).

290 See F. Neugebauer, *Deutung*; Robinson, 'The Petrine Epistles and Jude', *Redating*, 140–99;; Riesner, *Petrus-Brief*, 124–43; revised version of Riesner's paper forthcoming in C. P. Thiede (ed.), *Das Petrusbild in der neuren Forschung*, Wuppertal, 1986.

291 A detailed study by the present author on the historical setting and the literary tradition of 2 Peter is forthcoming.

292 A. M. Stibbs, *The First Epistle General of Peter* (Leicester, 1959), 175, suggests, by a different translation of 1 Pet. 5:12, that Silvanus was personally known to the recipients of the letter ('to you a faithful brother'). This would imply a missionary journey by Silvanus on his own.

293 So Selwyn, op. cit. n. 182, 10–12; Bauer, op. cit. n. 71, 357.

294 Their help in drafting the letter could also explain the differences between James' speech and the final version.

295 Nuances over against both 1 Pet. 5:12 and the Ignatius letters shown by Dionysius' letter to the Romans (quoted in Eusebius *HE* 4, 23:11, where he describes 1 Clement as . . . *dia Klēmentos grapheisan*, i.e. written by Clement as the authoritative representative of the Roman Church.

296 These conditions are described and analysed by Roller, 14–19. Ellis, *Dating*, 487–502, who accepts Silvanus as Peter's secretary without question (498), quotes Roller approvingly in his own comments on the use of 'co-workers' in the composition of NT letters.

    It is also worth noticing that Peter writes briefly (*oligon*) 'by' Silvanus—the use of this adverb in the context of writing (*graphō*) suggests that the role of a mere messenger is not intended—or can one 'briefly' travel all over Asia Minor?

297 Josephus, *Ant.* 20, 9:1.

298 Hegesippus, according to Eusebius (*HE* 2, 23:3) a member of the post-apostolic generation, but probably a contemporary of Tatian, c. AD 170, preserves an old tradition: 'He was called the Just (*dikaios*) by everyone, from the time of the Lord to our own'; and Hegesippus goes on to explain by what devout adherence to traditional temple worship, righteousness of character and asceticism he had deserved this epithet (Eusebius, *HE* 2, 23: 4–7). As this tradition tallies well with the picture of James one can construct on the basis of NT evidence itself, it appears entirely trustworthy. (Cf. Dunn, 256, etc.)

299 2 Thes. 1:4–8 is interesting also because it ends with fire: eschatology, in apostolic thinking, is connected with fire—both in terms of suffering and purification, and in terms of judgement and selection (cf. p. 112 above on the context of 2 Pet. 3:7–13; see also 1 Cor. 3:13, Ps. 66:10, Pr. 17:3; 27:21, Zc. 13:9; Mal. 3:2–3). Nothing could be more forced than seeing in 1 Pet. 1:7; 4:12 an allusion to the experience of the fire of Rome.

300 For a detailed analysis of the letter in this respect, Neugebauer, *Deutung*.

301 In Seneca's tragedy *Octavia*, written c. 62/63 (for date and authenticity see J. Schmidt, *'Octavia', Pauly's Real-Encyclopaedie der classischen Alterthums-Wissenschaft* (Stuttgart, 1937), 1788–99), Agrippina's shadow appears, foreboding revenge for the monstrous crime (*Octavia* 593–645).

302 See Suetonius, *Life of the Caesars* 6, 34:1–4. Nero had contributed to or committed other murders before—of Claudius in AD 54, carried out by Agrippina on his behalf or in his interest, of Britannicus in AD 55—but the murder of his own mother as recently as AD 59 was the most heinous of Nero's deeds that would have caught the public imagination during Peter's second stay. Suetonius, *Life of the Caesars* 6, 39:2, even quotes several satirical verses that were put up publicly over all Rome; in them, Nero, the singing 'Apollos', is attacked as a matricide, and the Romans are (mockingly) asked to flee the city.

303 For this and the following enumeration of occurrences, see Kelly, op. cit. n. 88, 188–89.

304 Only in the fourth and late fifth century is the word used twice more: Epiphanius, *Ankurōtos* ('The Anchored One') 12:5—cf. his *Panarion* ('Medicine chest') 66, 85:6; and Dionysius Areopagites, *Letter 8*.

305 See Zahn, op. cit. n. 285; Robinson, *Redating*; Riesner, *Petrusbrief*.

306 E.g. Bigg, op. cit. n. 285, 237–41; Bauckham, op. cit. n. 81, 285–87.

307 On the angels of 1 Cor. 11:10 as disregarded guarantors of the order of creation, cf. F. F. Bruce, *1 & 2 Corinthians* (London, 1971), 106; and Hengel, *Judentum*, 422–27.

308 See 1QSa 2:8–9; cf. Riesner, *Petrusbrief*, 135.
309 For earliest contacts between members of the Essene communities and the Christians, see (possibly) Acts 6:7 (cf. C. Spicq, 'L'épître aux Hébreux: Apollos, Jean-Baptiste, les Hellénistes et Qumran', *Revue de Qumran* 1 (1958/ 59), 365–390; Pixner; R. Riesner, 'Essener und Urkirche in Jerusalem', *Bibel und Kirche* 2/40 (1985), 64–76.
    For the Essene influence on the heretical teaching fought against by Paul (and Peter), see Schlatter, *Geschichte*, 222; Gunther, *St. Paul's Opponents;* Riesner, *Petrusbrief*, 136–37.
310 Cf. 2 Pet. 2:4 with Enoch 10:11–14; 91:15; 2 Pet. 3:6 with Enoch 83:3–5; see J. T. Milik, *The Books of Enoch, Aramaic Fragments of Qumran Cave 4* (Oxford, 1976).
311 Hengel, *Judentum*, 422–27; Riesner, *Jesus*, 291–97.
312 Cf. Riesner, *Petrusbrief*, 136–37.
313 Cf. Callaghan, *griegos*, 74–75 and plate 5; Thiede, *7Q*, 553, 559.
314 Cf. also Murphy – O'Connor, *Essenes*. It is possible that the heretics of Rev. 2:14, the Nicolaitans, are related to those of 2 Peter, as 2 Pet. 2:15 also refers to them as successors of Balaam; see Zahn, op. cit. n. 285, 102. Irenaeus (*Haer* 1, 26:3; 3, 11:1) preserves the trustworthy tradition that the Nicolaitans were so named after their founder and leader, Nicolas of Antioch, a Gentile who had become a Jewish proselyte before he was converted to Christianity —Acts 6:5! If he was one of the 'seven' with decidedly pro-'Greek' (hellenistic—*Hēllenistai*, Acts 6:1) 'qualifications'—we once again have a context of Greek or Graecized influence. (Cf. P.Géoltrain, 'Esséniens et Hellénistes', *Theologische Zeitschrift* 15 (1959), 241–54, on Essene influences on the 'Hellenists'). Not only are we thus, if these assumptions are correct, once more in the earliest stages of Christian development after Pentecost; Revelation might even have quoted 2 Pet. 2:15 as a handy reference for characterizing the Nicolaitans who troubled the church at Pergamon (cf. Zahn, op. cit. n. 285, 71, 102, 614). Cf. also Neugebauer, *Entstehung*, 20–22, on Essene influences in Asia Minor.
315 This obvious reliance of Jude on 2 Peter was already seen and cogently argued by Th. Zahn, op. cit. n. 285, II. 91–93, who also argues for the authenticity of Jude. Cf. Crehan, 148.
316 Recently again Ellis, 'Prophecy and Hermeneutic in Jude', in *Prophecy*, 223– 36; Bauckham, op. cit. n. 81, 14–16.
317 Demonstrated persuasively, with corroborative arguments, by Robinson, *Redating*, 197, and Ellis, *Prophecy*, 223–36.
318 The so-called 'Asian' style has been detected in parts of 2 Peter by A. Deissmann, *Bible Studies* (Edinburgh, 1901), 366–68 and others. Cf. Robinson, *Redating*, 197.
319 Although *exodus* could mean simply 'departure' (cf. pp. 157f. and n. 259 above on Irenaeus, *Haer*. 3, 1:2), here it clearly implies death, as it stands in the immediate context of both Jesus' prediction and of the Transfiguration story, where *exodus* also means death (cf. Lk. 9:31 and p. 48, above).
320 P72, the oldest extant papyrus of 2 Peter ('the most important textual witness' for the catholic epistles: Aland/Aland, 103), has the present tense, *spoudazō*, a reading corroborated by the Codex Sinaiticus and later by the fifteenth century minuscule 69. If p72 is taken seriously, then Peter is not speaking about some future action, but about something he is going to do immediately. And this would corroborate the old assumption (cf. p. 18 and n. 2, 259 above), that Peter refers to Mark's gospel. At first neutral he has

finally approved of it, and has for some time authorized copies; now he has another one made for the readers of his letter. (Cf. also Crehan, 146–47.)

One must not read too much into the identification (as yet only very tentative) of the Qumran fragment 7Q10 as 2 Pet. 1:15 (cf. note 313), but it is tempting to assume that the presence of 2 Peter next to the gospel of Mark in Cave 7 (for the certain identification of 7Q5=Mk. 6:52–53 see note 3 above) is yet another instance of the close links between the gospel and the letter, all the more so as it is precisely 2 Pet. 1:15 that appears to have been preserved—possibly attached to Mark as its apostolic authentication.

321　For a full analysis, cf. Green, 30–32.

322　Or two, according to the edition of the extant text by J. A. Fischer, *Die Apostolischen Väter* (Darmstadt, 1974), I. 227–265.

323　This is the form given by the most valuable witness, p72, together with the Ephraim Rescriptus C04 and the Porfirianus P025 as well as several minuscules. Cf. the analysis by Crehan, 145–46.

324　The letter has a remarkably good and early direct attestation, (cf. Kelly, op. cit. n. 88, 223–24), whereas 2 Peter, after early use by Roman authors (Clement, Hermas, Barnabas) has a more chequered career in the second century (cf. n. 287 above) and is established first not by the united opinion of church history, but by its manuscript tradition, which is partly shared by Jude and is connected neither with Rome nor with Asia Minor, but with the beginnings of the Coptic Church (the 9th century *Sahidic* manuscript, going back to an early third century version, Pierpont Morgan M572; cf. K. Schüssler, *Epistolarum Catholicarum Versio Sahidica* (Doctoral thesis, Münster, 1969); and the uniquely-important mid-third century p72; cf. C. M. Martini, *Beati Petri Apostoli Epistulae Ex Papyro Bodmeriana VIII Transcriptae* Milano, 1968)—a fact that presupposes a long and complex textual tradition.

325　*Homily on Joshua* 7:1, extant only in Rufinus of Aquileia's Latin translation (. . . *duabus epistolarum suarum personat tubis*), which had a deep influence on Gregory the Great (cf. Chadwick, *Early*, 108).

326　The existence of differences should not overshadow the fact that even here similarities are surprisingly numerous and impressive. Cf. Holzmeister; Green, 11–14.

327　Again, there is 'a remarkable degree of similarity': cf. Green, 14–23; Guthrie, op. cit. n. 32, 841–45.

328　This and the following dates are of necessity conjectures; they are preferred here to alternative suggestions not least because they appear to fit the extant evidence just that decisive bit better. No weight of 'proof' for the historicity of the events depends on them.

　　Cf. Edmundson, 203–05; W. Coleborne, 'A Linguistic Approach to the Problem of Structure and Composition of the Shepherd of Hermas', *Colloquium, The Australian and New Zealand Theological Review,* 3 (1969), 133–42.

329　See Edmundson, 191.

330　Robinson, *Redating*, 327–35.

331　So Cullmann, in his stimulating analysis of the letter, in *Peter*, 91–110.

332　Reicke, *Era*, 247. Cf. A. Fridrichsen, 'Propter invidiam. Note sur 1 Clem V', *Eranos* 44 (1946), 161–74.

333　Cf. Clement's letter itself, Tertullian (*Apol.* 5:3–4, *To the Nations* 1:7, *Scorpiace* 15), Eusebius *HE* 2, 25:5), Jerome, (*On famous men* 5), *et al.*

334 Cf. Ascension of Isaiah 4:3 (probably a very early text—AD 70?—which deserves renewed analysis not least because of its connections between Christianity and the Essenes. Cf. Robinson, *Redating*, 239–40, note 98; R. J. Bauckham, 'The Worship of Jesus in Apocalyptic Christianity', *NTS* 27 (1980/81), 322–41. Tertullian, *Scorpiace* 15, Lactantius, *On Divine Institutions* 4:21, *On the kinds of deaths of the Persecutors* 2:5–6, *Acts of Peter* 41, *et al.* Cf. also the allusion in Ignatius' letter to the Romans (c. AD 110) 4:3.

335 Cf. Eusebius, *HE* 2, 25:5.

336 See Dockx, 129–46; cf. Jerome, *On famous men*, 5.

337 For two representatives of the opposite positions, see J. W. Ph. Borleffs, 'Institutum Neronianum',*Vigiliae Christianae* 6 (1952), 129–45; and J. Zeiller, 'Institutum Neronianum. Loi fantôme ou réalité', *Revue d'histoire ecclésiastique*, 50 (1955), 393–99.

338 Suetonius begins by stating (16:2) that numerous prohibitions and sanctions were revived or introduced by Nero, and he cites the death sentence against the Christians with approval as one of them (he describes the Christians as people of a new and evil superstition, *gens hominum superstitionis novae ac maleficae*).

339 Tertullian even says that the persecution of the Christians outlasted Nero: while all other measures taken by Nero were obliterated with the memory of the man himself, the measures instituted against the Christians remained: *et tamen permansit erasis omnibus hoc solum institutum Neronianum*.

340 See also the late fourth century historian Sulpicius Severus, who knew the writings of Tacitus (he quotes him directly). In his *Chronicle* 2, 29:3, he links the Neronian persecution with the aftermath of the fire, mentions Nero's laws as a further consequence (*post etiam datis legibus religio vetabatur, palamque edictis propositis Christianum esse non licebat*), and reports the deaths of Peter and Paul as attendant circumstances of this further step (*tum Paulus ac Petrus capitis damnati; quorum unum cervix gladio desecta, Petrus in crucem sublatus est.*)

341 Cf. Mohrmann.

342 See Kirschbaum, 172–203.

343 See Kirschbaum, 48–94; Guarducci, *Ausgrabungen*; Walsh, 43–72; Lampe, 87–97.

344 M. Guarducci, 'Documenti del l° secolo nella Necropoli Vaticana', *Rendiconti della Pontifica Academia Romana di Archeologia* 29 (1956/57), 1–27; Kirschbaum, 20–28.

345 V. Capocci, 'Gli Scavi del Vaticano. Alla ricerca del sepolcro di S Pietro e alcune note di diritto funerario Romano', *Studia et Documenta Historiae et Juris* 18 (1952), 202–04; *id.*, 'Sulla concessione . . .'.

346 The precise place of execution is unknown. Although at first sight the Vatican Gardens are an obvious choice, Peter was not among the first victims of the mass executions taking place there. Different traditions in legend and art, as in crucifixion between two pyramids depicted on the fifteenth century main porch of Saint Peter, have led to different hypotheses. The latest and most original one, suggesting a site at the Campus Martius, on the Via Lata-Flaminia, is due to Demus-Quatember.

347 Cf. in particular *Martyrdom of Polycarp* 18:2–3!

348 This reconstruction of the events, as based on the available archaeological evidence, follows the results of Kirschbaum's analysis, 126. It is worth mentioning that in the immediate vicinity of Peter's burial place a simple, tile-covered tomb was discovered, the so-called Theta tomb, and that one of

the tiles is marked with a stamp dating it to the time of Nero. Cf. Guarducci, art. cit. n. 344; *Ausgrabungen,* 368–69.

349 For an analysis of this phenomenon and its consequences for the socio-political relationship between Christians and non-Christians in the mid-second century, see Lampe, 88–91.

350 This fragmentary stone from the red wall was first deciphered by A. Ferrua, 'La Storia del sepolcro di San Pietro', *La Civiltà Cattolica* 103 (1952), 25 and plate 3. The burden of proof for the (hypothetical) whereabouts of the bones was placed on this stone by Guarducci; see *Ausgrabungen,* 392–95.

351 For Guarducci's account of how she rediscovered what she believes are the bones of Saint Peter (and which can be seen today in the repository in the graffiti wall, encased in transparent plastic boxes) see *Ausgrabungen,* 396–405. For a careful analysis of her case, see E. Dassmann, 'Ist Petrus wirklich darin?' in Kirschbaum, 223–248. Cf. also the passionate backing of Guarducci's arguments by Walsh.

There are other questions which similarly cannot be fully resolved. Were (parts of) Peter's body transferred to San Sebastiano *ad Catacumbas* during the persecution under Emperor Valerianus in 258 (and back again under Constantine in c.330)? Which relics of Peter and Paul (if any) are preserved in San Giovanni in Laterano (cf. Guarducci, 342, *Ausgrabungen,* 406–14; Kirschbaum, 145–48, 205–22; cf. also Chadwick, *Pope Damasus* and *St. Peter*)? Concerning these we may remember the friendly aside of Delehaye: 'Not every relic that is above all doubt must be false . . .' (Cf. Dassmann, art. cit. n. 351, 245). Whatever conclusions we reach, they will not affect the questions raised in this book.

Index of Biblical References:
Old Testament and Apocrypha

Index of Biblical References:

New Testament

Index of Extra-Biblical References:

Persons, Authors and Anonymous Texts